THE AMERICANS OF URUMIA

Iran's First Americans and their
Mission to the Assyrian Christians

Hooman Estelami
Fordham University

Editor: Benjamin Kaufman

First published by Bahar Books, LLC
www.baharbooks.com

ISBN: 978-1-939099-84-6
This book is printed on acid-free paper.
Printed in the United States of America

To the Memory of My Mother ... Parvin Anvar-Estelami
(September 10, 1939 – July 31, 2010)

THE
AMERICANS
OF URUMIA

TABLE OF CONTENTS

PREFACE

The fact that Americans were living and working in Iran as early as the 1830s is unimaginable to many. Except for a handful of Orientalists and Middle East scholars, the general public lacks awareness about the long history that exists between the two countries. The hostile postures that have been at play for over four decades have made it difficult to remember that there were times when war, oil, and trade were not the contexts for the formation or breakdown of relations between the United States and Iran.

America's first residents in Iran did not settle down in the main population centers. Instead, they chose to live and work in some of the most remote, rugged, and inhospitable parts of the country. They settled near the Turco-Persian border in the city of Urumia in northwestern Iran. They were private citizens whose lives were focused on the Assyrian Christian population, which was concentrated in the Urumia region. Their missionary labors were spearheaded by Justin Perkins, an educator and theologian from Massachusetts, who in 1834 moved to Persia. He was followed by Asahel Grant, a physician from upstate New York. Dozens of other Americans followed Perkins and Grant, many of whom formed their families in Urumia, raised their children there, grew old, passed away, and were laid to rest in Urumia. Generation after generation of Americans considered Urumia as their home.

The Americans of Urumia were a unique group. They lived in an Iran, which at that time, had no strategic value for America. As such, their relationships with the Persians reflected exchanges that were not tainted by political and economic agendas. They were highly educated, most having graduated from some of America's best colleges and universities, many with doctorate and medical degrees. They wrote beautifully and frequently. Their life experiences and observations have been preserved in the form of biographies, memoirs, correspondences, and missionary logs, consisting of thousands of pages of writings, which are accessible to us today. These writings, alongside photographs and archives maintained by various historical societies, university libraries, and digital collections, provide a glimpse of the conception point of the two countries' relations.

I must confess that the writing of this book was an evolutionary process. At first, the goal was to develop a collection of archived photographs from the late nineteenth century and early twentieth century Persia to provide readers with the visual sensations of Persia in that time period. Through this process, I encountered portrait images of Howard Baskerville, an American who was killed in Tabriz in 1909. Baskerville was fighting alongside Persians resisting the Russian encirclement of Tabriz. The project soon evolved into developing a better understanding of other Americans who lived in Iran at that time. Baskerville turned out to be the tip of the iceberg. Baskerville was preceded by dozens of Americans who had come to live and work in northwestern Persia decades earlier. It is these early Americans who became the focus of this book, with special attention given to four of them: Justin Perkins, Asahel Grant, Joseph Plumb Cochran, and William Ambrose Shedd.

I have many people to thank for supporting me on this journey. First and foremost is my wife, Nazanin. I am lucky to be married to her. Without any pretensions, I must acknowledge that she is the most supportive spouse one could ask for. She has been patient, as this multi-year project has taken up a great deal of our time (as well as our living space; as I write, our entire dining room table is covered with stacks of about one hundred books being consulted before the final publication of the book). She is a constant source of moral and intellectual support, and I owe her a great deal for her patience, encouragement, and love through the years.

I am deeply thankful to several of Dr. William Ambrose Shedd's descendants who kindly shared with me their personal experiences and perspectives: Celia Barker Lottridge, Jonathan Barker, and Carolyn Mason. My conversations with them, as well as their generosity in granting me access to one of Dr. Shedd's unpublished manuscripts, provided me with invaluable insights into Dr. Shedd and other American missionaries in Urumia. They gave me a boost of inspiration to advance this work. In addition, I am thankful to Dr. Thomas Ricks, who has frequently helped me understand the intricacies related to the American presence in northwestern Persia. His careful reading of the manuscript and his constructive suggestions are deeply appreciated. I must also express my gratitude to Gordon Taylor, the author of the most definitive biography of Dr. Asahel Grant, for sharing with me his thoughts and suggestions and providing me with helpful guidance on related resources. Much gratitude is due to Arthur Kover, who kindly and encouragingly read an early draft of this manuscript. His reflections helped me better articulate specific critical points in the manuscript regarding the missionaries' motivations and contributions in Urumia. Arthur's perspective on intellectual inquiry and his openness to various approaches to research fosters growth in anyone fortunate enough to know him. Furthermore, I am thankful to Ben Kaufman for the outstanding editorial support on this book. His careful and critical reading of the manuscript and his constructive suggestions have been instrumental to the quality of the work.

I am grateful to my home institution of nearly three decades, Fordham University, for having provided a supportive intellectual base for my academic research and writing. Fordham's view of the academic world is not restricted by the traditional boundaries forced upon academics in many other institutions. In the spirit of the inquisitive mindset fostered at Fordham, many years ago, I asked the question: *Who were the first Americans to live in Iran?* I am indebted to Fordham for having created the intellectually productive environment in which I was able to answer this important question by writing this book.

I must also express my deep gratitude to the Presbyterian Historical Society (PHS) in Philadelphia. The PHS archives are meticulously maintained by some of the most capable and caring professionals in the field. Had it not been for the high standards with which they maintain the digital and physical archives of the PHS, much of the work in this book, especially as it relates to the photographs included, would not have been possible. It is primarily because of the PHS that the readers in this book do not have to imagine the visual sensations experienced by the Americans who lived in Urumia, but can, in fact, see it for themselves.

This book is intended for both academic and non-academic readers. For non-academics, it provides a picture of how the initial contacts between Americans and Iranians were formed during the nineteenth and early twentieth century. For academic readers interested in further exploring the historical events discussed in this book, additional resources are provided as footnotes and reference lists at the end of every chapter.

It is essential to acknowledge that many of the images included in this book are sourced from black and white photographs printed over a century ago. These original prints have decayed over time and were digitally revived. Even with the best attempts to bring these images back to life using digital enhancement tools, the visual quality is admittedly less than perfect. As a result, some of the images will lack contrast and clarity, as one might expect. However, I felt that for the reader, being able to visually experience history in these pictures is essential, despite their imperfections.

A couple of clarification points need to be made concerning the choice and spelling of the names used in this book. "Persia" is frequently used in this book in preference for "Iran" since the latter was only adopted officially in 1935. With the exception of specific cases placing issues or topics in a modern (post-1935) context, "Persia" will be used. Similarly, the terms "Ottoman" and "Turkey" will be used interchangeably. However, the former will be used more frequently as the Ottoman Empire was in place during the period under study in this book.

In terms of addressing the Assyrian Christian population, the term "Nestorian" was used by the American missionaries in the first few decades of their entry into Persia. As will be discussed in this book, this term is not the preferred form of addressing the modern Assyrian population in Iran and worldwide. As much as possible, only in the timeframe and context in which the American missionaries used the term "Nestorian" in their writings will this reference be used, and a general preference to use "Assyrian" will be evident in the text. In terms of the names of locations and individuals, many variations in spelling are evident in Western writings. As such, in most cases, I have tried to remain consistent with the spelling adopted by the majority of authors. It is also important to recognize that the term "Kurd" has been used somewhat carelessly by some of the early writers at a time when little research existed on the cultural, artistic, and linguistic richness and diversity of the Kurdish people. The Western interpretation of the Kurds during the nineteenth century was a stereotypical one in which they were typically portrayed as backward, savage, and illiterate. The historical roots of this population and its cultural richness, which modern writers such as Wadie Jwaideh, David McDowall, and Martin van Bruinessen have uncovered, were unknown to Orientalists and the American missionaries during the nineteenth century. As such, interested readers are encouraged to examine contemporary research on Kurdish culture, art, literature, social traditions, independence aspirations, and the political forces which influenced them during the nineteenth century and the years leading to the First World War.

In terms of the sources of facts and figures used, each chapter contains a full list of references and recommended readings at the very end. For the four missionaries profiled, greater reliance is given on the biographies written by those who labored, lived with, or personally knew these missionaries. For Justin Perkins, the biography written by his son, Henry Martyn Perkins, titled *Life of Reverend Justin Perkins*, published in 1887, is used as a source. For Asahel Grant, greater reliance has been given to the words of his missionary colleague, Thomas Laurie, who in 1853 authored *Dr. Grant and the Mountain Nestorians*. For Joseph Plumb Cochran, Robert Speer's biography of Cochran, titled *The Hakim Sahib*, published in 1911, is used as a source. For William Ambrose Shedd, reliance has been given to Mary Lewis Shedd's book, *The Measure of a Man*, published in 1922. In addition to these, to gain a more comprehensive perspective, sources that provide contemporary assessments on the lives, actions, and accomplishments of these four missionaries have also been used in each chapter. Interested readers are therefore encouraged to consult the sources cited in each chapter for additional study. The sources of the photographs, maps, and sketches used in this book are also listed at the end of the book as a separate section. Interested readers are invited to examine the book's website *Urumia.com* for additional resources.

This book is dedicated to the memory of my mother, Parvin Anvar-Estelami. She passed away over a decade ago. Yet, her loss is felt by me every day. Not a day goes by that I do not think of her or am not reminded of the pain of the loss. She embodied the spirit of kindness, generosity, selflessness, and care for others. She was not only a giving, forgiving, and loving person but also had a fantastic sense of humor and was one of the most positive people I have ever known. She was and still is a role model to me, and I miss her very much. Her vision of life is alive in those who follow the same mottos through compassion, generosity, caring, and kindness.

I hope that in the same spirit of kindness and compassion, this book helps us appreciate the fact that despite the modern state of hostility between the United States and Iran, the relationship did not start this way. During the period covered in this book, America was trusted by Persians far above any European nation. Through the decades, the relationship between the two countries evolved, and misunderstandings, differences, and tensions developed. I have tried my best to convey the historical facts as accurately as possible and have steered away from my own editorial input. The book provides a glimpse of history, long forgotten by Americans and Iranians. Reviving the memories of a past long gone may enlighten a path to a brighter future.

Chapter 1

IRAN'S FIRST AMERICANS

The United States and Iran have been in a confrontational posture with each other for decades. Following Iran's Islamic Revolution of 1979, and the occupation of the American embassy in Tehran, in November of that year, formal diplomatic relations between the two countries have since been severed. The anti-American sentiments that characterized Iran's Islamic revolution revealed the large ideological gaps that separate the two countries. Decades of tensions in the form of military skirmishes, proxy wars, and economic sanctions have contributed to the expanding gap. The general state of the relations between the two countries appears as something beyond repair.

Despite the long history of hostilities and the constantly recurring prospects of war between Iran and the United States, little is known about the very beginning of the relationship between the two nations. Public knowledge as to how the first contacts between the citizens of the two countries took place is generally lacking. As will be seen in this book, the initial contacts between Americans and Persians date back nearly two centuries. They were initiated in the first half of the 19th century, through the activities of a handful of Americans who traveled to Persia (the name of Iran prior to 1935) as Christian missionaries. The commencement of their activities took place in a remote region of the country in what is now the province of West Azerbaijan. Their activities in this region lasted until the end of the First World War and were concentrated in a rugged area to the west of Lake Urumia, bordering Turkey.

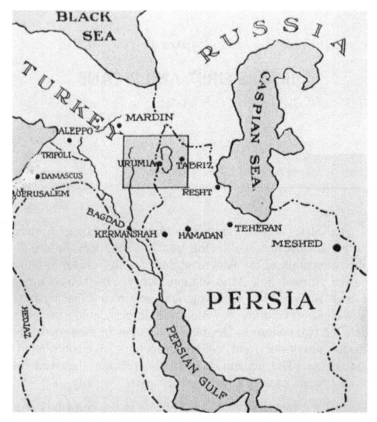

The Urumia Mission Field (square area; from Mary Lewis Shedd's *The Measure of a Man,* 1922)

An important aspect of the history of American-Iranian relations is the unique role that the American missionaries played in initiating the relations. To most scholars and laypeople, it is an unknown fact that the early missionaries, initially under the guidance of the American Board of Commissioners for Foreign Missions (ABCFM), began serving in Persia as early as 1834. In December of 1870, ABCFM transferred its role in Persia to the Board of Foreign Missions of the Presbyterian Church in the United States of America. Their activities in Urumia were halted due to the atrocities of the First World War, which affected the Urumia region with horrific human losses due to repeated military invasions of the area by foreign powers, famine, and the mass flight of the population. While the American missionaries continued their work in Persia after the First World War until the termination of relations between the two countries in 1979, there is much to be learned about the early phases of their activities in Urumia where their work began.

Given that America's first footprints in Persia were in Urumia, it is important to have an accurate understanding of what America's pioneering activities and their underlying motivations were. The accomplishments and mistakes of the American missionaries shed light not only on what was or could have been achieved in what seems like a distant past, but also what the modern opportunities for improved relations may be between the United States and Iran. History cannot be changed or denied. However, the recognition of the work initiated nearly two centuries ago, leading to cultural, educational, and medical work in Persia, is essential for developing a full understanding of the history of US-Iran relations.

American missionary activities in Persia were pioneered by a missionary named Justin Perkins. Perkins was the very first American citizen to take up residence in Persia permanently. He arrived in Tabriz, in northwestern Persia, in August of 1834, and was joined a year later by a fellow missionary physician named Asahel Grant. The two moved to Urumia in November of 1835, and their pioneering steps resulted in an influx of American missionaries to this area. Their activities aimed to serve the Assyrian Christian population of the region. Most of this population was centered in the city of Urumia and its surrounding plains, and the mountainous regions to the west of the city, within and beyond the Turco-Persian border.

Justin Perkins, Iran's First American Resident (c. 1860s)

Although no accurate census figures existed at the start of America's mission in Urumia, Persia's total population was estimated to be approximately 12 million. Urumia was a small town of about 25,000 inhabitants. Of these, 600 were Assyrian Christians. Within Urumia and the surrounding plain, which expanded from Lake Urumia to the east of the city to the high mountains in the Turkish-Persian border region to the west, there were approximately 40,000 Assyrian Christians, many living in hundreds of villages in this area. Another 110,000 were believed to reside in the Kurdish mountains, beyond the Turkish border.[1]

---

[1] For relevant statistics, see Perkins (1861), *Missionary Life in Persia*, pp. 79, 85, 94, 100.

Urumia and Surrounding Regions (c. 1863)

The Lake Urumia region was, and still is, a fertile agricultural area. At the commencement of American missionary activities, it was known for producing wheat, rice, cotton, tobacco, grapes, cherries, apricots, apples, pears, quinces, peaches, plums, melons, and nuts.[2] Even today, it is considered to be one of the most productive agricultural regions of Iran. The Urumia plain is bounded on its eastern side by Lake Urumia, and to its north and west by rising mountain ranges, which then and now are primarily populated by Kurdish populations, residing in small villages scattered across the high mountain slopes. Perkins described Urumia upon his arrival as such:

---

[2] Perkins (1843), *A Residence of Eight Years in Persia*, p. 7.

The district of Oroomiah is in the western part of Azerbaijan, the north-western province of Persia. It consists of a magnificent plain, situated at the eastern base of the Koordish mountains, and extending from them to the beautiful lake of the same name. The *lake* of Oroomiah is about eighty miles in length and thirty in breadth, lying in direction a little to the west of north and east of south. Its waters are very salty, perhaps as much so as the waters of the Dead Sea. No fish are found in it; but fowl, particularly the duck and flamingo frequent it in great numbers. The plain of Oroomiah is about forty miles in length, lying upon the central section of the lake, and in its broadest part, is about twenty miles wide. Imposing branches of the Koordish mountains sweep down quite to the waters of the lake, at the extremities of the plain, enclosing it like a vast amphitheater. This great plain, with the adjacent declivities of the mountains, comprising an area of about six hundred square miles, contains at least three hundred and thirty villages.[3]

When Perkins and Grant arrived in Urumia, they found it to be populated by a mix of inhabitants with a fascinating diversity of religious and ethnic backgrounds. These included Shi'ite and Sunni Moslems, Assyrian Christians (also referred to as "Nestorian" Christians), Armenian Christians, Jews, and Zoroastrians. Urumia had a unique standing as a significant population center for Assyrian Christians throughout the region. This was due to the diversity of the population of the Urumia plain. For centuries, people of different backgrounds lived close to each other in relative peace and collectively benefited from the prosperity found in the Urumia plain due to its fertile soil, an abundance of water supplies, and high agricultural output. With the large population of Assyrians beyond the Ottoman border, and with the border being unguarded and unmarked, traveling back-and-forth between the Ottoman regions and Urumia was typical.

---

[3] Note the difference in the spelling of Urumia, which was in use by the early American missionaries.

The Urumia Plain with Lake Urumia Visible at a Distance (c. 1892)

Justin Perkins and Asahel Grant were the first two American missionaries in Persia. Dozens of other American missionaries and their families were deployed to Persia in the decades that followed. The uniqueness of Perkins and Grant is that they were America's first two residents in Persia and the initiators of much of the early contacts between the two nations. At the turn of the twentieth century, and in the years leading to the commencement of the First World War, two other missionaries, Joseph Plumb Cochran and William Ambrose Shedd, were the leading missionaries in Urumia. They witnessed the ratcheting up of tensions and violence in the area, arising from tribal tensions involving the Kurds, the Assyrians, and the Armenians, which blended with regional conflicts involving the Persians, the Ottomans, the British, and the Russians.

Cochran and Shedd were unique in their own ways since they were themselves born in Persia, spoke multiple local languages, and were deeply embedded in the culture and norms of the locals. This made their actions, writing, and perspectives highly informative. They had unique insights into the mindsets of the local Persians, Kurds, and Assyrians, and rendered an early American perspective on Persia and her people. For this reason, in this book, these four missionaries — Perkins, Grant, Cochran, and Shedd — will be profiled. We will trace their backgrounds and upbringing, their life experiences and accomplishments, and their perceptions and opinions on historic events that they witnessed or were part of.

The early days of American presence in Iran are fundamental to the development of a better understanding of the modern state of the relationships between the two nations. Perkins and Grant came to Persia at a time when the United States had no economic or military interests in the area whatsoever. No formal diplomatic relations between the two countries had been established, and oil had not yet been discovered in the region. There were no official representatives of either country present at the other, and America often relied on European allies, most notably Britain, to represent its interests in Persia. Persia simply did not present any strategic interests to America, and as such, the nature of American engagement under the umbrella of the American missionaries was neither political nor economic.

Perkins and Grant and the American missionaries that followed them in later years had come to serve the needs of the local Assyrian Christian population by providing medical, religious, and educational services. These services were also extended to non-Christians. During the eight decades following the commencement of the Urumia mission activities in 1835, the accomplishments of the Mission, in terms of the number of people it touched and the scale of services provided, are simply impressive. By 1836, the Urumia School for Boys (also referred to as the "College for Boys") was established. By 1838, a boarding school for girls, later named the Fiske Seminary, became operational. The Lancastrian teaching method used by the Urumia mission station was an innovation never seen before in Persia. It allowed the scaling up of educational services in the Urumia region so that each student would be able to become a teacher of the future, thereby enabling exponential growth in instructional capacity in the education system introduced by the missionaries.

By the end of the nineteenth century, the education system organized and managed by the Urumia mission consisted of nearly one hundred schools in the city of Urumia and the Assyrian villages in the Urumia plain.[4] In 1839 the Mission's printing press began operating in the city of Urumia. It was the first of its kind and provided for the

---

[4] Consult Ameer (1997), *Yankees and Nestorians,* for a detailed analysis and history of the accomplishments of the Urumia mission station on educational initiatives.

production of educational material on a scale that could not have been produced through any other means available at that time. In 1880 the Westminster Hospital of Urumia, modeled after American hospital systems, was built and became the very first modern hospital and medical college in all of Persia.

Understanding the nature of the initial encounters between Americans and Persians in the nineteenth century is important, not only as an academic historical inquiry, but also for achieving practical clarity regarding today's state of affairs. These encounters, which began with the arrival of Perkins and Grant in Urumia in 1835, came to a halt in 1918 due to the atrocities of the First World War and the Ottoman occupation of Urumia. However, during these eight decades, dozens of Americans served in Urumia, forming and raising their own families. Their children, born in Urumia, continued the tradition, many serving as missionaries in Urumia and elsewhere in Persia. This unique community of Americans created a multi-generational legacy of America's early presence in Persia, which is worthy of recognition, remembrance, and critical analysis.

Urumia Mission Station Missionaries and Family Members in 1904

References and Related Readings

Ameer, John Pierre (1997). *Yankees and Nestorians: The Establishment of American Schools Among the Nestorians of Iran and Turkey, 1834-1850.* (Doctoral Dissertation). Harvard University.

Armajani, Yahya and Thomas M. Ricks (1986). *Middle East: Past and Present.* Englewood Cliffs, NJ: Prentice-Hall.

Daniel, Elton L (2012). *The History of Iran.* Santa Barbara: Greenwood.

Elder, John (1960). *History of the American Presbyterian Mission to Iran: 1834-1960.* Literature Committee of the Church Council of Iran.

Guilak, Hooshang (2011) *Fire Beneath the Ashes: The United States and Iran: A Historical Perspective 1829-1947.* Xlibris Publishing

Kinzer, Stephen (2010). *Reset: Iran, Turkey and America's Future.* New York: Henry Holt and Company.

Malick, David G. (2008). *The American Mission Press: A Preliminary Bibliography.* ATOUR Publications.

Perkins, Justin (1861). *Missionary Life in Persia: Glimpses of a Quarter of a Century of Labors Among the Nestorian Christians.* Boston: American Tract Society.

Perkins, Justin (1843). *A Residence of Eight Years in Persia Among the Nestorian Christians.* Andover: Allen, Morrill & Wardell.

Chapter 2

DEVELOPMENT OF WESTERN AWARENESS OF THE ASSYRIAN CHRISTIANS

In the early 1800s, America's evangelical ambitions in the Middle East were formed under the guidance of the American Board of Commissioners for Foreign Missions (ABCFM). The ABCFM began as a joint effort by Presbyterian, Congregationalist, and Dutch Reformed denominations in the United States.[5] Its goal in Persia was to set up a mission station to serve the religious, educational, and medical needs of the Assyrian Christian population (also referred to as "Nestorian" Christians) of northwestern Persia. The Mission was referred to as the "Mission to the Nestorians."[6]

---

[5] The Dutch Reformed denomination discontinued its association with the ABCFM in 1857 since the Reformed church believed it could independently train missionaries and raise the needed funds on its own (see Herman Harmelink' research: "The Ecumenical Relations of the Reformed Church in America," *Journal of Presbyterian History*, 1967, Vol. 45, No. 2, pp. 71-94.). The Presbyterians and Congregationalists divided the mission field in December of 1870, with the Presbyterians, under the Board of Foreign Missions of the Presbyterian Church in the United States of America, taking responsibility for Persia, and the Congregationalists leading the ABCFM's efforts in Ottoman territories.

[6] The term "Nestorian" is what Assyrian Christians were initially referred to by the early American missionaries. Depending on the context and time period being

The world's awareness about the very existence of this unique population of Christians was limited at that time, and it grew primarily due to the work of a handful of Westerners conducting archeological and military intelligence work in the area of ancient Mesopotamia (modern-day northern Iraq). This population, which resided in the remote mountainous areas of a region covering what is now western Iran, eastern Turkey, and northern Iraq, was unknown to the Western world until the early part of the nineteenth century.

An Assyrian (Nestorian) Family in the Kurdish Mountains (c. 1890s)

Claudius James Rich's Encounters with Mountain Nestorians

The Western world's initial realization of the presence of a population of Assyrian Christians in the Kurdish mountains of Persia and Turkey was triggered during archeological excavations being conducted by the British in the Ottoman territories near Persia in the early years of the nineteenth century. Claudius James Rich, a British linguist who specialized in Oriental languages, was working for the British East India Company as an intelligence officer in the area of the ancient city

---

discussed, "Nestorian" and "Assyrian" will be used interchangeably, though the latter is the preferred form in this book.

of Nineveh. In his fieldwork, Rich began to recognize ancient artifacts in the fields where he was operating. He began to collect his finds and conducted archeological excavation work of his own. This led to the uncovering of the remains of ancient civilizations, some of which had been mentioned in Biblical texts.

Rich's excavation work had two effects. First, the artifacts which he had uncovered energized the Christian world by reviving Biblical stories, for which, prior to that time, no archeological evidence had been found. His discoveries helped strengthen long-held religious beliefs regarding civilizations inhabiting Babylonia and Mesopotamia in the centuries preceding Christianity's rise. Second, in the course of his archeological activities, Rich came into contact with a previously unknown population of Christians, who at that time resided in remote mountainous villages, unnoticed to most of the world.

An Assyrian (Nestorian) Village in the Highlands of the Kurdish Mountains (c. 1890s)

Being a trained linguist and skilled in an array of Oriental languages, including Arabic, Turkish, Persian, Aramaic, and Hebrew, Rich correctly noted that the language spoken by these Christians was Aramaic — the same language spoken by Jesus and the apostles. Rich's descriptions of the discoveries were compiled in a book titled *Memoir on the Ruins of Babylon*, which was published in 1811. It primarily received attention among British scholars of the time. Americans were, for the most part, unaware of Rich's work. However, his work triggered interest among a small number of British intellectuals about the unique population of Christians which he had encountered in the highlands. The fact that for centuries these Christians had been hidden from the view of the Western world deserved closer attention among those interested in the history of Christianity. Some believed them to be the Lost Tribes of Israel. After his death in 1821, Rich's journals were published under the title *Narrative of a Residence in Koordistan and the Site of Ancient Nineveh* (published in 1836).

The Smith and Dwight Expedition and the Merrick Inquiry

Claudius Rich's archeological finds, his discovery of Nestorian (Assyrian) Christians, and his observation regarding the linguistic connections between their spoken language and the language spoken by Jesus remained unnoticed by the American Christian community for several years. However, it attracted the attention of the British serving in the Ottoman Empire. In 1826, the chaplain of the British embassy in Constantinople (modern-day Istanbul), Reverend Robert Walsh, published his notes, gathered from personal observations and second-hand accounts, regarding the existence of ancient Christian sects in the lands on both sides of the Tigris river. In this article, published in the *Missionary Herald* (a periodical of the American Board of Commissioners for Foreign Missions), Walsh highlighted the urgency "that American missionaries in Syria will ere long to be able to obtain more certain and full information respecting the condition and character of this people."[7]

Due to Walsh's writing and his persuasion of his fellow American clergy, the Nestorian Christian population was brought to the attention of the ABCFM. In the spring of 1830, two ABCFM missionaries, Eli Smith and Henry Dwight, were commissioned by the ABCFM to conduct a feasibility study of the region for setting up ABCFM mission stations.[8] Their expedition covered Syria, Armenia, Asia Minor, and

---

[7] *Missionary Herald* (1826), p. 120.

[8] For a summary of Smith and Dwight's explorations, consult *Looking for the Armenians: Eli Smith's Missionary Adventure, 1830-1831* by Margaret R. Leavy.

Persia, and was subsequently compiled as a study with the title: *Missionary Researches in Armenia*. During their travels, Smith and Dwight visited the Urumia region, but they had to forgo visiting the city of Urumia for fear of the plague. Instead, they visited the various villages in the surrounding Urumia plain for a total of nine days.

Despite the shortness of their visit, and their inability to enter the city of Urumia, they found the Urumia region to be of prime potential for the ABCFM. The reason was the large number of Nestorian Christians in this region, which Smith and Dwight felt were in need of revival through religious instruction, literacy initiatives, and medical services. They found that the Nestorians with whom they spoke were highly receptive to such forms of assistance from the Americans. The Nestorians' welcoming response created a positive impression on the two American missionaries.

Smith and Dwight concluded that among all the Christian populations in Turkey, Armenia, and Persia that they had visited, the Nestorians of the Urumia region would be the most promising recipients for ABCFM assistance. They recommended that a mission field be centered in the city of Urumia, despite not having been able to enter the city during their short visit. In his report to the ABCFM, Eli Smith stated that: "I never felt a stronger desire to settle at once as a missionary among any people I have ever seen."[9] The expedition by Eli Smith and Henry Dwight identified the Urumia region as the prime location for setting up an ABCFM mission station. This was due to the strategic and geographic advantages related to Urumia, as well as the openness and receptivity that Smith and Dwight felt among the Nestorians of the Urumia plain.

A second inquiry was commissioned by the ABCFM in 1834 to explore the prospects of missionary and evangelical work among Moslems in Persia. This inquiry was to investigate the possibility for their conversion to Christianity. The expedition was led by another American missionary, James Lyman Merrick, who was accompanied by two German missionaries as they visited Persia's major population centers such as Shiraz, Isfahan, and Tehran. Merrick and his companions found the Moslems of Persia unreceptive to Christian evangelism. This was a realization that was further reinforced by the

---

[9] Smith (1833), *Researches in Armenia*, Vol. II, p. 253.

fact that the three missionaries' lives were endangered multiple times during the course of their travels. Writing while he was in Isfahan and reflecting on his experience, Merrick concluded: "At Tehran the prospect of missionary labor was but faint star light, here at Isfahan it is clouded midnight."[10] With the unfavorable assessment given by Merrick regarding setting up mission operations in Persia's major population centers and the contrastingly favorable assessment of Smith and Dwight regarding Urumia, the determination of the ABCFM to focus on Urumia was further strengthened.

Archeological Work by Layard and Botta

Interest in Christian missionary work was further fueled by a growing volume of archeological finds in the area of Mosul, in what is now northern Iraq. In the 1840s archeological excavations by the British archeologist Austen Henry Layard and French diplomat Paul-Émile Botta in this area uncovered the remains of the ancient Assyrian capital of Nineveh. The excavation work of Layard, which also brought him in contact with Nestorians who lived in the area at the time of his excavations, helped him recognize the historical significance of these people. He wrote that Nestorians "are indeed as much the remains of Nineveh and Assyria, as the rude heaps and ruined palaces."[11] The archeological discoveries of Botta and Layard created greater desire by European nations to understand and explore this region.

For the American missionaries, these discoveries were significant as they were further reinforced by their own discovery of artifacts in the Mosul region by Asahel Grant. In the early-1840s, Grant had personal encounters with Layard and Botta, who showed him some of their archeological finds. On his journeys through the mountain ranges north of Mosul, Grant had also identified and documented artifacts and ancient structures which he had come across.[12]

The Europeans' grand motivation in Mesopotamia was to gain presence in this region of the world and uncover archeological treasures, most of which were eventually transported and housed in

---

[10] Elder (1960), *History of the American Presbyterian Mission to Iran*, p. 6.
[11] Layard (1867), *Nineveh and its Remains*, Volume I, p. 5.
[12] Laurie (1856), *Dr. Grant and the Mountain Nestorians*, p. 210.

Western museums. In contrast to this materialistic motivation, a spiritual motivation triggered by these discoveries was the validation of Biblical stories and the discovery of ancient civilizations whose descendants, having converted to Christianity centuries earlier, still lived in the area. As such, the desire to develop relations with people of this ancient civilization involved several Western countries, including America, Britain, France, Switzerland, and Germany.[13]

The Legend of Henry Martyn

It is important to note that American interest in establishing a mission station in Persia was also attributed to a British named Henry Martyn. Martyn was an Anglican priest, who became a chaplain for the British East India Company in 1806. He was assigned to ministerial duties for British soldiers based in India. Similar to Claudius Rich, Henry Martyn had linguistic aspirations, and in his case, he took on the task of translating the New Testament into Farsi (the common language of most Persians) and Urdu. While in India, he produced his Urdu translation and the first draft of his Farsi translation of the New Testament. In 1811 he traveled to Persia to refine and complete his Farsi translation with the help of a native Farsi speaker. His work stands out since his translation is the very first case of the New Testament being made accessible to Persians in their own language. The written exposure of Persians to Christian theology was made possible through Henry Martyn's work.

Henry Martyn was notable for his persistence in presenting Christianity's messages to the governing class and Moslem clergy in the major Persian cities he visited. These included Shiraz, Isfahan, and Tabriz. Although there was much resistance to his efforts and he was not well received in Persia, his persistence, in light of his failing health and weak physique, was exemplary to many in the American missionary community. One notable follower was Justin Perkins, the very first missionary assigned to Persia by the ABCFM, as noted earlier. Perkins not only mentioned Henry Martyn as a source of personal inspiration for his own missionary work, but also named one of his children after Henry Martyn.

---

[13] Yeselson (1956), *United States-Persian Diplomatic Relations: 1883-1921*, p. 7.

In his second book published in 1861, Perkins mentioned an encounter which he had with a Chaldean bishop in the Salmas district (approximately 100 miles north of Urumia) in 1858, who had met Henry Martyn.[14] The bishop provided Perkins with a personal account of the time he and Martyn had spent together in the Salmas area. Furthermore, Smith and Dwight, in their travel through Tabriz in 1830, met a British physician who had treated Henry Martyn nearly a decade earlier, while Martyn was on his way from Persia to Turkey. The doctor had told Smith and Dwight that Martyn was suffering from malaria-like symptoms at the time of his departure from Tabriz. Henry Martyn subsequently died due to illness in northeastern Turkey. Interestingly, the second American missionary to arrive in Persia and join Justin Perkins, Asahel Grant, had similar sentiments towards Henry Martyn. Grant mentioned Henry Martyn as his inspiration in his ABCFM missionary application papers, and eventually, he, too, named one of his sons Henry Martyn.[15]

References and Related Readings

Ainsworth, William F. (1842). *Travels and Researches in Asia Minor, Mesopotamia, Chaldea, and Armenia* (Vol I & II). London: John W. Parker.

Ameer, John Pierre (1997). *Yankees and Nestorians: The Establishment of American Schools Among the Nestorians of Iran and Turkey, 1834-1850.* (Doctoral Dissertation). Harvard University.

Elder, John (1960). *History of the American Presbyterian Mission to Iran: 1834-1960.* Literature Committee of the Church Council of Iran.

Emhardt, William and George M. Lamsa (1926). *The Oldest Christian People.* Eugene: Wipf & Stock.

Harmelink, Herman (1967). "The Ecumenical Relations of the Reformed Church in America," *Journal of Presbyterian History,* Vol. 45, No. 2, pp. 71-94

Karimi, Linda C. (1975). *Implications of American Missionary Presences in 19th and 20th Century Iran. Masters Dissertation.* Portland State University.

---

[14] Perkins (1861), *Missionary Life in Persia*, footnote on p. 187.
[15] Laurie (1853), *Dr. Grant and the Mountain Nestorians*, p. 27.

Laurie, Thomas (1853). *Dr. Grant and the Mountain Nestorians*. Boston: Gould and Lincoln.

Layard, Austen (1867). *Nineveh and its Remains*. London: John Murray.

Leavy, Margaret R. (1992). *Looking for the Armenians: Eli Smith's Adventure, 1830-1831*. New Haven: The Connecticut Academy of Arts and Sciences.

Malick, David G. (2008). *The American Mission Press: A Preliminary Bibliography*. ATOUR Publications.

Missionary Herald (1826). "Christians Called Chaldeans," pp. 120-121.

Perkins, Justin (1861). *Missionary Life in Persia: Glimpses of a Quarter of a Century of Labors Among the Nestorian Christians*. Boston: American Tract Society.

Rich, Claudius J. (1836). *Narrative of a Residence in Koordistan, and on the Site of Ancient Nineveh*. London: James Duncan.

Smith, Eli (1833). *Researches of the Rev. E. Smith and Rev. H.G.O. Dwight in Armenia: Including a Journey Through Asia Minor, and into Georgia and Persia, with a Visit to the Nestorian and Chaldean Christians*. Boston: Crocker and Brewster.

Stewart, John (1928). *Nestorian Missionary Enterprise: The Story of a Church on Fire*. Edinburgh: T.&T. Clark.

Yeselson, Abraham (1956). *United States-Persian Diplomatic Relations: 1883-1921*. New Brunswick: Rutgers University Press.

Chapter 3

THE NESTORIANS

The term "Nestorian" refers to a unique Christian minority that in the 1800s resided primarily in the mountains and plains overlapping modern-day northwestern Iran, eastern Turkey, northern Iraq and northeastern Syria. This population was much larger centuries ago and thinned down considerably in numbers due to genocide and mass migration following the atrocities of the First World War. Nestorian Christians also resided in southwestern India and were present in northern China centuries earlier.

The appellations "Nestorian," "Assyrian," and "Syrian" have been used by various authors to refer to this unique group of Christians, who were followers of Nestorius, the bishop of Constantinople in the fifth century AD. Nestorian Christians have historically preferred to be called "Assyrian" Christians or "Syrian" Christians, rather than "Nestorian", since there was a stigma associated with Nestorianism conflicting with the Church of Rome in some of its theological foundations. Note that "Syrian" is simply an expressed abbreviation for "Assyrian" and not a reflection of the population being associated with Syria.[16] Depending on the time period, one appellation or the other was more prevalent among the American missionaries, and in this book, all three will be used at various points, depending on the time period and

---

[16] Consult Joseph (1961), pp. 3-21 for the complexities surrounding the various appellations. The term "Assyrian" became more widely used starting from the 1880s, partially due to its frequent use by the Archbishop of Canterbury (Gaunt 2006, p. 16).

the norms of communications used in the missionary writings at that time.[17]

The Fall of the Assyrian Empire

The interchangeability of "Nestorian" and "Assyrian" from a historical point of view relates to the history and eventual downfall of the Assyrian Empire, and the resulting geographic resettlement of the population of Assyria prior to the rise of Christianity. When the Assyrian Empire collapsed in 610 BC, the leading figures of the empire, including royalty, priests, warriors, and the wealthy, escaped to the Kurdish mountains. These mountains, which had originally served as their summer resorts to escape the heat of the Nineveh Desert, became their permanent refuge in times of hostility.[18]

The Kurdish Mountains (from Wigram & Wigram's *The Cradle of Mankind,* 1911)

---

[17] Whenever possible, "Assyrian" rather than "Nestorian" will be used in this book to respect the norms and preferences of modern times.
[18] Emhardt and Lamsa (1926), *The Oldest Christian People,* p. 20.

In the highlands of the Kurdish mountains, these Assyrians were able to escape the treacheries of persecution, war, and invasion attempts by the Roman and Persian armies, who, in addition to their attacks on the Assyrians, were also in battle with each other. The high elevation and rough terrain of the Kurdish mountains made them practically impenetrable for large invading armies. For centuries, the Assyrian population that settled in the Kurdish mountains found peace in these secluded regions of the world.

The Rise of Eastern Christianity

In the year 66 AD, a Jewish rebellion in Jerusalem against their Roman rulers broke out. The rebellion was crushed by the Romans. Members of the newly formed Jewish Christian Church fled eastward to the city of Pella in the upper Jordan valley.[19] There, they were able to continue practicing their faith, developing it into the earliest form of Christianity. Beyond the eastern borders of the Roman Empire, Christianity found followers in the Persian Empire, giving rise to the Eastern form of Christianity. Although the early Christians continued their work to grow the base of the faith, Christianity was a religion that was harshly persecuted for over two centuries within the boundaries of the Roman Empire.

However, to the east of the Roman Empire, Christianity was being proselytized in Persia as early as 100 AD. At that time, the dominant religion in Persia was Zoroastrianism. Christianity was tolerated in Persia, and by 225 AD, the foothold of Christianity in Persia extended from the Kurdish mountains to the Persian Gulf. Many Persian Christians at that time were converts from Zoroastrianism or children of converts.[20] Their presence was welcomed by Persian rulers since Christians were at that time being persecuted by the Romans, and shared with the Persians their adversarial position toward Rome.

Although the Persians were initially receptive toward Christians due to their anti-Roman views, their receptivity declined with the Christianization of Rome. Persian authorities became concerned that Persia's Christian subjects may feel greater loyalty toward Rome. This

---

[19] Diarmaid MacCulloch (2011), *Christianity: The First Three Thousand Years,* p. 106.
[20] Stewart (1928), *Nestorian Missionary Enterprise,* p. 5.

became a pressing concern when in 324 AD, the Roman emperor Constantine declared Christianity as the formal state religion of the empire. The Christianization of the Roman Empire led to growing Persian suspicions about the Christians residing in Persian territories. It resulted in the persecution of the Persian Christian population, and in some cases the complete displacement of Christian societies. The peak of these persecutions took place under the rule of the Persian king Shapor II around 350 AD. Persia's Christians had to take refuge in the secluded mountainous regions of Kurdistan to avoid persecution. Despite the difficulties arising from their displacement, they grew the base of Christianity among the Assyrians who had moved to the highlands of the Kurdish mountains centuries earlier, desiring in similar ways to escape persecution by the Persians and the Romans.

Given the long history of hostilities between the Persians and Romans, it became necessary for Persian Christians to distinguish their faith from the Roman form of Christianity. This was a necessity in order to prevent further persecution by Persian rulers. Creating a distinction also helped crystalize and define the boundaries of what is referred to as the "Church of the East", with the term "East" being in reference to the relative geographic location of its followers in relation to the eastern boundaries of the Roman Empire. As such, "Church of the East" initially referred to the followers of Christianity within the Persian Empire.

Although the geographic identification of the Church of the East was within Persia, and although the Roman and Persian Empires were adversaries, the Church of the East and the Roman Church co-governed until the second half of the 5th century. This was done through councils of bishops, which deliberated on church governance matters. However, the theological views of the bishops in the east were considerably different from those of Rome on some of the most fundamental aspects of the faith. Co-governance proved to be a challenge.

Eastern Christians were considerably independent of Rome in their theological views and religious practices. The unification of Christianity between population centers in the east and those within the Roman Empire was difficult due to the fact that the Persian and Roman Empires were in constant conflict. Furthermore, there were significant physical distances separating Eastern and Roman Christians due to the uninhabitable lands separating their population centers, such as the

Syrian Desert. The geography of the region made travel and regular contact between the two Christian worlds difficult.

However, the most significant gap between Eastern and Roman Christianity was not geographic but theological. As Emhardt and Lamsa argue: "In the West, Christianity had to face many natural difficulties growing out of the proneness of the Greek mind to philosophical analysis, and the jealousy felt by the Romans to any claim that did not conform to their program of imperialism or lend itself to legalistic codification."[21] As such, the traditions and theological views of Christianity developed in the four centuries following its rise were notably different in the eastern portions of the Roman Empire, compared to those in the western parts of the empire.

Nestorius

It was during the 5th century AD that the separation between east and west and the need for clarifying the theological distinctions of the Church of the East from those of the Church of Rome became clear. The need for articulating the theological differences was due to growing hostilities between bishops in eastern parts of the Roman Empire and those to the west. In 428 AD, Nestorius, a Greek-born graduate of the Theological School of Antioch, became the bishop of the Roman Church in Constantinople. He was a highly accomplished Christian scholar and teacher. Despite his high standing as a bishop, Nestorius raised questions about some of the most fundamental views of Roman Christianity.

Nestorius questioned the theological grounds of what was being taught in other population centers in the Roman Empire, especially as it related to the teachings of Cyril, the bishop of Alexandria. The two men simply did not see eye-to-eye. Their differences had deep historical roots in Christian theology. As Emhardt and Lamsa point out:

> There is no doubt that the basic principles of Nestorius' teachings were taken from the works of Diodore of Tarsus and Theodore of Mopsuestia. Both were great theologians and teachers in the school of Antioch, which openly opposed the allegorical and theoretical teaching of Alexandria.

---

[21] Emhardt and Lamsa (1926), *The Oldest Christian People,* p.39.

Consequently, such statements as 'Mary is the Mother of God' were too confusing for acceptance by the Antiochian theologians who followed the Syrian tradition. Such utterances, when translated into Syriac, define the Person of Christ weakly. The Syriac word for Son is 'Bar,' derived from the word 'Bara,' meaning to create. When therefore, God was said to be son of Mary, the Christian doctrine of the deity appeared to be reduced to the level of a mere form of Paganism. Nestorius said, 'I cannot speak of a God being two or three months old.' In his letter to Pope Celestine, Bishop of Rome, he said, 'If the Godhead of the Son had its origin in the womb of the Virgin, then it was not a Godhead like that of the Father, and He who was born could not be homoousios with the Father, which was just what the Arians denied Him to be.' They said that if God was born, then there was a time when He did not exist.[22]

As Emhardt and Lamsa noted above, these views were not uniquely attributed to Nestorius and had been expressed by other Christian theologians, some of whom were his own teachers. However, due to his newly gained status as the bishop of Constantinople, Nestorius was more clearly heard by the public. His words resulted in theological divisions and conflicts among bishops in various cities within the Roman Empire. This earned him the attention of the Church of Rome, causing great concern. Having raised the above challenges about traditional theological positions of Roman Christianity, Nestorius was called upon to defend himself in the Council of Chalcedon, attended by bishops of all the major cities where Christianity was practiced. The Council condemned Nestorius, and he was deposed and exiled to Egypt, where he died.

The decision by the Council of Chalcedon to condemn and exile Nestorius was viewed as unacceptable by eastern bishops. This was the breaking point whereby the Church of the East became a theologically and politically distinct entity from the Church of Rome. In 484 AD, the Church of the East adopted Nestorian's doctrines and formally separated itself from the Roman Church. Over the next century, the followers of Nestorius became known as "Nestorian Christians." They were shunned and persecuted by Rome and Roman Christians.[23] They

---

[22] Ibid., pp. 51-52.

[23] This is one reason why, at the time of the arrival of the American missionaries in Persia, the Assyrians preferred not to be addressed as Nestorian.

eventually had to migrate eastward to Persia. Given that their religion was no longer affiliated with the Roman Empire and in fact conflicted on certain theological grounds with the Roman version of Christianity, Persia was a natural place for them to resettle.

The Kurdish mountains, where many of their fellow Persian Christians had already settled alongside the Assyrians who had settled there centuries earlier, is where the followers of Nestorius migrated to. Over time, the Kurdish mountains began to hold a large population of Nestorian Christians due to the migration of Christians from the Roman Empire and the conversion of the local Assyrian population to Nestorian Christianity. As evident from the above, strictly speaking from a chronological perspective, the Church of the East preceded Nestorian Christianity. However, due to their shared geography, similarity in beliefs, and the eventual adoption of Nestorian principles by the Church of the East, the two became so closely associated that they are, for most practical purposes, treated synonymously today.

The Christian influence on the Assyrian population residing in the Kurdish mountains accounted for the indigenous growth of Christianity in Persia at that time. This influence grew following the migration of the followers of Nestorius to the area and the formal adoption of Nestorian principles by the Church of the East. The geographic congregation of these population groups explains the modern-day interchangeable nature of "Nestorian" and "Assyrian" (and its shortened version "Syrian") when referring to this unique Christian minority. The migration of Eastern Christians to the mountains instead of the open plains was largely for defensive reasons, as the high elevations and the rough terrain prevented invaders from reaching them. Their settlements in high elevations made them difficult to reach, thereby protecting them from persecution — the very reason that the Assyrians had also escaped to the same area centuries earlier.

With the formal adoption of Nestorian principles by the Church of the East, the prospects of Persian Christians being persecuted by their Persian rulers diminished. In their mountain settlements, Nestorian Christians prospered as a population. They were able to practice their faith while maintaining a sustainable existence. One of the most remarkable aspects of this time period was the Nestorians' own zeal for missionary work. The range of their evangelical efforts took Nestorian missionaries as far east as China, Siberia, India, and Afghanistan, and west to Cyprus and Egypt.[24]

The Rise of Islam

The arrival of Islam in Persia in the seventh century was not an impediment to Nestorian Christians. As Islam advanced in Persia, where the dominant religion was Zoroastrianism, it found itself an ally in Persia's Christians. This is because in expanding into Persia, Islam was replacing Zoroastrianism, with which Persian Christians had drastic differences. At certain points in time, Christians in Persia had been persecuted by orders of Zoroastrian high priests, resulting in the Christian flight into the highlands. It has been suggested that the Prophet Mohammad's early exposures to Christianity, before the proclamation of Islam as a religion, was through indirect contacts with Eastern Christians. [25] As such, Christianity was recognized and viewed with respect by the Prophet Mohammad.

Under Islam, by the words of the Prophet Mohammad, Christians and Jews were to be protected subjects. Under these rules of protection, they could choose to become Moslems or to remain of their own faith. If they decided to remain of their own faith, they could continue to practice their religion and enjoy a degree of autonomy, as long as they paid a protection tax ("jizya"). The formal expression of how non-Moslems would live under Moslem rule became clearer in 717 AD, under the rule of the Umayyad caliph, Umar II (Umar ibn Abd al-Aziz) and is referred to as the Pact of Umar. It spelled out a set of conditions that non-Muslims had to follow in Islamic-ruled lands.[26] With respect to appearance in public, the Pact described matters such as how non-Muslims should dress, travel, and build their homes, and forbade them from bearing weapons. With respect to the justice system, the Pact addressed issues such as property rights for non-Moslems and how disputes between non-Moslems and Moslems were to be settled. It also forbade proselytization efforts by non-Moslems to attempt to convert Moslems, and forbade the building and repair of houses of worship. Regarding the value of non-Moslem lives in an Islamic society, the

---

[24] Emhardt and Lamsa (1926), *The Oldest Christian People*, p. 65.

[25] Shedd (1904), *Islam and the Oriental Churches*.

[26] Davidson (1956), *The Hatt-i-Humayn of 1856 and the Climate of its Reception*.

Pact placed the physical protection of non-Moslems under Moslem control and provided guarantees as long as non-Moslem subjects strictly abided by the principles set forth by the Pact of Umar.

The Mongols

The fate of Eastern Christians was bound to change as Mongol rulers replaced Abbasid Moslem rulers and changed the conditions in which Nestorian Christians lived under their rule.[27] While Christians were not ill-treated in the early parts of Mongol rule, the prospects for Christians in all Mongol occupied lands diminished in the later parts of the Mongol era, especially under the rule of Tamerlane.

Nestorians found a need to retreat back into the Kurdish highlands, where the vicious and violent forces of Mongol armies could be avoided. As such, from the 15th century until the early part of the 19th century, when they were rediscovered by Westerners, Nestorian Christians retained an existence in the elevations of the Kurdish mountains, where they kept out of sight of the entire world.

Nestorian Demographics

Reflecting back on the days of his arrival in Urumia, Justin Perkins described the Nestorians as such:

> The Nestorians of Oroomiah, which is a part of ancient Media, situated in the north-western province of modern Persia, to whom our labors have hitherto been primarily directed, are simple-hearted peasants, humble in their worldly circumstances, being subject to Mohammedan rulers, by whom they are more or less borne down, though they naturally possess high, independent feelings, and are restless under their oppression. Those dwelling in the adjacent, rough Koordish mountains, which are part of ancient Assyria, are a wild, rude people, leading a more precarious life, mostly with their flocks, being

---

[27] During the early decades of the Mongol conquests, the Mongols were not Moslems and therefore did not follow the guidance provided through Islamic principles and the Pact of Umar with respect to the protection of Christians.

less subject to systematic exaction; but until lately, in constant apprehension and danger of being overrun and sacked by their more numerous and powerful neighbors, the Koords, except the inhabitants of two or three almost inconceivably rough mountain districts, who, by the aid of the rocky ramparts that surround them, and their muskets and daggers, which they always wear or keep near them, maintained a kind of desperate independence of the marauding Koordish chiefs, who in turn had long resisted the control of the Turkish government.[28]

As may be evident from Perkins' description, at the time of his arrival, the Nestorians seemed to have peaceful but uneasy relations with their Kurdish neighbors in the mountains.[29] They were also confined with restrictions affecting non-Moslems residing under Moslem rule, as one would expect from the conditions set forth by the Pact of Umar. The tensions between the Nestorians and the Kurds, and the Nestorians' challenges in elevating their social and economic status were evident in the very first observations made by Perkins. These challenges would continue to characterize the nature of the tense relationships between the Nestorians and their neighbors for decades after Perkins' writing.[30]

The geographic distribution of the Nestorian population at the time of the arrival of the missionaries was in three distinct regions.[31] One group was located in the plains of Urumia and the Salmas district (to the north of Urumia) in northwestern Persia, in what is now the West Azerbaijan province of Iran.

---

[28] Perkins (1861), *Missionary Life in Persia,* pp. 35-36.

[29] Note also the varied spelling of "Kurdish" used by Perkins.

[30] It is important to recognize that Perkins' view of the Kurds (or as he spells it, "Koords") was from the perspective of the Nestorians who were, for the most part, neighborly yet tense in their interactions with the Kurds. The views of the Kurds, as an ethnic minority seeking its own identity and independence, especially within the Ottoman Empire in the nineteenth century, were not the focus of the missionaries. The Nestorians and the American missionaries in Urumia were however, greatly affected by forces of Kurdish nationalism, which is an important topic researched by Orientalists and will be discussed later in this book. It would be difficult to fully comprehend the dynamics of American missionary work in Urumia without recognizing the impact of Kurdish nationalist aspirations affecting the Ottoman Empire and the neighboring areas of Persia.

[31] Joseph (1961), *Nestorians and their Muslim Neighbors,* p. 23.

The second group consisted of Nestorians living in the Persian mountains to the west of Urumia and in the Hakkari mountains of Turkey, beyond Persia's western border. Despite the large size of this population group, it was a relatively unknown group to the Western world. As described in the earlier passage by Perkins, the mountain Nestorians were rough and primitive, compared to the Nestorians of the city of Urumia. The locations where the Nestorians of the Turkish Hakkari mountains lived were situated in high elevations, out of reach, and were generally dangerous for travel. Furthermore, tribal conflicts and lawlessness in the area made it especially dangerous to visit the mountain Nestorians of Turkey. However, despite the majority of the mountain Nestorian population residing in Turkey rather than in Persia, this population was important to the American missionaries in Urumia, as the Nestorian patriarch resided among the mountain Nestorians of Turkey.

A Nestorian Mountain Village
(c. 1890s; note the missionaries' triangular tent set up on top of the first house)

The third population group of Nestorian Christians resided to the south of the Hakkari mountains, in the plains of Mosul (which is now part of Iraq). The mountain Nestorians and those living in and around Mosul were living within Ottoman territory and therefore outside of the official scope of the Urumia Mission.[32] Mosul had a diverse population with a great deal of ethnic and religious representation (various Christian denominations, Jews, Moslems, Yazidis, and Zoroastrians), and a rich history matched with comparable archeological treasures. As such, it was of great attraction to Western explorers in the nineteenth century.

It is important to point out that within the three areas, described above, where the Nestorians lived, other Christian populations were also present. These included Armenian Christians, who resided mostly to the north of the Hakkari region, and Chaldean Christians who were present in all three regions and consisted of Nestorians who generations ago had converted from Nestorianism to Catholicism.[33]

Population estimates of Nestorians vary by source and time. Perkins (1843, pp. 8-11) estimated that at the time of his arrival to the Urumia area, there were approximately 150,000 Nestorians living in the Ottoman territories, and about 30,000-40,000 lived in the Persian territories. Within the city of Urumia, for which he estimated a population of 25,000 inhabitants (of all religions), he believed that there were about 600 Nestorians and 2,000 Jews. These estimates are impossible to confirm, since census systems were not in place in Persia or the Ottoman Empire at that time.

Over time, the size of the Nestorian population declined due to regional and world conflicts. Stewart (1928) estimated that at the time of the start of the First World War, somewhere between 100,000 to 200,000 Nestorians lived in the Ottoman Empire and Persia. He estimated that this figure had dropped to only 40,000 in the decade following the war, due to genocide, famine, disease, war casualties, and the mass flight of Nestorians from the area to avoid violence and persecution.

---

[32] In later years, some of the American missionaries from Urumia traveled to these areas and served in this region, despite the fact that it was not part of Persia.

[33] Readers are encouraged to examine *Mosul and its Minorities* by H.C. Luke for a detailed account of the diversity of religious and ethnic groups residing in Mosul.

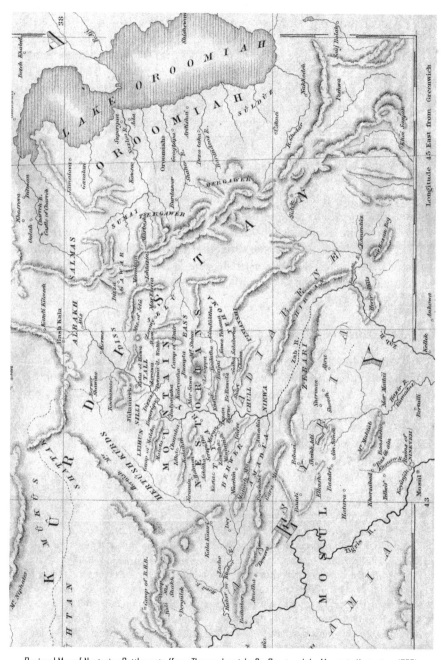

Regional Map of Nestorian Settlements (from Thomas Laurie's *Dr. Grant and the Mountain Nestorians*, 1853)

Ameer provides similar overall estimates and suggests that at the start of WWI, the size of the Nestorian Christian population living in the Turkish mountains was approximately 105,000, and the number of those living in the plains of Mosul was around 5,500.[34] The size of the population of the Nestorians in the Urumia plain (including the city of Urumia) at that time was estimated by Ameer to be about 30,000 — a figure close to what Perkins had estimated upon his arrival to Urumia in 1835.

Emhardt and Lamsa estimated that only about 15,000 of the pre-WWI Nestorian inhabitants of the Urumia plain returned to this area in the years immediately following the war.[35] Many had permanently relocated to other population centers in Persia, such as Tabriz, Hamadan, and Kermanshah, and large numbers had perished during WWI. Others had fled Persia altogether and were stationed in refugee camps established by the British in the Mosul region, and some eventually immigrated to the United States and Britain.

The Nestorian Ecclesiastical Organization

In terms of the ecclesiastical system of the Nestorians, at the very head of the church is the Nestorian patriarch. The patriarch is commonly referred to as "Mar Shimon" ("Mar" being a title of respect in the Syriac language meaning "my lord", and "Shimon" meaning Simon; Mar Shimon meaning "Lord Simon").[36] The hierarchy of the system started with Mar Shimon at the very top, followed by (in descending order of significance): metropolitans, bishops, archdeacons, priests, and deacons.[37] At the time of the commencement of the Urumia mission,

---

[34] Ameer (2008), *Assyrians in Yonkers,* pp. 78-79.

[35] Emhardt and Lamsa (1926), *The Oldest Christian People,* p. 129.

[36] Gaunt (2006), *Massacres, Resistance, Protectors: Muslim-Christian Relations in Eastern Anatolia During World War I,* p. 8; In the missionary writings and Western literature in the nineteenth century and the early part of the 20th century, the designation "Mar Shimon" (also spelled "Mar Shimun" by some authors; named after the Shimun dynasty) is invariably used to refer to the Nestorian patriarch in charge, with little or no reference to the Patriarch's personal name. Once a patriarch had passed away and a new patriarch was in place, the same designation of "Mar Shimon" was used to refer to the new patriarch, at times with the additional reference to their first name added at the end.

[37] Perkins (1843), *A Residence of Eight Years in Persia,* p. 18.

Mar Shimon resided in the Kurdish mountains of Turkey, in the village of Quchanes.[38] There were 18 bishops under him, four of whom were based in Urumia. The bishops could be responsible for supervising as many as 30 villages and their clergy.[39]

Mar Shimon was the ecclesiastical head of Nestorian Christians. However, not only did he have spiritual authority over his subjects, but he also had temporal authority, which means that he could pass judgment on secular and non-spiritual matters of his people.[40] There were however, many restrictions and conditions applicable to Mar Shimon. As the patriarch, he was never to marry and had to remain celibate for life. From his childhood, he had to follow a strict diet and abstain from consuming meat. As a grown man, he was never to shave his beard. Since the patriarch was to remain celibate, he would have had no children of his own, and upon his passing, his oldest nephew would become the next patriarch, and in the absence of a nephew, it would have been his oldest unmarried brother. As such, the patriarchate would be passed down from uncle to nephew, generation after generation. When the American missionaries arrived, the lineage of patriarchy had been in place since the sixteenth century.

One of the norms in Nestorianism was that in addition to the patriarch, all of the other clergies at or above the level of bishops were also to remain celibate and refrain from eating meat. In terms of religious ceremonies and church decorations, Nestorians were simple, as expressed by Justin Perkins in his first encounters with them:[41] "The religious belief and practices of the Nestorians are much more simple and scriptural than those of other oriental Christians." They did not believe in image-worship in their churches and did not practice auricular confessions. The architectural design of their churches were simple and basic, often consisting of stone buildings with few if any windows and small entranceways.

---

[38] Also spelled Kuchaness, Kuchanes, Qudshanis, Qodchanis, and similarly sounding variations. This village is now renamed Konak, located in the Hakkari province of modern-day Turkey.

[39] For the time period covered in this book, the Nestorian patriarchs were as follows: Abraham (1825-1861); Reuben (1861-1903); Benjamin (1903-1918).

[40] Emhardt and Lamsa (1926), *The Oldest Christian People*, p. 58.

[41] Perkins (1843), *A Residence of Eight Years in Persia*, p. 20.

A Nestorian Church and its Congregation (c. 1890s)

As much as Perkins respected the Nestorians and their rich history and culture, there were aspects of Nestorian traditions that he had difficulty with in his early encounters. These included a singular emphasis on fasting, as well as other dietary restrictions, as for example evident in the following passage:

> Their periodical fasts, consisting of restrictions to vegetable diet, for example, many of the people would sooner die than violate. Declarations to that effect have been repeatedly made to our physician, when he has prescribed chicken soup for the sick, which they would most perseveringly refuse, because prescribed on days when their church canons restrict them to vegetable diet.[42]

---

[42] Perkins (1861), *Missionary Life in Persia*, p. 37.

Americans' Initial Impressions of the Nestorians

The initial interactions of Eli Smith and Henry Dwight with the Nestorians of the Urumia plain were encouraging. The two missionaries had found that the Nestorian population was, in general receptive to American missionary support. Smith and Dwight recognized a great need for the educational, religious, and medical services that the ABCFM could offer. The recognition for these needs was further reinforced by the observations of Justin Perkins in his own early encounters with the Nestorians in 1834. However, in describing the state of the Nestorians in the early days of his interactions with them, Perkins appeared highly critical, writing:

> Of the meaning of regeneration, even their most intelligent ecclesiastics seemed to know nothing; and their works were not found perfect before God. The plain commandments of the Decalogue — those against falsehood and the violation of the Sabbath in particular — were wantonly and almost universally broken.... And falsehood, among all classes seemed to be much more habitual than telling the truth, and when there was not even the poor apology of a pretext for preferring falsehood to truth. Intemperance, too, was fearfully prevalent. Their temptation to this vice is great, — their fertile country being like one great vineyard, and furnishing wine almost as cheap as its springs of water.[43]

He wrote in not too flattering ways, reflecting on how he saw the population of people that he had been tasked to serve:

> The Nestorians are still, to a painful extent, under the influence of human, and many childish, traditions. They attach great importance to their periodical *fasts*, which are about as numerous as in the other Eastern churches, often to the neglect of integrity and purity of heart, and even of external morality. The vice of lying is almost universal, among both ecclesiastics and people. Intemperance is very prevalent. The Sabbath is, to a great extent, regarded as a holiday. And profaneness and some other vices are very common. Indeed, the mass of this people seem literally to have a *name to live, while they are dead*.[44]

---

[43] Perkins (1843), *A Residence of Eight Years in Persia,* pp. 37-38.

[44] Ibid., pp. 21-22.

As one reads these descriptions of the Nestorians by Perkins, it appears that his views on the state of the Nestorians were harsh, critical, and even demeaning. It is important however, to recognize that Perkins was writing for an American audience. The readers of his words were primarily Protestant Christian Americans who were members of church congregations supporting the ABCFM, both inspirationally and financially. For them, the idea of an American mission station in remote lands, supported by their donations, would be more favorably justified if clear weaknesses in the population being served could be articulated. As such, while Perkins' observations may have been factually correct, there is also the possibility that his articulation of the weaknesses he saw among the Nestorians had been intentionally overcritical to meet the aspirations of ABCFM's donors in America.

What was indisputable in Perkins's observations was the urgent need to address illiteracy among the Nestorians. This stemmed from the absence of a written form for the spoken dialect of the language which the Nestorians of Urumia spoke. The language which they spoke was a modified version of ancient Syriac, which was a forgotten language not used in its original form for centuries. The modern version had been modified informally by the Nestorians over the centuries and reshaped through their interactions with other local languages, such as Farsi, Arabic, Turkish, and Kurdish. Furthermore, the spoken language of the Nestorians of Urumia, due to its evolutionary changes, had no written form. The degree to which it was modified over the centuries was so extensive that it seemed to have become a language of its own. However, as it had evolved, it failed to have a written rendition and formalized grammatical laws. In describing the concerns over illiteracy, Perkins wrote:

> Education, when we reached the Nestorians, was at an ebb almost as low as vital religion. None but their ecclesiastics could even read; and but very few of them could do more than chant their devotions in an unknown tongue — the Syriac, a modern dialect of which is their spoken language, while neither they nor their hearers knew anything of the meaning.[45]

---

[45] Perkins (1861), *Missionary Life in Persia*, p. 41.

As evident from the above passage, the two ABCFM missionaries who were sent to explore the needs for a mission station in Urumia, as well as Perkins, who was assigned to establish this mission station, had recognized the urgent need for improving literacy levels among the Nestorians. However, the efforts that the American missionaries were about to undertake in the years following these initial interactions, engaged them at much deeper levels. These efforts eventually included the establishment of a massive school system in the Urumia plain and beyond. They also resulted in the creation of a written form and the grammatical principles for the modern Syriac dialect used in Urumia, the establishment of a printing press, wide-reaching efforts to provide medical services, and the construction of Iran's first medical college in Urumia.

References and Related Readings

Ainsworth, William F. (1842). *Travels and Researches in Asia Minor, Mesopotamia, Chaldea, and Armenia*. London: John W. Parker.

Ameer, John Pierre (2008). *Assyrians in Yonkers.* Piscataway: Gorgias Press.

Davidson, Roderick (1956). "The Hatt-i-Humayn of 1856 and the Climate of its Reception" in *Reform in the Ottoman Empire (1856-1876).* Princeton: University Press.

Emhardt, William and George M. Lamsa (1926). *The Oldest Christian People.* Eugene: Wipf & Stock.

Gaunt, David (2006). *Massacres, Resistance, Protectors: Muslim-Christian Relations in Eastern Anatolia During World War I.* Piscataway, NJ: Gorgias Press.

Joseph, John (1961). *Nestorians and their Muslim Neighbors.* Princeton: Princeton University Press.

Luke, Harry C. (1925). *Mosul and its Minorities.* London: Martin Hopkinson & Company.

MacCulloch, Diarmaid (2011). *Christianity: The First Three Thousand Years.* New York: Penguin Books.

Perkins, Justin (1861). *Missionary Life in Persia: Glimpses of a Quarter of a Century of Labors Among the Nestorian Christians.* Boston: American Tract Society.

Perkins, Justin (1843). *A Residence of Eight Years in Persia Among the Nestorian Christians.* Andover: Allen, Morrill & Wardell.

Rockwell, William W. (1916). *The Pitiful Plight of the Assyrian Christians in Persia and Kurdistan.* New York: American Committee for Armenian and Syrian Relief.

Shedd, William A (1904). *Islam and the Oriental Churches: Their Historical Relations.* Philadelphia: Presbyterian Board of Publication and Sabbath-School Work.

Stewart, John (1928). *Nestorian Missionary Enterprise: The Story of a Church on Fire.* Edinburgh: T.&T. Clark.

Wigram, W. A. (1910). *An Introduction to the History of the Assyrian Church or the Church of the Sassanid Persian Empire, 100-640 A.D.* London: Society for Promoting Christian Knowledge.

Wigram, W. A. and E.T.A. Wigram (1914). *The Cradle of Mankind.* London: Adam and Charles Black.

Chapter 4

THE AMERICAN BOARD OF COMMISSIONERS
FOR FOREGIN MISSIONS

To understand the American missionary zeal in the nineteenth century, one needs to examine the motives behind the formation of the American Board of Commissioners for Foreign Missions (ABCFM), the First Great Awakening, and the Second Great Awakening. The First Great Awakening dates back to the middle of the eighteenth century, and is most closely associated with Calvinist views of Christianity. It emphasized the philosophical view of determinism, which postulates that human actions and outcomes are predetermined at birth. Given imperfections and weaknesses in human nature, it asserted that although people are born sinners, they can achieve salvation through confession, prayer, and good deeds. The First Great Awakening helped create a sense of religious revival among the population of the English colonies in America. One of the reasons for the populist excitement that it generated was that it emphasized that religious practice does not need to be institutionalized. It should instead be a personal and emotional experience, connecting one with God. The First Great Awakening made religious practice engaging and accessible to the masses.[46] Despite the religious revival created, the effects of the First Great Awakening in terms of the participation level of the public had begun to dissipate toward the middle of the eighteenth century.

---

[46] MacCulloch (2011), *Christianity: The First Three Thousand Years*, pp. 755-765.

The Second Great Awakening, which came to life in late eighteenth century and the early part of the nineteenth century, was a response to the need for greater religious participation by the masses. It came about at a time when America had achieved independence from Great Britain and was geographically expanding. The United States had begun to expand rapidly, and there was a need among the population of settlers for spiritual and religious enlightenment. As such, the Second Great Awakening was characterized by the mobilization of clergy from various Protestant denominations, who would travel from settlement to settlement to advance the messages of their denomination and encourage conversions.[47]

A primary characteristic of the Second Great Awakening was the desire to ensure that Christianity is accessible to the masses. The abolition and temperance movements were partially motivated by the changing national mindset advocated during the Second Great Awakening. So was the notion of bringing religious education to remote areas of the country, and to underprivileged populations of America. Often religious services were offered regardless of race, and were given to both freed and enslaved individuals in the days prior to the abolition of slavery in America. American Indians, frontier settlers, and eventually, as the movement grew, populations outside America grew in relevance to the movement.

The Second Great Awakening also advocated the importance of women in advancing the cause of Christianity. The growing reliance on female preachers and missionaries became a defining characteristic. In addition, given that a fundamental view associated with the movement was that the prophecy of Christianity had not yet been achieved, there was an expectation for the return of Christ to bring peace and enlightenment to humanity. Therefore, an apocalypse was anticipated. This anticipation increased the missionary fervor among America's various Protestant denominations, to advance the cause of Christ, convert non-believers, and to prepare the world for the expected return of Christ. The timing of the apocalypse was believed to be in the mid-1800s, creating an urgent need at the turn of the nineteenth century, for new evangelical organizations and expansive missionary operations.[48]

---

[47] Hutchison (1993), *Errand to the World.*

[48] Knight (1994), *Millennial Fever and the End of the World: A Study of Millerite Adventism.*

The task at hand was to advance the message of Christianity to non-believers, in order to save their souls before the anticipated apocalypse.

The Formation of the ABCFM

At the start of the nineteenth century, there was an urgent felt need among some of America's Protestant denominations for advancing Christianity globally. This need was motivated by the mindset of the Second Great Awakening. Missionary societies began forming, one of which was the American Board of Commissioners for Foreign Missions (ABCFM), established in 1810. Similar movements were already underway in Europe, and had given rise to the formation of the Missionary Society of London in 1799 and the British & Foreign Bible Society in 1804.[49] Missionary societies were also formed in France and Germany, with passion and drive matching those of the ABCFM in America.

The ABCFM was formed by students, alumni, and associates of Williams College (Massachusetts) and Andover Theological Seminary (now Andover Newton Theological School at Yale University). Its founders were inspired by the Second Great Awakening, the belief in Christian revival, and the felt need for the expansion of Christianity to foreign lands. Since foreign expansion was a massive undertaking, it could not be efficiently achieved by any one Christian denomination. As such, ABCFM's efforts and resources were collective, across several Christian denominations, making it a non-denominational entity.

Three denominations with similar theological foundations and social mandates collaborated in the early formation and functioning of the ABCFM: Congregationalists, Presbyterians, and Dutch Reformed. The combination of efforts of these denominations under the unified umbrella of the ABCFM enabled them to share resources and reduce overlap in missionary labor. In the years that followed, the ABCFM mission stations were set up around the globe, including in India, Sri Lanka, Thailand, Greece, Turkey, Syria, Persia, and South Africa. This geographic expansion was in line with one of the guiding principles of the Second Great Awakening, related to the expansion of Christianity to non-believers in foreign lands.

---

[49] Joseph (1961), *Nestorians and their Muslim Neighbors,* p. 40.

From its headquarters in Boston, the ABCFM grew to become the most substantial American humanitarian organization of the nineteenth century. Its dominance in the humanitarian field was evident in its abundant financial resources, a large number of missionaries and staff deployed to countless mission stations and outposts worldwide, its vast geographic range, and the masses of humanity it served around the globe. The ABCFM possessed an effective fundraising organization, through which church congregations in America regularly provided the donations needed to finance its operations at home and abroad. All of the funds were received through private donations, and no funding from the American government was provided to support it.

ABCFM Funding and Administration

As John Ameer has noted, the funding that the ABCFM provided to the Nestorian mission station in Urumia was quite favorable on a relative basis to the funding provided to the other mission stations around the world, especially when considering the comparatively small size of the Nestorian population. Furthermore, the level of commitment of the ABCFM to the Urumia mission station grew over the years.[50] In 1838, the Mission received 3% of ABCFM's total funding. By 1842, this figure had grown to 6%, amounting to three times the funds allocated to ABCFM's missionary operations in China, twice the amount of funding for its Cherokee missions, and six times the amounts allocated to New York State's Indian missions. The ABCFM also had a well-managed recruitment system for identifying and recruiting driven and well-educated missionaries from theological seminaries in America. One of the notable characteristics of the missionary recruitment efforts of the ABCFM, which relates to some of the guiding principles of the Second Great Awakening, was the critical role of women in advancing Christianity, as evident by the large number of female missionaries that joined the organization.

Once funding and mission staffing were in place, the ABCFM had a methodical approach for supervising each mission station's activities through regular reporting requirements by the mission station heads, and individual missionary reports. One of the many important

---

[50] Ameer (1997), *Yankees and Nestorians,* p. 30.

contributions of the ABCFM to the study of history in the regions of the world in which it operated was that it encouraged its missionaries to correspond with the headquarters in Boston regularly. Given that the missionaries were well-educated graduates of some of America's top colleges, the depth and volume of their writings have been instrumental in advancing our understanding of the history of the people which they served.

The accumulated volume of written content, in the form of missionary reports, books, and archival material, has formed a treasure trove for understanding the activities of the mission stations and the history of the social groups with whom the American missionaries interacted. This is especially important since the missions primarily served underprivileged societies that often lacked literacy and the resources needed to create their own historical records. The monthly publication by the ABCFM called the *Missionary Herald*, starting from the early 1800s, helped capture the essence of early missionaries' interactions with the societies they came into contact with. The *Missionary Herald* was also used as a communication tool with the congregations of churchgoers in America, to keep them informed on the activities and accomplishments of each mission station, and to keep American churches engaged and aware of the ABCFM's efforts around the globe.

In the context of Persia, as in many other mission fields, the ABCFM's instructions to the missionaries was to not challenge the norms of the population they were to serve. In the specific context of the Nestorians of Persia, the missionaries were instructed to not attempt to create an independent church, but rather to help the Nestorians achieve religious revival within the context of the Nestorian Church. The support provided by the missionaries to the Nestorian Church was to open the path for religious revival among the Nestorians. The missionaries would act as enablers of faith by raising the literacy level of the population and providing medical and evangelical services.

While the strengthening of the Nestorian Church was the original intent of the ABCFM, the eventual outcome on many grounds was quite different. During the second half of the 19th century a breakup of the Old Nestorian Church ensued, and a new church called the Syrian Evangelical Church was formed. At approximately the same time, the ABCFM became primarily a Congregationalist organization. The

Dutch Reformed denomination became an independent missionary body in 1857.[51] Furthermore, the ABCFM's operations in Persia were transferred in December of 1870 to the Board of Foreign Missions of the Presbyterian Church in the United States of America (PCUSA), headquartered in New York City. Therefore, from 1871 onward, all of the American missionaries in Persia functioned under the guidance of the Presbyterian Board of Foreign Missions (PBFM).

The Mission to the Nestorians

Following the 1830-31 expedition of Smith and Dwight, the ABCFM found itself uniquely interested in Persia's Nestorian population for a range of reasons. As noted earlier, there was the suggestion of a Biblical connection, reinforced by the fact that the Nestorians spoke a dialect of Aramaic, which was the language spoken by Jesus and his disciples. Furthermore, the location of the Nestorian settlements in Mesopotamia reinforced Biblical stories, which were fundamental to Christian theology and history. In the first half of the nineteenth century, the geographic location where Nestorian settlements were found suggested a connection between Nestorians and the earliest Christian settlements and created great excitement in the Christian world.

The belief in the existence of a Biblical link was expressed by explorers and Orientalists early on. For example, Asahel Grant, the pioneering missionary physician from the Urumia mission station, was convinced that in his expeditions in the mountainous regions west of Urumia and in the Kurdish mountain ranges of Turkey, he had encountered Nestorians who were direct descendants of the Ten Lost Tribes. According to the Old Testament, the Ten Lost Tribes were Israelites that were taken captive by the kings of Assyria in ancient times.[52] Grant's assertion of a link to the Ten Lost Tribes was based on the similarities in rituals, traditions, physical appearance, and ways of life, between what is described in the Bible and the Nestorians he had encountered in the mountains.

---

[51] Harmelink (1967), *The Ecumenical Relations of the Reformed Church in America*.
[52] 1 Chron. 5:26 and 2 Kings, 15:5, 29 (see Perkins 1843, p. 2).

Grant believed in this theory so strongly that in 1841 he published a book titled *"The Nestorians, or, The Lost Tribes,"* in which he articulated his observations related to this possible link. However, the basis of Grant's theory, that the Nestorians were connected to the Lost Tribes due to perceived similarities between Nestorians and Jewish populations of the region, was almost immediately challenged. Among those refuting his theory was Justin Perkins, his close missionary colleague, as well as renowned Orientalists of the time. Those opposing Grant's theory emphasized that the similarities that Grant had used as the basis for his theory were observable among many different population groups in the Near East, and could not be considered definitive evidence of a link between the Nestorians and the Ten Lost Tribes.[53] Although Grant's theory was refuted, it persisted for decades, as some scholars continued to hint at the possibility of such a link.[54]

Despite the unproven theories of a Biblical link between the Nestorians and the Lost Tribes, there were many objective and rational reasons as to why the Nestorian population was a good choice for ABCFM support. In the context of American Protestants, the expedition by Smith and Dwight had suggested to them that the Nestorians were a more promising group for the ABCFM to work with, since other Christian populations of the area, such as the Chaldeans and the Armenians, were more set in their ways and less likely to be influenced by American missionary efforts. In the view of the ABCFM, the Nestorians seemed to be relatively more open to receiving missionary aid and guidance from America.

Furthermore, there was a sense of compatibility between Nestorian religious practices, and those of many Protestant denominations in America. In fact, on several occasions, the American missionaries and the ABCFM reports referred to them as the "Protestants of Asia."[55] This was partially driven by the simplicity in religious practice which was a characteristic of the Nestorian Church and a common characteristic of Protestant religious practices at that time in America. "Protestant simplicity" is how Justin Perkins characterized Nestorians' religious

---

[53] Joseph (1961), *Nestorians and their Muslim Neighbors*, p. 16.

[54] Emhardt and Lamsa (1926), *The Oldest Christian People*, pp. 21-22.

[55] Perkins (1861), *Missionary Life in Persia*, p. 107.

practices.[56] For example, Nestorian churches were designed with architectural simplicity. Also, Nestorian religious practices abhorred image-worship and auricular confessions, and forbade excessive consumption of alcohol. The simplicity of Nestorians' religious practices put them in close proximity to American Protestants, and in contrast with the Roman Church, with which the American missionaries competed in several missionary fields in the region.

The ABCFM was also impressed by the early history of Nestorians, dating back over a thousand years, when missionary zeal characterized Nestorianism. As mentioned earlier in the discussions related to the early history of the Nestorian Church, soon after being peacefully settled in Persia, the Nestorians began their own missionary endeavors. These endeavors took them as far away as Siberia, Japan, China, India, Cyprus, and Egypt. Although the Nestorians that the American missionaries encountered in the nineteenth century no longer exhibited missionary aspirations, the missionary history of the Nestorian Church had a strong appeal to the ABCFM. It suggested the possibility that once the Nestorian population of Persia is reinvigorated, they may revive their missionary traditions, further advancing the ABCFM's degree of influence in the region.

By strengthening the Nestorian Church and providing educational and medical services, the leadership of the ABCFM believed that they might be able to mobilize a movement among the Nestorians, to advance Christianity in the Urumia region and beyond. The ABCFM believed that the strategic location of the Nestorian settlements, surrounded by Moslems of the Ottoman Empire and Persia could possibly make Nestorians a force in advancing Christianity in the region. Smith and Dwight found Nestorians to be open-minded toward followers of other religions. Therefore, they thought that Nestorians could be influential among other religious minorities in the area as well as the Moslem population.

It is important to recognize that while the original population of interest for missionary work was the Nestorians, the conversion of Moslems to Christianity had also been given consideration by the ABCFM. This eventually proved to be impossible since Islamic principles strictly forbid a Moslem from converting to any other

---

[56] Ibid., p. 86.

religion. In fact, shortly after Smith and Dwight were assigned to explore the Nestorian population of the Urumia region, another American missionary, James Lyman Merrick, visited the major cities of Persia to explore the prospects to proselytize the Persian Moslem population. His exploratory labors, which nearly cost him his life, indicated that the likelihood of success for proselytization initiatives with the Moslem population would be nil.

The Nestorians, at the time of the arrival of the first American missionaries, were a disadvantaged population. Most were poor, illiterate, and in need of medical and educational services. The legal system in place in Persia at that time did not put Christians on equal footing with their Moslem neighbors. Although the imbalance was partially remedied in the final years of the nineteenth century, mostly through European influence and the establishment of Church-based legal boards, the need to provide a greater level of social balance and economic equity for the Nestorians helped justify the ABCFM objective of aiding the Nestorians of the Urumia region.

As may be evident from the above discussion, it is important to be reminded that American interests in aiding the Nestorians of Persia were guided by religious and social motives. There were no economic or political motives at play. There were no natural resources such as oil or minerals that could justify American presence in the area, and Persia's geography represented no strategic or military interests to America. In fact, at that time, America itself was preoccupied with the challenges of its own expansion as the country grew westward. The idea of pursuing a presence in Persia was not of national interest to America. Therefore, funding for the Nestorian Mission, as well as other mission stations run by the ABCFM around the globe, was secured entirely through private donations from American churchgoers, and no financial resources from the American government were sought or used. America's missionary efforts in Persia were apolitical in nature.

References and Related Readings

Ameer, John Pierre (1997). *Yankees and Nestorians: The Establishment of American Schools Among the Nestorians of Iran and Turkey, 1834-1850.* (Doctoral Dissertation). Harvard University.

Emhardt, William and George M. Lamsa (1926). *The Oldest Christian People.* Eugene: Wipf & Stock.

Harmelink, Herman (1967), The Ecumenical Relations of the Reformed Church in America," *Journal of Presbyterian History,* Vol. 45, No. 2, pp. 71-94.

Hutchison, William R. (1993). *Errand to the World: American Protestant Thought and Foreign Missions.* Chicago: The University of Chicago Press.

Joseph, John (1961). *Nestorians and their Muslim Neighbors.* Princeton: Princeton University Press.

Knight, George R. (1994). *Millennial Fever and the End of the World: A Study of Millerite Adventism.* Nampa, ID: Pacific Press.

MacCulloch, Diarmaid (2011). *Christianity: The First Three Thousand Years.* New York: Penguin Books.

Perkins, Henry Martyn (1887). *Life of Rev. Justin Perkins, D.D.: Pioneering Missionary to Persia.* Chicago: Woman's Presbyterian Board of Missions of the Northwest.

Perkins, Justin (1861). *Missionary Life in Persia: Glimpses of a Quarter of a Century of Labors Among the Nestorian Christians.* Boston: American Tract Society.

Chapter 5

URUMIA

The city of Urumia, which is the center of a region by the same name, is located to the west of Lake Urumia. Lake Urumia is a shallow salt lake.[57] It is believed that in the early days of Christianity, St. Thomas visited the shores of Lake Urumia, on his way to India and converted some of the locals to Christianity. Archeological finds from the area date as far back as 20th century BC. The region is believed to be the birthplace of Zoroaster, the founder of the ancient Persian religion of Zoroastrianism. At the time of the arrival of the American missionaries, Urumia was the largest city in what is now the West Azerbaijan province of Iran. It continues to have economic and socio-cultural prominence, being the capital of the province and its largest population center.

---

[57] Samuel G. Wilson, in 1895, estimated the average depth of the lake to be between 12 to 16 feet, with its deepest point being 46 feet deep. The depth of the lake has since decreased due to evaporation and reduced water intake. The salt concentration in the lake is so high that it has no fish.

A View of the City of Urumia (c. 1890s)

There are varied spellings of the name of the city, including Ooroomeeyah, Orūmīyeh, Oroomiah, Ooroomiah, Urmia, Urumia, Urmi, Oroomia, Urmiah, Urūmiyeh, Urumiyyih, Urumiyya, Urmiyeh, and Urumiya. There are very few cities in the world that have a greater number of variations in the spelling of their names. The differences in spelling have to do with different pronunciations of the name, which varied greatly due to the ethnic, linguistic, and religious diversity of the Urumia plain, with a range of different dialects for each language.

Given the varied backgrounds of those with whom Westerners came into contact and the various mother tongues of the Westerners themselves, the spelling and associated pronunciation have changed quite a bit over time. Over the years, different writers have used a range of different spellings: Asahel Grant used "Ooroomiah"; Justin Perkins, David Stoddard, and Thomas Laurie used "Oroomiah"; Joseph Plumb Cochran, William Shedd, Abraham Yohannan, and John Elder used "Urumia"; John Joseph used "Urmiyah"; Wadie Jwaideh and David McDowall used "Urumiya"; Martin van Bruinessen used "Urmiyeh"; Heleen Murre-van den Berg and Michael Zirinsky used "Urmia." In modern Iran, "Urmia" is the officially used English spelling.

In this book, "Urumia" is the adopted spelling for two reasons. First, it is the spelling that correctly corresponds to the most common way the name is pronounced in modern Iran. Secondly, it is the spelling adopted by Abraham Yohannan, who was a professor of Oriental languages at Columbia University and a former resident of Urumia. Yohannan's knowledge of the languages of the region, his own experience as someone who grew up and lived in Urumia, as well as his academic standing as a scholar in Oriental languages at Columbia University, would render his choice of spelling to be the most fitting for the time period under study in this book.

In terms of the meaning of "Urumia", the prevailing view is that the name dates back to the 9th century BC and the Kingdom of Van. The linguistic roots of the name were researched by Burrow. Burrow concluded that Urumia is related to the word "Urmi" meaning wave, from Indo-Iranian roots, and the meaning of the word is "watertown."[58] Given that the location of Urumia is next to a large lake and that the Urumia plain is rich with water resources such as streams, springs, and rivers flowing down mountain ranges, this definition would be quite fitting. The city was renamed Rezaiyeh during the Pahlavi dynasty (1925-1979) but was renamed back to its original name after the Islamic Revolution of 1979.

The nearest major city to Urumia is Tabriz, which is the capital of the modern-day East Azerbaijan province of Iran. Tabriz was the seat of the crown prince of Persia at the time of the arrival of Justin Perkins. At that time, since no bridge over Lake Urumia had been constructed, travel from Tabriz typically required one to circle around the northern shores of the lake, making for a journey of about 150 miles on foot, horseback or carriage.[59] Boating on Lake Urumia was also possible, and toward the end of the nineteenth century small cargo boats operated on the lake. Today, with the construction of the bridge connecting Tabriz to Urumia, the traveling distance is cut to approximately 90 miles. The main villages surrounding Urumia during the early missionary days were Seir, Geog Tapa, Ardishai, Gulpushan, and Ada. Urumia is located at an altitude of 4,300 feet above sea level and is surrounded to its west by rising mountain ranges.

---

[58] Burrow (1973), *The Proto-Indoaryans*, pp. 139-140.
[59] Perkins (1887), *Life of Rev. Justin Perkins,* p. 17.

An Assyrian (Nestorian) Family in Urumia (c. 1890s)

Today, the population of the city of Urumia is approximately one million. However, at the time of the arrival of the American missionaries in 1835, Urumia was a city of only about 25,000 residents. At that time, the city's circumference was about 4 miles of mud walls and ditches. In terms of building construction, most homes were constructed of unburnt brick.

In characterizing the climate of the area, Perkins wrote: "The climate of Oroomiah is *naturally* one of the finest in the world. It resembles, in its temperature, the climate of our Middle States. Unhappily, however, *artificial* causes are at work which render it decidedly unhealthy, — particularly to foreigners."[60] By "artificial causes," Perkins was referring to poorly planned water drainage systems and stagnant water pools for agricultural use, resulting in the

---

[60] Perkins (1843), *A Residence of Eight Years in Persia,* p. 8; note "Oroomiah" as the different spelling used by Perkins.

outbreak of epidemics such as cholera, typhoid fever, and malaria.[61] These put the lives of Urumia's residents at great risk over the years, contributing to thousands of lost lives.[62]

In describing the plain between Lake Urumia and the mountains to the west of Urumia, Laurie wrote: "A highly fertile plain gently slopes from the mountains to the lake, comprising an area of about five hundred square miles, and dotted with not less than three hundred villages. These vary in population from one hundred to one thousand inhabitants."[63]

One of the most significant villages to the American missionaries was the village of Seir, located to the southwest of Urumia. Here, about six miles from Urumia, Perkins constructed a residential compound for the missionaries. Perkins' original intent for establishing residential facilities for the missionaries at Seir was to provide a safe haven for them during the heat of the summer. Summer heat, combined with poor environmental conditions resulting from water-borne diseases related to agricultural practices, was a contributor to disease in the city of Urumia.

Health concerns were far more prevalent during the summer months since irrigation waters, the flooding of rice paddies, and the use of water pools for agricultural purposes helped host mosquito larvae resulting in the outbreak of malaria. Poorly planned water drainage systems increased the incidence rate of other forms of water-borne diseases such as cholera and gastrointestinal infections. With the lack of water treatment methods, the incidence rate of such illnesses rose considerably during summer. Seir provided a sanctuary for the missionaries from these diseases during the summer months, and eventually turned into a year-round compound regularly utilized for residential and educational purposes by the Urumia mission station.

---

[61] All of which were diseases with no effective medical remedies and no reliable diagnosis methods at that time. For example, the cause of malaria was unknown to the medical community until the late nineteenth century.

[62] Almost all deaths among the American missionaries and their families were directly attributed to such diseases.

[63] Laurie (1853), *Dr. Grant and the Mountain Nestorians,* p. 59.

Flooded Rice Fields in the Urumia Region (c. 1890s)

The Village of Seir (c. 1911)

Similar to most other cities, Urumia was divided into different neighborhoods depending on the residents' ethnicities and religions. The Nestorians had their own neighborhood, separating them from the Moslem and Jewish neighborhoods. Roughly 600 Nestorians lived in the city in 1835, when Perkins and Grant arrived. Laurie describes Urumia as such: "The flat-roofed houses are mostly built of mud or sun-burnt bricks, and are enclosed with high walls of the same material. The more wealthy have beautiful gardens attached to their dwellings, where the family can enjoy themselves, secure from all intrusions."[64] Laurie estimated that a population of approximately 20,000 Nestorians lived in some 300 villages surrounding Urumia, within a range of about 50 miles from the city.

The Urumia plain is agriculturally fertile. At the time of Perkins' arrival, it produces a wide range of crops such as apples, grapes, melons, plums, cherries, peaches, pears, and grapes. In describing the climate and natural environment of Urumia, Perkins wrote:

> It is naturally good, but is rendered unhealthy by artificial causes. The constant evaporation in summer from its myriads of irrigated fields — almost the entire surface of the district, consisting of a plain of nearly a thousand square miles in extent being repeatedly flooded, (and the rice fields constantly so,) to water the soil during the warm months of the year, — is one such cause; and another and still more prolific one is the almost limitless extent of its annual vegetation. A country so charming, — stretching more than fifty miles along the beautiful lake, and back from it to the base of the lofty Koordish mountains, — so bright under the effulgence of its gorgeous sun and pure heavens, and rejoicing under its thrifty growth of abundant crops, presents to the eye so much the aspect of an Eden as almost to preclude the idea of sickness and pain. But the foreigner is soon forced to feel that its brilliant skies and balmy breezes, beautiful and grateful as they are, are still pregnant with the elements of disease and death.[65]

The above passage emphasizes the beauty of the Urumia plain, but also the health risks associated with living there. The choice of Urumia as a mission field, and the addition of a medical component to its operations was a pioneering achievement for the ABCFM. The medical

---

[64] Ibid., p. 60.
[65] Perkins (1861), *Missionary Life in Persia*, p. 45.

services of the Mission spearheaded many of its other activities in Urumia and elsewhere in Persia, and helped create good relations with the population of the region. The health services of the Mission were instrumental in creating positive exchanges with the locals, as these services were badly needed. They also helped support the health and wellbeing of the missionaries themselves, who were at constant risk of contracting a range of deadly diseases. As Laurie stated: "But the missionary physician is also useful in prolonging the lives of his associates; and, if ever there was a station where a physician was needed for that purpose, that station is Oroomiah. Situated far in the interior, out of the reach of other educated physicians, it is also peculiarly unhealthy."[66]

In the 1830s the ABCFM began recruiting missionaries for the specific task of serving the newly discovered Nestorian Christian population of the region. The intensity and drive of the ABCFM, which had mobilized the American effort in Urumia, was eventually joined by similar efforts from other nations, as the Urumia region became host to missionaries from France, Britain, Germany, and Russia during the second half of the nineteenth century.

As John Joseph succinctly articulated: "There was perhaps no missionary field in the world where there were so many rival Christian forces at work as were found in Urmiyah at the beginning of this [twentieth] century, all struggling to get predominance among the few people."[67] Therefore, while in the early part of the nineteenth century, Urumia may have been an undiscovered city for Westerners, by the end of the century it was a competitive arena for Westerners attempting to engage with, serve and influence the Assyrian (Nestorian) population of the city, the Urumia plain and the surrounding mountains.

---

[66] Laurie (1853), *Dr. Grant and the Mountain Nestorians,* p. 70.

[67] Joseph (1961), *Nestorians and their Muslim Neighbors,* p. 123; note "Urmiyah" as the spelling used by John Joseph.

References and Related Readings

Burrow, T. (1973). "The Proto-Indoaryans," *The Journal of the Royal Asiatic Society of Great Britain and Ireland*, No. 2, pp. 123-140.

Joseph, John (1961). *Nestorians and their Muslim Neighbors*. Princeton: Princeton University Press.

Laurie, Thomas (1853). *Dr. Grant and the Mountain Nestorians*. Boston: Gould and Lincoln.

Perkins, Henry Martyn (1887). *Life of Rev. Justin Perkins, D.D.: Pioneering Missionary to Persia*. Chicago: Woman's Presbyterian Board of Missions of the Northwest.

Perkins, Justin (1861). *Missionary Life in Persia: Glimpses of a Quarter of a Century of Labors Among the Nestorian Christians*. Boston: American Tract Society.

Perkins, Justin (1843). *A Residence of Eight Years in Persia Among the Nestorian Christians*. Andover: Allen, Morrill & Wardell

Wilson, Samuel G. (1895). *Persian Life and Customs*. New York: Fleming H. Revell Company.

Chapter 6

JUSTIN PERKINS

Justin Perkins was the very first American to take up residence in Persia. He was also the first missionary to open up Persia as a missionary field for Americans. Following his footsteps, in the decades that followed his arrival, dozens of missionaries came to Urumia from America. His pioneering work also led to more mission stations being established in other parts of Persia. The innovations that Perkins introduced to the education system, through the implementation of the Lancastrian teaching method, made it possible to expand educational services in the Urumia region rapidly, on a scale unachievable through other means.

One of Perkins' many contributions was the development of a written form for the dialect of the Syriac language spoken by the Nestorians of the Urumia region. This spoken dialect was considerably different from the classical form of Syriac known to linguists and Orientalists at that time, which was of no practical use to the Nestorians of Persia. The establishment of a script and grammatical principles for spoken Syriac, achieved by Perkins and his colleagues, facilitated the formal education of the Nestorian population of Persia. This significantly improved the literacy rate in the Persian Nestorian population, and led to the development of a modern schooling system in the Urumia region. Furthermore, the establishment of the Urumia mission station resulted in an influx of educators and missionary physicians from America. Through the work of other American missionaries that followed Perkins, Western advancements were introduced to Persia in the areas of public health and education.

Perkins was born on March 5, 1805, in West Springfield, Massachusetts, to William and Judith Clough Perkins. As a child, in addition to schoolwork, he would spend a considerable part of his days farming, as would be expected of children in his time living in rural areas. Born during the period of the Second Great Awakening, Perkins was influenced by the messages of this movement. He had an awakening experience when he was eighteen years old, raising in his mind the question of what God intended for him to achieve in life. At the age of twenty, Perkins decided to become a Congregational minister and sought an education that would prepare him for the ministry by entering Amherst College.

At Amherst, he was an energetic and focused student. According to his classmates, because of his intense focus on schoolwork and strong work ethic, he slept only about four hours at night. His high energy level, constant commitment to his studies, and his endless drive earned him the title of the "twenty-four-hour boy" by his classmates at Amherst.[68] Amherst College not only provided Perkins with solid educational foundations, but also gave him the opportunity to meet visionaries and missionaries, with great effect on his vision of what can be achieved through missionary work. While at Amherst, he attended a speech by Eli Smith, who was visiting Amherst, to speak about the importance of missions and missionary work. Smith eloquently described to Amherst students the missionary prospects of America in Persia and the Ottoman Empire. Smith had a strong impact on Perkins as his words became a source of inspiration for the young Amherst student to pursue missionary work.

Among the other important people that Perkins came into contact with at Amherst was Mary Lyon, a revolutionary in American female education. In later years, she established two colleges: Wheaton Female Seminary and Mount Holyoke Female Seminary, both of which remain in place today (Wheaton College and Mount Holyoke College), in the state of Massachusetts.

Similar to Perkins, Lyon was born into a family of farmers, and as a child, had spent a great part of her time on the farm. As a young adult, she became a school teacher and gradually grew up in academic ranks and opened her own school. Later in life, she was approached by Laban Wheaton, an affluent lawyer and former Congressman, who commissioned her to establish Wheaton Female Seminary. She then proceeded to establish Mount Holyoke Female Seminary in South Hadley, Massachusetts. Her vision of what was necessary in women's education in America was manifested in the innovative curriculum and organization of Mount Holyoke.

Perkins and Lyon had engaging conversations about educational theories and methods. These were topics which would absorb both their lives in the following years, with Perkins leading the charge in

---

[68] Perkins (1887), *Life of Rev. Justin Perkins: Pioneer Missionary to Persia,* p. 10.

establishing an education system in Urumia, and Lyon eventually establishing Mount Holyoke Seminary. The conversations with Mary Lyon had a lasting impact on Perkins, since many of the accomplishments in female education achieved by Perkins and his missionary colleagues in Urumia decades later, directly reflected what Mary Lyon had pioneered in America. She believed that education should be affordable for all, rather than just being accessible to the wealthy, and that the rigor and content of female education should match that of male education.[69]

Lyon also advocated that the curriculum for female students should help them break away from the boundaries of their traditional roles in society as maintainers of households. Instead, it should focus on training women to become teachers and visionaries of the future. The model that Lyon established in Mount Holyoke was to be replicated by many other women's colleges in the years to come, including Vassar College (New York) and Wellesley College (Massachusetts). Her vision was informed by one of the guiding principles of the Second Great Awakening, related to the increased role of women in a wide range of societal roles, and a break from the traditional boundaries which social norms had forced upon women at that time. In the years following her initial conversations with Perkins, Lyon's Mount Holyoke Seminary came to have a great influence on the Urumia mission and the ABCFM. Five of the ABCFM female missionaries destined for Persia were graduates of Mount Holyoke Seminary.

The educational environment at Amherst College, as well as the gifted and driven individuals Perkins crossed paths with, had life-changing effects on him. He graduated from Amherst with honors in 1829, then taught at Amherst Academy and, in the following year, became a student at Andover Theological Seminary. At the commencement speech in 1832, upon receiving his degree from Andover, Perkins spoke on the theme of "The Obligation of Literature and Science to the Enterprise of Missions," a topic which would shape much of his life and future missionary endeavors.[70]

After completing his degree at Andover, he returned to Amherst College for one year to serve as a tutor. In January 1833, he was

---

[69] Fiske (1870), *Mary Lyon: Reflections of a Noble Woman.*
[70] Perkins (1887), *Life of Rev. Justin Perkins,* p. 81.

commissioned by the ABCFM to become a missionary. The pressing need of the ABCFM, motivated by the explorations of Smith and Dwight, was the establishment of a mission for the Nestorians of Urumia. Perkins was given the lead role in this undertaking, and was asked to embark on this mission in September of that year.

Perkins became an ordained minister in the summer of 1833 and in July of that year, only a few weeks before deployment to his mission field, he married Charlotte Bass. It was customary for the ABCFM to encourage male missionaries being deployed to distant fields to marry before their deployment. This practice became evident in future missionary assignments as well, where in many cases missionaries would marry within a few months of being assigned to a foreign mission field. Thomas Laurie, a missionary colleague of Perkins and Grant, explained this practice as such: "If the experience of modern missions has settled anything, it has settled the principle that a good wife is essential to the usefulness, and even the continued life, of the missionary. The heathen themselves have noticed that he who is alone is easily discouraged, and led to abandon his post."[71]

On September 8, 1833, Justin Perkins was provided with his missionary instructions from the American Board of Commissioners for Foreign Missions. The instructions were delivered to him in the chapel of Andover Theological Seminary. Eli Smith also received his instructions from the ABCFM that same night at Andover. The instructions provided to Perkins were quite lengthy and detailed.[72] They highlighted the importance of being an observer and an explorer, and respecting the norms and customs of the Nestorians. They also emphasized the need to respect the locals, and to not attempt to modify the religious practices of the Nestorians. They also asked Perkins to maintain an open-minded approach to providing assistance to this population, in whatever way best seen on the ground, once he had established the mission station in Urumia.

Unfortunately for Perkins, on the same night that he and Smith had received their instructions from the ABCFM, he fell ill. He developed a high fever and was low on energy. He became weak to the point that made it impossible for an unusually energetic person like him to walk.

---

[71] Laurie (1853), *Dr. Grant and the Mountain Nestorians*, p. 30.
[72] Perkins (1843), *A Residence of Eight Years in Persia*, pp. 28-30.

This was clearly of great concern to him since he had carefully planned his voyage to Persia, so as to leave on the same ship that Smith was boarding from Boston Harbor.[73] Fortunately for Perkins, due to poor weather conditions, the ship's departure was delayed, and Perkins' health improved slightly during that delay. However, he was still very weak and unable to walk on his own. Perkins requested his doctor to permit him to be transported on the back of a horse-drawn wagon to Boston so that he could board the departing ship and join Smith.

His doctor reluctantly complied, and Perkins, accompanied by his wife, was rushed by carriage to Boston Harbor. He was still so weak that he had to be carried onto the deck of the ship. The captain of the ship, upon seeing Perkins' poor state, said: "We shall very soon have to throw that man overboard."[74] The drive and positiveness that his classmates in Amherst had noted, earning him the title of "twenty-four-hour boy," were evident in his persistence to board the departing ship, under highly unfavorable conditions.

With an illness that could have potentially killed him had he not been on land, the risk-taking and optimism that Perkins showed is reflective of the uniquely positive perspective he brought to many of life's experiences. His sense of optimism, a faith that all will be fine, combined with a desire to push forward despite unfavorable odds, characterized Perkins and the majority of the American missionaries that eventually served in Urumia. Without such a positive attitude, survival, and effective labor under inhospitable conditions would have been difficult and draining. Once the ship had sailed, Perkin quickly recovered. Given that Perkins had met Smith as an honored guest speaker visiting Amherst, and given the inspirational effects that Smith had on him, the ability to spend time with Smith was immensely valuable to him. The long voyage allowed Perkins to benefit from Smith's wisdom and insights on matters related to missionary work, specifically related to the Nestorians of the Urumia region, with whom Smith had interacted during his expedition of 1831.

---

[73] Smith was destined for his mission in Syria, and the ship the two were to take was from Boston to Malta.

[74] Perkins (1861), *Missionary Life in Persia*, p. 14.

References and Related Readings

Fiske, Fidelia (1870). *Mary Lyon: Recollections of a Noble Woman.* London: Morgan, Chase and Scott.

Laurie, Thomas (1853). *Dr. Grant and the Mountain Nestorians.* Boston: Gould and Lincoln.

Perkins, Henry Martyn (1887). *Life of Rev. Justin Perkins, D.D.: Pioneering Missionary to Persia.* Chicago: Woman's Presbyterian Board of Missions of the Northwest.

Perkins, Justin (1861). *Missionary Life in Persia: Glimpses of a Quarter of a Century of Labors Among the Nestorian Christians.* Boston: American Tract Society.

Perkins, Justin (1843). *A Residence of Eight Years in Persia Among the Nestorian Christians.* Andover: Allen, Morrill & Wardell.

Chapter 7

THE COMMENCEMENT OF
THE URUMIA MISSION

The ship carrying Perkins, Smith, and their wives took nearly six months to make it from Boston to Constantinople. At that time, trans-continental travel was done using sailing ships, as steam-powered ships were not yet in commercial use. They reached Constantinople in the winter of 1833. Smith and his wife were headed to Malta and parted with the Perkins, who remained in Turkey until the spring of 1834. With the cold winter weather, the couple's long stay in Turkey was in anticipation of improving weather conditions in late spring. With the arrival of spring, they traveled to Erzurum, a caravan town mid-way between Trebizond and Lake Van. However, before the commencement of the final stretch of their land journey, news came of potential dangers on the roads ahead. Robbers had attacked a caravan of travelers headed to Persia. The Perkins' original travel plans to Urumia would be risky under such circumstances. Therefore, the couple was advised to travel through the Russian-held territory of Georgia rather than the Kurdish mountains of Turkey.

While travel through Georgia was expected to be safer than the bandit stricken mountains of eastern Turkey, the eventual experience seemed to be quite the opposite. In August of 1834, at the Georgian border, the couple was detained by Russian border guards. The Russian officials at the entry point declared most of the Perkins' belongings as contraband and sent their belongings back to Erzurum. Their passports were also declared as insufficient for travel. The couple, therefore, had to camp at the border for several days until the needed paperwork could be processed. Once the paperwork at the Georgian entry point was cleared, they were able to continue their voyage toward the Persian border. However, similar issues awaited them when attempting to leave Georgia to cross the border with Persia. The Russian border guards at the Persian border did not consider their passports to be valid for crossing the border and detained them at the river Aras, which separated Russia from Persia.

The difficulties that the Perkins were experiencing passing through Russian territory may have been partially attributed to the Russian Orthodox Church's discomfort with having western missionaries approach Christian minorities in the region.[75] Regardless of the reason, the delay was affecting the health of Charlotte, who was pregnant with the couple's first child. The summer temperatures were quite high, and her health was quickly deteriorating. Justin Perkins was able to procure the help of a Persian government official who was passing through on the same road that the Perkins had set up their tent. This official who was headed to Tabriz agreed to deliver a note from Perkins requesting assistance from the British ambassador in Tabriz, Sir John Campbell.

Campbell, having received the message from Perkins, immediately notified the Russian ambassador. The two collaboratively made arrangements for the entry of Perkins and his wife into Persia. A caravan was dispatched by the British to facilitate the Perkins' passage to Tabriz. In the meantime, Perkins was able to negotiate his way with the Russian border officials on his own before assistance could arrive. The couple crossed the Persian border. The caravan dispatched by the British met up with them in the Persian mountains and took the couple back to Tabriz, where they arrived on August 23, 1834.

Three days after the couple's arrival in Tabriz, Charlotte gave birth to the couple's first child. She had a difficult delivery and was unconscious for several days. Much to the Perkins' sorrow, their baby girl was unwell and died within months of her birth. She had been named Charlotte, after her mother, and was the first of the six children

---

[75] In the decades that followed, especially toward the end of the nineteenth century, Persian Christians became of great interest to the Russian Orthodox Church. This was partially motivated by Russia's desire to increase its political influence in Persia.

that, in the coming years, the couple would lose due to a range of illnesses.[76] Their sorrow was to become a common theme among other American missionary families that followed them to this region of the world. American missionary children often suffered from illness, and many died as infants in Persia.[77]

During the time that they were in Tabriz, a new Persian king was crowned in Tehran. Fath-Ali Shah, who was the second king in the Qajar dynasty, had ruled Persia during some of its most challenging times and through two wars with Russia. Both wars had resulted in significant territorial losses for Persia. Fath-Ali Shah passed away in October of 1834 at the age of 62. His grandson and chosen heir, Mohammad Mirza became the next Qajar king of Persia.

Two months after settling in Tabriz, Perkins visited Urumia for the first time. This was uncharted territory, since the expedition by Smith and Dwight in 1831 had been restricted to certain parts of the Urumia plain and the two American missionaries had not been able to enter the city of Urumia due to the outbreak of the plague. In the village of Gavalan, approximately 30 miles north of the city of Urumia, Perkins met a man by the name of Mar Yohannan.[78] He was a Nestorian bishop of Urumia. In his diaries, Perkins noted that Yohannan was the very first Nestorian that he ever shook hands with. This handshake eventually led to years of collaboration between the two men.

Yohannan told Perkins that he had met Smith and Dwight in 1831, on their visit to the area. Perkins, realizing the depth of Mar Yohannan's understanding of the Nestorians of the region, had a great need to seek his advice and wisdom, and to learn from him about the culture and language of the Nestorians.

---

[76] Their only surviving child was Henry Martyn Perkins, who moved to America for his education and eventually authored a concise and authoritative biography of Justin Perkins, published in 1887.

[77] An insightful statistic produced by Taylor (2008, pp. 109-110) is that of the 59 gravestones in the Seir cemetery where the Urumia missionaries buried their loved ones, 41 belong to missionaries' children, and most were under the age of three.

[78] "Mar" being a religious title in Nestoriansim, meaning "my Lord." Mar Yohannan's first name was John. He was one of four Nestorian bishops of the Urumia plain, his area of responsibility being the northern sections of the plain.

Mar Yohannan

Yohannan accompanied Perkins as he toured the Urumia region. He also agreed to join him in Tabriz and temporarily moved there to become Perkins' personal tutor. He taught Perkins vernacular Syriac and familiarized him with the customs and traditions of the Nestorians of the region. Yohannan also brought with him Priest Abraham as an assistant. He was an 18-year-old priest from the village of Geog Tapa, the largest Nestorian village in the Urumia plain. Despite his young age, Priest Abraham had mastery of both classical and vernacular Syriac. This proved instrumental in helping Perkins create a written form of the spoken Syriac dialect of Urumia.

The wisdom of Perkins in identifying and recruiting Nestorians with knowledge and authority was critical. Through the tutoring which he received from Yohannan and Abraham, he began his own personal development and learning, and became acclimated with the Nestorians, their culture and language. During this time, Perkins was able to learn the Syriac language from Mar Yohannan, and awaited the arrival of an American missionary physician by the name of Asahel Grant and his wife, Judith Grant. Asahel Grant was an accomplished physician from upstate New York, and his wife was a linguist. The Grants arrived in Tabriz in October of 1835.

The arrival of Grant was instrumental to the initiation of activities of the American mission in Persia. Grant assisted Justin Perkins in negotiating favorable conditions for the commencement of Mission activities in Urumia. With Grant's medical skills, the local population of Urumia, as well as the Persian government officials, found the prospects of an American mission station highly attractive. This gave the two missionaries leverage in establishing the conditions under which the Mission would operate in Urumia.

One week after the Grants' arrival in Tabriz, Perkins and Grant left for Urumia. The British consulate in Tabriz provided them and their wives with travel documents and protection guarantees. They were welcomed by the governor of Urumia, who gave them temporary lodging. To secure their permanent place of residence and mission station in Urumia, Grant had secured a reference letter from the governor of Tabriz addressed to the governor of Urumia. This is one way that Grant's services as a capable physician (in this case in having provided medical services to the governor of Tabriz during Grant's short stay in Tabriz) helped pave the path for setting up the mission station in Urumia. Within one week, they had secured a house in Urumia.

In November of 1835, the Perkins and the Grants took up residence in Urumia and began the operations of the Urumia mission station. Grant began to provide the Mission's medical services, and Perkins commenced work on the educational mandates of the Mission. The house they had secured was in the part of the city which was bordering the Nestorian and Moslem neighborhoods: "The house itself had a garden attached, and a court, shaded with trees, where ladies could enjoy the air, without the annoying publicity of walking through an oriental city. The whole is protected by a high mud wall."[79]

By January of 1836, Perkins had prepared the basement of his residence as a schoolroom to begin the Mission's educational work. The

---

[79] Laurie (1853), *Dr. Grant and the Mountain Nestorians,* p. 45.

school opened with only seven students. By the following day, enrollment had increased to 17, and by the summer, it had reached 40 students.[80] Regarding the issue of literacy and religious education, reflecting back on the days of his arrival in the field, Perkins wrote:

> None but their ecclesiastics could even read; and but very few of them could do more than chant their devotions in an unknown tongue — the Syriac, a modern dialect of which is their spoken language, while neither they nor their hearers knew any thing of the meaning.[81]

The school was unique in that it was the first of its kind in Persia to use the Lancastrian model of teaching. This system emphasized a structured approach to education, with a hierarchy of students. The older and more senior students were first taught in a classroom setting by a master instructor. The remaining students were then grouped into small learning groups, each led by one of the more senior students who had been taught directly by the master instructor.

This system enabled the more senior students to become instructors for students that were junior to them.[82] The classroom layout was partitioned to provide separate learning spaces for different groups. The junior students would move from one learning space to another as they mastered each topic, one learning space at a time. This highly efficient system of education was first established by the British to serve the rapidly growing educational demands of the population in the colonies. It was relatively new at the time of the commencement of the Urumia mission's operations, having only been used in practice since 1805.[83]

There were several unique benefits gained by using the Lancastrian approach to education. It allowed for one master instructor to teach a very large number of students, by splitting the class into smaller learning groups, each of which would be instructed by a senior student. This enabled significant efficiency gains in the education system, by reducing the overhead and instructional costs of education.

---

[80] Ibid., p. 75.

[81] Perkins (1861), *Missionary Life in Persia*, pp. 41-42.

[82] Joseph Lancaster (1821), *The Lancastrian System of Education*.

[83] Cubberley (1919), *Public Education in the United States*.

The Mission Seminary (painting by Justin Perkins; c. 1836-1843)

The training of senior students (so that they themselves can become master instructors) allowed for the rapid expansion of the system. The school system could be geographically expanded and new schools could be opened using these newly minted master instructors in a relatively short period of time. Geographic expansion was critical from the perspective of the Mission, since the offering of educational services in a large number of Nestorian villages in the Urumia region was a critical objective of the Mission. Reflecting on this, Perkins wrote: "Its object, from the first, was to raise up pious teachers and preachers."[84]

Priest Abraham who, as mentioned earlier, had accompanied Perkins back to Tabriz to assist him in learning Syriac, served as the master instructor for the newly opened school. Perkins served as the school's superintendent. Within the first year, the Mission opened three primary schools in three large villages. The number of schools eventually grew to exceed 60 schools in nearly 60 villages in the following years.[85] One of the most significant challenges in combating illiteracy in Urumia was that there was no written form for the dialect of the Syriac language used in Urumia.

---

[84] Perkins (1861), *Missionary Life in Persia,* p.43.
[85] Ibid., p. 110.

Urumia Female Seminary Graduate (dressed in white at the schoolhouse entrance)
and Her Students in the Kurdish Mountains (c. 1905)

School Children in a Village School in the Urumia Plain (c. 1905)

Perkins described the unique nature of the Syriac dialect spoken in the Urumia region as such:

> The *vernacular* language of the Nestorians, is a modern dialect of the ancient Syriac, much barbarized, by inversions, contractions and abbreviations, and by the introduction of a great number of Persian, Koordish and Turkish words, each class prevailing respectively, in a particular district, in proportion as it is situated near to the people using either of those languages. Though thus corrupted, however, as now spoken by the Nestorians, the body of the language comes directly from the venerable ancient Syriac, as clearly as the modern Greek comes from the ancient.[86]

He further elaborated on the challenges of creating a written form for an evolved language, which to the best of his knowledge at that time had no written form, or agreed upon grammatical rules:

> Very little attempt has been made to reduce the vernacular language of the Nestorians to *writing*, until we commenced our missionary operations. The ancient Syriac being a dead language, and entirely unintelligible to the people until studied as a learned tongue, it seemed to us, at the outset, quite indispensable to the due accomplishment of our object, to make their modern dialect the medium of written, as well as of oral, instruction.[87]

Perkins and Priest Abraham proceeded to develop a written form of the spoken Syriac language and formalized its grammatical structure.[88] In aiding them to teach the written form to their students, reading cards were used for class instruction. It is essential to point out that Perkins' understanding about the lack of a written form for the spoken form of Syriac in Urumia was not informed by the fact that a written form had already been developed for the dialect of Syriac spoken by Nestorians in the Mosul area.[89] However, given the differences between the two dialects, the written form of the Mosul dialect was of little use to the population of Nestorians in Urumia.

---

[86] Perkins (1843), *A Residence of Eight Years in Persia*, p. 12.

[87] Ibid., p. 13.

[88] The grammatical rules were later refined and formally structured by David Tappan Stoddard.

[89] Murre-van den Berg (1996), *The Missionaries' Assistants*, pp. 3-17.

The establishment of the written form for vernacular Syriac was critical for producing the educational material needed in the schools, as well as the production of religious texts needed to advance the Mission's religious services. As a result, in the first year of the Mission's operations, a considerable amount of Perkins' time was dedicated to the development of the written form of modern Syriac — a linguistic contribution for which he is widely recognized. He was also preoccupied heavily with other Mission tasks, including teaching English, preaching, and manual labor.[90]

References and Related Readings

Cubberley, Ellwood P. (1919). *Public Education in the United States.* Boston: Houghton Mifflin.

Lancaster, Joseph (1821). *The Lancastrian System of Education.* Baltimore: Lancastrian Institute.

Laurie, Thomas (1853). *Dr. Grant and the Mountain Nestorians.* Boston: Gould and Lincoln.

Murre-van den Berg, Heleen (1999), *From a Spoken to a Written Language: The Introduction and Development of Literary Urmia Aramaic in the Nineteenth Century.* Leiden: Nederlands Instituut Voor Het Nabije Oosten.

Murre-van den Berg, Heleen (1996). "The Missionaries' Assistants: The Role of Assyrians in the Development of Written Urmia Aramaic," *Journal of the Assyrian Academic Society*, 10(2), pp.3-17.

Perkins, Henry Martyn (1887). *Life of Rev. Justin Perkins, D.D.: Pioneering Missionary to Persia.* Chicago: Woman's Presbyterian Board of Missions of the Northwest.

Perkins, Justin (1861). *Missionary Life in Persia: Glimpses of a Quarter of a Century of Labors Among the Nestorian Christians.* Boston: American Tract Society.

Perkins, Justin (1843). *A Residence of Eight Years in Persia Among the Nestorian Christians.* Andover: Allen, Morrill & Wardell.

Stoddard, David T. (1855). *Grammar of the Modern Syriac Language.* New Haven: American Oriental Society.

Taylor, Gordon (2008). *Fever & Thirst: An American Doctor Among the Tribes of Kurdistan, 1835-1844.* Chicago: Academy Chicago Publishers.

---

[90] Perkins (1887), *Life of Rev. Justin Perkins: Pioneer Missionary to Persia,* p. 21.

Chapter 8

EARLY EXPANSION OF
THE URUMIA MISSION

Within the first year of commencing operations, the work of the Urumia mission station was well received by the Persian government. The presence of the Americans was also well received by the local Moslem population. One of the facts that made the Moslem residents of Urumia receptive to the American missionaries was that both Perkins and Grant, due to their religious convictions and the lessons of the Second Great Awakening regarding temperance, were opposed to the consumption of alcohol. This was a fundamentally important point in the eyes of Moslems, who had up until that time assumed that all Christians consumed alcohol. Islam strictly forbids alcohol consumption by Moslems. It was a pleasant surprise for the local Moslems to have finally found Christians who agree with them on this matter of great importance in Islam. The following extract of a letter written by a local official to Perkins further demonstrates the welcoming effects of the Mission's views on temperance:

> Our Moolah wished me to find, in the gospel if it was forbidden
> to drink wine. We looked into the gospel translated into the

Persian language, and we found it written in 1 Cor. 6:10, that no drunkard shall inherit the kingdom of God.[91]

Given the warm reception by the locals, the Mission's resources and offerings grew over the years. Albert Holladay and William Stocking joined the Mission in 1837, along with their wives (Anne Holladay and Jerusha Stocking). Holladay was from Virginia and a graduate of the University of Virginia. His language skills were impressive and included Latin, French, Spanish, Italian, and Greek. He was also mathematically inclined. These skills were critical in the role he would play in the Missions' educational initiatives. Stocking was from Connecticut. He completed preliminary college-level studies while in America and continued his theological studies when he came to Urumia, under the guidance of Perkins.[92]

In 1838, Britain and Persia went to war over disputed territories including what is now modern-day Afghanistan. Diplomatic relations between the two countries were cut off. This meant that the support that the Urumia mission station had received from the British diplomats in Tabriz would no longer be available. In its early years, the Mission relied a great deal on British diplomatic resources for such things as securing of travel documents, diplomatic representation, medical assistance, and postal service. Now, with the departure of the British diplomats from Persia, the Mission was in a vulnerable position. However, reassurances of safety were expressed by the governor of Urumia. Furthermore, the Russian Consul in Tabriz provided assurances and offered to grant formal protection for the Americans, as needed.

In 1838 the Urumia mission station's scope of educational services was expanded, and the female seminary was opened, much due to the labors of Judith Grant. However, within less than a year, in January of 1839, the mission suffered greatly due to her death. Her loss was so deeply felt by Perkins and his wife, that they named their daughter Judith Grant Perkins in her honor.

In the autumn of 1839, Willard Jones and his wife Miriam arrived. In 1840, Austin Wright, a missionary physician, and Edward Breath, a printer, joined the Mission. Wright was from Vermont. He had

---

[91] Perkins (1861), *Missionary Life in Persia*, p. 73.

[92] He became an ordained minister while in Urumia.

completed part of his studies in Dartmouth College before attending the University of Virginia to study medicine. Wright had an instrumental role in the medical services of the Mission. Wright's role eventually became more significant, while Grant was visiting the Kurdish mountains in the Ottoman Empire and on furlough in America. Wright also took on the lead role in the Mission's medical work in the years following the passing of Grant.[93]

One of the most outstanding yet understated missionaries to join the Mission was Edward Breath. Unlike most other American missionaries, Breath had no formal college education and was a printer's assistant while in America. However, his contributions to the educational and literacy accomplishments of the Mission were perhaps one of the most significant among all missionaries ever to have set foot in Urumia. He introduced printing to the Mission and, by doing so, made it possible to advance the Mission's literacy mandates significantly. The printing press, which he introduced to Urumia, was unique in the entire region and unmatched in quality and output capacity. Because of the printing press technology introduced by Breath, thousands of book copies and millions of pages were produced for use by the schools established by the Mission in the Urumia plain and beyond.

Breath's background contributed to his passion to make such a significant impact, thousands of miles away from home. He was born in New York City. He worked as a printer for an abolitionist newspaper and was a companion of the famous abolitionist, Reverend Elijah Lovejoy. In fact, Breath was by Reverend Lovejoy's side when the reverend was shot and murdered by a pro-slavery mob in Alton, Illinois in 1837. Breath considered this experience to be a life-changing moment that gave him a sense of purpose for his future missionary endeavors. The printing press arrived in Urumia alongside Breath in November of 1840. It was in boxes, massive, and heavy. Unlike most other printing presses at that time, it was custom-manufactured to be in smaller pieces, so that it can be transported on the back of animals and

---

[93] Consult Perkins (1865), *The Beloved Physician: A Sermon Occasioned by the Death of the Rev. Austin H. Wright, M.D.*

reassembled at the press location. It was assembled within days of arriving in Urumia and began operating shortly thereafter.[94]

The first printings were test prints (all in small caps) of a prayer in ancient Syriac. Breath painstakingly cut the modern Syriac type fonts (developed by Perkins and his assistants for the dialect of Syriac used in Urumia) for the press. By March 1841, in addition to printing in ancient Syriac, the press was able to print in modern Syriac.[95] The formation of a written form of modern Syriac and the ability to print in large volumes were critical to the Mission's success. Printing helped increase the level of literacy among the Nestorians on a scale unimaginable through any other means. Education, both in secular and religious forms, could be administered through the books printed by the press. This reduced the burdens and human resource needs of the Mission, allowing it to operate more efficiently and expanded its reach with the limited resources at its disposal.[96] By 1841, one of the major accomplishments of the Mission, primarily achieved through the works of Justin Perkins and priest Abraham, was the translation of the New Testament into modern Syriac. This, in combination with the establishment of the printing press, made the mass distribution of the New Testament to the Nestorian population possible.

The death of Judith Grant in 1839 and the passing of the Perkins' son (also named Justin) later in that year made it necessary for the Mission to prioritize the health of its own people. The suffering that the missionaries and their families were experiencing due to the loss of loved ones to a range of illnesses was commonly shared. During the time that Charlotte and Justin Perkins were mourning the loss of their son, they received a condolence letter from Grant. At that time, Grant was also mourning the loss of his own wife, Judith, and had since traveled to Mosul and in his letter acknowledged the shared pain: "You and I are called to drink often of the cup of affliction."[97] The shared sadness of losing loved ones to various illnesses made it more pressing to set up a "health retreat" away from the city of Urumia, especially for the summer.

---

[94] See Malick (2008), *The American Mission Press: A Preliminary Bibliography,* p. 9.
[95] Coakley (1995), *Edward Breath and the Typography of Syriac*
[96] For a summary of the Urumia press output in its early years, see Henry Martyn Perkins (1887), *Life of Rev. Justin Perkins: Pioneer Missionary to Persia,* pp. 40-55.
[97] Laurie (1853), *Dr. Grant and the Mountain Nestorians,* p. 117.

The Urumia Mission Station Printing Press (c. 1905)

The exceptionally hot summer temperatures of the city, combined with water-borne diseases such as malaria and cholera, made Urumia a very unhealthy place for living during the summer months. Other disease symptoms that frequently afflicted the missionaries and their families in Urumia were high fever and ophthalmia (burning inflammation of the eyes). It was believed that the occurrence of these illnesses would be greatly reduced by leaving for higher elevations in the summer.[98]

It became clear to Perkins that it was essential for the Mission to have a retreat outside of Urumia. This retreat was eventually built in the

---

[98] Perkins (1861), *Missionary Life in Persia,* p. 45.

village of Seir, six miles south-west of the city.[99] At the higher elevations of Seir, cooler temperatures prevailed. Its distance from large bodies of agricultural water that could host deadly diseases, made Seir a healthier environment for the missionaries and their families during the summer months. Perkins closely supervised the construction tasks and the retreat was completed in 1841. For decades after its construction, Seir served as a summer retreat and as a residential compound for many missionaries and their families who found the climate and environment more hospitable than that of Urumia.

By 1841, having resided in Persia for a total of eight years and upon the completion of the construction of the Seir retreat, Perkins felt a need to visit America. Part of his motivation was to recruit more missionaries for the Urumia mission station. However, the return was also due to the failing health of his wife. Recognizing that a change in the environment may be necessary for her, the ABCFM directly instructed Perkins to return to America. At that point, the family consisted of Charlotte, Justin, and their 13-month old daughter Judith, whom the couple had nicknamed the "Persian Flower."

Mar Yohannan had expressed great interest in seeing the New World. While Perkins did not persuade or dissuade him from making the journey, the ultimate decision as to whether or not Yohannan would be able to make the trip, was with his father. Despite his high status as a bishop of Urumia, Yohannan had to seek his father's blessing for this trip, which was reluctantly given. On their journey back to America, the Perkins were therefore joined by Yohannan.

By Yohannan joining the departing party, it became possible for those in America to interact with someone from the faraway lands of Persia's Nestorians. People in America were able to experience first-hand who the Nestorians were. Once in America, Yohannan accompanied Perkins on his tours of different churches and college campuses. By doing so, he would provide validation for the accomplishments of the Urumia mission station. This not only allowed Perkins to justify the cause of the Urumia mission effectively, but it

---

[99] With the southward expansion of the city of Urumia over the years, the current distance between the southern limits of the city and the village of Seir is approximately two miles.

was also of great help in his efforts to recruit missionaries with a passion for serving in Persia.

The party left Urumia on July 5, 1841. They followed very much the same path taken nearly a decade earlier by the Perkins to travel to Urumia. On their way, they stopped in Constantinople. Judith Perkins learned to walk on board the ship that took them from Constantinople to New York. They arrived on January 11, 1842, just in time for an ABCFM meeting. Perkins had always been known for his punctuality. His punctuality on this one occasion, arriving from half-way around the world, just in time for this ABCFM meeting in New York City, must have impressed his missionary colleagues.

References and Related Readings

Coakley, John F. (1995). "Edward Breath and the Typography of Syriac," *Harvard Library Bulletin*, 6(4), 41-64.

Laurie, Thomas (1853). *Dr. Grant and the Mountain Nestorians*. Boston: Gould and Lincoln.

Malick, David G. (2008). *The American Mission Press: A Preliminary Bibliography*. ATOUR Publications.

Murre-van den Berg, Heleen (1999), *From a Spoken to a Written Language: The Introduction and Development of Literary Urmia Aramaic in the Nineteenth Century*. Leiden: Nederlands Instituut Voor Het Nabije Oosten.

Perkins, Henry Martyn (1887). *Life of Rev. Justin Perkins, D.D.: Pioneering Missionary to Persia*. Chicago: Woman's Presbyterian Board of Missions of the Northwest.

Perkins, Justin (1865). *The Beloved Physician: A Sermon Occasioned by the Death of the Rev. Austin H. Wright, M.D.* New York: Edward Jenkins.

Perkins, Justin (1861). *Missionary Life in Persia: Glimpses of a Quarter of a Century of Labors Among the Nestorian Christians*. Boston: American Tract Society.

Chapter 9

"A RESIDENCE OF EIGHT YEARS IN PERSIA"

During the visit to America, Perkins wrote his first book: *A Residence of Eight Years in Persia*. In it, he provided an inside glimpse of life in Persia. It was beautifully written and contained Perkins' own hand drawings, which captured the visual sensations of the landscape, places and people that he had come across.[100] The challenging conditions and the time constraints under which Perkins had written the book are noteworthy. The self-discipline of Perkins as an author would be the source of envy for any aspiring author today. His ability to multi-task partially explains why he had been given the nickname of "twenty-four-hour boy" by his classmates during his college days at Amherst. He described the circumstances under which he wrote the book, while in America, as such:

> I copied about one-fourth of the volume, on our homeward passage. My circumstances, after reaching this country, could hardly have been more unfavorable for prosecuting the task, remaining, as I did, but a day or two in a place, with two exceptions of a week, during the first nine months, and being called upon, almost constantly, to attend public meetings, in company with the Nestorian bishop who came with me. I have sometimes written an hour at a public house, while waiting for a

---

[100] The publication of this book in 1843 was preceded by the 1841 publication of *Nestorians, or, the Lost Tribes,* written by Perkins' closest missionary associate at that time, Asahel Grant.

stage-coach; at other times, in the cabin of a steamer, among scores of passengers; and have often revised my manuscript, while travelling in rail-road cars.[101]

A Residence of Eight Years in Persia was published in 1843. It has served as a resource for Orientalists seeking an understanding of the early encounters between Americans and the various groups living in the Urumia area at that time, for nearly two centuries. Authorship of this book created a context for Perkins to expand his scholarly and missionary conversations with interested audiences. During the visit to America, he gave numerous speeches in colleges and theological seminaries in northeastern United States, communicating the cause of the American missionaries in Persia and promoted the ABCFM. He was also in pursuit of energetic and passionate missionaries to join him and his colleagues in Urumia. Yohannan accompanied Perkins on many of these visits, mostly in major cities in New York and Massachusetts.

Among the colleges visited was Mount Holyoke Seminary, a women's college in Massachusetts, established by Mary Lyon. In his earlier years as a student at Amherst College, Perkins had been introduced to Lyon, who eventually established Mount Holyoke Seminary. In those days, the two had extensive conversations on educational philosophies and pedagogy. In later years, Lyon successfully implemented many of her innovations regarding female education in America through the schools she established.

Many of the female ABCFM missionaries destined for Persia and the Ottoman Empire emerged from Mount Holyoke. Perkins' visit to Mount Holyoke sparked the interest of one person in particular, Fidelia Fiske. Fiske was a Congregationalist with firm religious convictions and one of the first graduates of Mount Holyoke Seminary. She had a passion for becoming a missionary from an early age, influenced by her uncle, Pliny Fisk, who had served as a pioneering ABCFM missionary in Egypt and Palestine.[102] When she met Perkins at Mount Holyoke,

---

[101] Perkins (1843), *A Residence of Eight Years in Persia,* page VI.

[102] Note the varied spelling of the last name. A book published in her name two years after her death has her last name spelled as "Fisk." Justin Perkins referred to her as "Miss Fisk." Her gravestone in Shelburne Center Cemetery in Massachusetts has her last name engraved as "Fisk." However, the Female Seminary named after her in

Fiske was a faculty member and the designated successor to Mary Lyon.[103] However, with her passion for missionary work, and the personal encouragement of Lyon, Fiske decided to join the Mission in Urumia. She would eventually have monumental effects on female education in Urumia and Persia, by replicating some of Lyon's ideals, which had been successfully implemented at Mount Holyoke.

The visits to the various churches and college campuses paid off. During the one-year time period that Perkins and Yohannan promoted the missionary cause, they were able to recruit additional missionaries for the Urumia mission. All would join them on their return journey to Urumia. One such missionary was David Tappan Stoddard, who Perkins met while touring Middlebury, Vermont. According to Stoddard's biographer, Joseph Thompson, upon meeting Stoddard: "Dr. Perkins at once felt that this earnest young preacher was the man he was in quest of for Oroomiah."[104] Stoddard had experienced an awakening while a student at Yale and believed in his destiny as a missionary.

Stoddard, however, also had serious hesitations about missionary life, as he wrote on the same night he had first met Perkins: "This evening Solomon and I have made a very pleasant call on Mr. and Mrs. Perkins, who are here on a flying visit. Mr. Perkins is quite anxious that I should go with him to Persia. I promised him that I would consider the matter, though I hardly think I shall go any where as a missionary." According to Thompson, the following day, in another correspondence, he elaborated on the source of his hesitation being his failing health:

> Mr. Perkins pressed me to take the subject into prayerful
> consideration, and I rather promised to do so. It seems to me,
> however, that I can be more useful at the West than in the
> missionary field. The only question about which I feel in great
> doubt is, whether my health will enable me to labor efficiently
> in *either* of these portions of the harvest. I can preach twice a

---

Urumia is called the "Fiske" Seminary. Missionary writings in later years spell her last name as "Fiske."

[103] Ameer (1997), *Yankees and Nestorians,* p. 75.

[104] Thompson (1858), *Memoir of the Rev. David Tappan Stoddard, Missionary to the Nestorians,* p. 89.

day with considerable ease, but after all I have not much
physical vigor, and I fear that two sermons a week, with
lecturing, and the innumerable duties of a pastor, will soon wear
me out.[105]

Stoddard was still undecided about committing himself to the
Mission and left Perkins without agreeing to join the Mission. It was
only by chance, when Perkins and Stoddard were attending an ABCFM
meeting in Norwich, Connecticut, that they were assigned to the same
room in the lodging location where they were staying. Rooming
together, Perkins was able to further the conversation, and it was after
this third meeting between the two men that Stoddard accepted the
invitation to join the Urumia Mission. His primary reason for accepting
the invitation was that he felt that his faith called for him to commit
himself to the missionary cause in Persia.

In addition to Stoddard's unquestionable faith, there were other
good reasons why Perkins desired Stoddard to join him. Stoddard was a
well-read, well-educated, and knowledgeable man. He was a scientist
by training and a graduate of Yale with honors. His abilities as both a
teacher and a researcher in the sciences were well recognized by those
at Yale. In fact, in choosing a missionary life, he gave up an offer for a
stable and comfortable lifestyle as a professor at Marietta College. It is
this level of intellectual power combined with the strength of devotion
that Perkins was looking for. As it turns out, Perkins was correct in his
assessment of Stoddard, since in the years that followed, Stoddard
succeeded in formulating the grammatical structure for the vernacular
Syriac. This accomplishment was of fundamental significance to the
Mission's mandate of formalizing the linguistic structure of the Urumia
dialect of Syriac, and propelled the Mission's literacy objectives
forward.

Return to Urumia

After a stay of about one year in America, the Perkins family decided
to return to Urumia. Fiske, Stoddard and his wife Harriette, and a newly
recruited missionary named Catherine Myers (who later married Dr.
Austin Wright in Urumia), joined the Perkins (Justin, Charlotte and
Judith) and Yohannan on the voyage to Urumia. They departed on
March 1st, 1843, from the port of Boston, heading for Smyrna

---

[105] Ibid., p. 90.

(modern-day Izmir, Turkey). Three weeks later, on March 24, Stoddard, writing a letter to a relative, described the typical day on board the ship:

> Perhaps you would like to know how our time is occupied, hour by hour. We are systematic. After rising in the morning we spend the time before breakfast, if any time remains, in reading the Scriptures. We get up about half-past six, and it takes about twice as long to dress as on shore, especially for the ladies. If you are disposed to think we are late risers, you will recollect that we are frequently disturbed in our rest by the rolling of the vessel, and the running to and fro of the sailors. Moreover, there is no place to sit in, when one is up, for the mates are busy washing down the decks, and the house on deck is not very comfortable. When breakfast is over, and Harriette and I have read our Bible, we study Turkish till ten o'clock.... At ten o'clock we all meet and spend an hour in reading Geology. It is very desirable that we should have a pretty good knowledge of this science, for we are going over one of the most striking geological countries in the world, and a country, too, very little explored.... After Geology comes our recitation in Turkish, Mr. Perkins being the teacher. This fills up the interval till dinner. At half-past one we again assemble to read. The latter part of the afternoon each one spends as he pleases, but it is usually occupied by our whole company in writing letters to absent friends. At six o'clock we meet still again, to spend a half-hour in singing. Several of our number have never learned to sing, and Mr. Perkins is very desirous they should learn. I do not wonder at it; for a missionary, of all other, should have this qualification. You will be glad to know that we are making very tolerable improvement, and that even I have hopes of being able at last *to sing*. Our singing is followed by our devotions, at which we expound the Scriptures, sing a hymn and pray. Then a part of the reminder of the evening we read D'Aubigne's History; The rest we spend in social converse. Our hour for retiring is from nine to ten.[106]

The party arrived in Smyrna in April of 1843, and after a short stay, they took a steamer ship to Trebizond, where they arrived in May. From there, they proceeded overland to Urumia. Stoddard's letters to his family members further elaborated on the land journey, as in the

---

[106] Ibid., pp. 110-112.

case of the following passage addressed to his brother regarding the Turkish portion of the voyage:

> Would you know how we look as we set out? Well, then, you shall see. Our party consists of seven, besides Mr. Perkins's little girl. Each of us has a horse and an American saddle. After us comes a horse loaded with our tents, then several more with Turkish chests, full of provisions. Then strung over the backs of animals are our cooking utensils and our luggage. Little Judith [Mr. Perkins's little girl] rides in a basket, which I have covered with a large calash to protect her from the sun. In the rear are two men — one a Jew — the other an Armenian; they are to aid us on our journey. As we wind up the narrow lanes of the city, see the Turkish women — all vailed except a single eye — peeping forth full of curiosity at the strangers. If you will follow us to the end of our first day's journey, you will see us pitching our tents by the side of a little stream, in a beautiful valley. Our attendant will bring our eggs, and crackers and butter, and dried tongues, and way-worn and hungry, we shall sit down to our grassy table. On the morrow, *Inshawlaw* (if God please), you shall see us beginning to ascend lofty mountains, and look down on some of the most enchanting scenery that the eye ever gazes on. Indeed the whole of this country is a Paradise.[107]

Upon returning to Urumia in June 1843, Perkins continued his work by supervising the translations into Syriac of many important texts. Mrs. Perkins gave birth to a boy on December 21, 1843, which the couple named Henry Martyn Perkins. He was named after the pioneering Anglican priest who had visited Persia nearly half a century earlier, and had produced the very first Farsi translation of the New Testament.

Perkins and Stoddard took on the primary responsibility for translating a large number of texts from English to modern Syriac. The fruits of their labors include the full translations of the New and Old Testaments completed in 1846 and 1852, respectively, as well as many commentaries on Biblical texts, including the books of Genesis,

---

[107] Ibid., pp. 119-120.

Exodus, and Daniel. Starting from 1849, the Mission also began the publication of *Rays of Light*, a monthly magazine for the Nestorian population of Persia, and one of the first magazines to ever be published in all of Persia. In all of these literary efforts, the help of Nestorian assistants was vital.[108] In addition to Yohannan and Priest Abraham, non-clergy Assyrian assistants aided in translation, writing, and printing tasks.[109]

In addition to translation work, Justin Perkins continued to preach and carry out his ministerial duties. Early in 1844, his closest and earliest missionary colleague, Asahel Grant, died while visiting Mosul. Grant was away from Urumia for a considerable length of time on the Ottoman side of the border, and had not been to Urumia since the summer of 1842. He had escaped from Turkey's Hakkari mountains to Mosul due to the war and violence in the region. In Mosul, while taking care of the refugees, Grant contracted typhus fever, and passed away on April 24th. Perkins was, therefore, unable see Grant for many years before Grant's passing.[110]

In 1847, the Boys' Seminary was moved from the city of Urumia to the village of Seir. The new location was the Mission's grounds in Seir, which Perkins had first established in 1841. The Seir location grew over the years and became a residential and educational facility. The following year, changes on a larger scale took place in Persia. The Qajar king, Mohammad Shah, died in 1848 from natural causes. The heir chosen by Mohammad Shah before his passing was his son, Naser

---

[108] Murre-van den Berg (1996), *The Missionaries' Assistants: The Role of Assyrians in the Development of Written Urmia Aramaic*.

[109] Note that the terms "Assyrian" and "Nestorian" are interchangeably used. In the early years of the Urumia Mission (and in fact in the very naming of the Mission formally being the "Mission to the Nestorians" or the "Nestorian Mission"), the more commonly used designation by the missionaries was "Nestorian." However, due to the fact that Nestorius was considered an outcast by the Roman Church, Nestorians generally preferred the use of the designation "Assyrian" instead. As such, respecting this preference and with increased sensitivity of the missionaries on this matter, as the years moved forward, missionaries began to use "Assyrian" more frequently, as will also be the case in this book.

[110] During these years, while Asahel Grant was away from Urumia, Dr. Austin Wright was at the head of the Mission's medical services.

al-Din, who became the next Qajar king of Persia at the age of seventeen.[111]

Due to his long reign of five decades and his personal ambitions and shortcoming, Naser al-Din Shah's policies and actions greatly impacted Persia. While he attempted to modernize Persia, he fiscally strapped the country into binding concessions with Russia and Britain and weakened Persia's independence. His weaknesses as a person and a ruler contributed to Persia's economic and military decline during the nineteenth century. Despite his many shortcomings, throughout his reign, Naser al-Din Shah was supportive of American missionary efforts.

References and Related Readings

Ameer, John Pierre (1997). *Yankees and Nestorians: The Establishment of American Schools Among the Nestorians of Iran and Turkey, 1834-1850.* (Doctoral Dissertation). Harvard University.

Becker, Adam H. (2015). *Revival and Awakening: American Evangelical Missionaries in Iran and the Origins of Assyrian Nationalism.* Chicago: University of Chicago Press.

Murre-van den Berg, Heleen (1996). "The Missionaries' Assistants: The Role of Assyrians in the Development of Written Urmia Aramaic," *Journal of the Assyrian Academic Society*, 10(2), pp.3-17.

Perkins, Justin (1865). *The Beloved Physician: A Sermon Occasioned by the Death of Austin G. Wright, M.D. Preached to the Families of the Nestorian Mission at Oroomiah, Persia*, Feb. 8th, 1865. New York: Edward O. Jenkins.

Perkins, Justin (1843). *A Residence of Eight Years in Persia Among the Nestorian Christians.* Andover: Allen, Morrill & Wardell.

Thompson, Joseph P. (1858). *Memoir of the Rev. David Tappan Stoddard, Missionary to the Nestorians.* Boston: American Tract Society.

---

[111] He reigned until his assassination in 1896.

Chapter 10

"THE PERSIAN FLOWER"

Judith Grant Perkins, the "Persian Flower"

In late summer of 1852, the Perkins family, consisting of Justin, Charlotte, their daughter Judith and their son Henry Martyn, embarked on a journey to the Kurdish mountains north of Urumia. During the trip, Judith contracted cholera. She began to exhibit clear symptoms of the disease when the family was in the outskirts of the village of Zorava (Zurabad), to the northwest of Khoi, nearly 200 miles away from Urumia. They were out of reach of any form of medical help and camped overnight outside of the village. A request for drinking water was denied by the villagers due to prejudice. Without essential medical help and drinking water, Judith passed away on September 4, 1852. She was only twelve years old.

Judith was the love of the Perkins. Her loss had a heavy toll on the family. She was so precious to the family that a missionary colleague of the family wrote a biography of her, honoring her life. It was published in 1853 and appropriately titled *The Persian Flower*.[112] Judith had a special place in the Perkins' hearts. She had missionary aspirations of her own, a desire to attend Mount Holyoke Seminary, and was an avid reader and organ player. She was full of passion, inspiration, and talent.

For decades after her passing, every year, the Perkins celebrated Judith's birthday on August 8th. Despite the pain of losing his beloved daughter, and the fact that the villagers near their encampment refused to provide them with the drinking water essential to Judith's survival, Perkins forgave them. Instead of expressing anger, he prayed for their souls. His reaction demonstrated his depth of conviction in the principle of forgiveness, so central to his faith.

The passing of Judith was especially devastating to Mrs. Perkins. Being far from her homeland and in a turbulent environment had affected her health.[113] During the 1850s, Persia became a less hospitable place for family life. In 1856, the Anglo-Persian War began. The war, which had been sparked due to disputes over the city of Herat (in modern-day Afghanistan), resulted in the deployment of British war

---

[112] Although the book was published anonymously, its authorship has been attributed to Thomas Laurie.

[113] For an informative account of the effects of the passing of Judith and other Perkins children on Charlotte Perkins, see Taylor (2009), *Deep Waters: Life and Death in the Perkins Family, 1834-1852*.

ships to the Persian Gulf. While it ended in April of 1857 with a peace treaty, the war clearly demonstrated Persia's military weaknesses and reinforced British domination of Persia. Britain effectively used its growing power over Persia for decades to come in forcing concessions and territorial claims. During the Anglo-Persian War of 1856, the diplomatic protection which the missionaries enjoyed under the umbrella of the British consul in Tabriz was no longer available to them. The absence of such protection was a source of concern, and during that time period, Russia had offered the Americans its protection.

Given Judith's passing and the growingly unstable political climate of Persia, by 1857 the Perkins made a decision for Charlotte and Henry Martyn to return to America. This change was deemed necessary to ensure physical and emotional health for Mrs. Perkins, and to provide a stable environment for Henry Martyn's education. They left Urumia in September of 1857. Perkins followed his family's return to America the following year, leaving Urumia in the summer of 1858.

It is important to recognize that by the time Justin Perkins began his return journey to America, the Urumia mission station's activities and physical facilities had significantly grown. This was a testament to Perkins' abilities as a visionary and a leader. In the nearly two decades that the Mission had been in place, its facilities had grown to include the Girls' School (eventually renamed the Fiske Seminary), located in the city of Urumia. It also included the Boys' School situated in the village of Seir (six miles from Urumia's southern boundaries at that time). The Mission also had a fully operational printing press in the city. Furthermore, the Mission supported nearly one hundred schools throughout the Urumia region and provided healthcare services to those of all faiths.

Perkins arrived in Boston in December of 1858 and remained in America for four years, returning to Persia at the end of 1862. During his stay, America began a period of great change. Abraham Lincoln became President in March of 1861, and the American Civil War fought over the issue of slavery began. Perkins visited England that year, where he gave speeches advocating the missionary cause and discussed the disgraces of slavery. He also preached his sermon titled *Our Country's Sin*. This was a sermon which he had delivered several years earlier, during an Independence Day celebration, to the families and associates of the Mission in Urumia. The contents of this sermon and its relationship to the anti-slavery movement in America are noteworthy. Among the expressions of Perkins in *Our Country's Sin* was the acknowledgment of the great need for change in American attitudes on slavery:

> I hold that our beloved native country is in the most imminent peril from the fearful system of American slavery, of falling into deep national disgrace, and calling down upon itself the signal judgments of heaven, and thus blighting, for a long period, the purest and the highest hopes of a suffering world.[114]

On other occasions while in England, Perkins had expressed his views of civil unrest in America: "That God has taken the monstrous evil of sin and slavery in hand and designs to shake it down by civil war, as the proximate if not the immediate agency, I have not the shadow of a doubt."[115] What Perkins articulated in *Our Country's Sin* was an expression of the abolitionist segment of many Protestant denominations in America at that time. The need for a clear expression of its views on abolition had, in fact, challenged the Prudential Committee of the ABCFM, which had resisted openly and unequivocally condemning slavery.[116] It feared the loss of financial donations from congregations that favored slavery. The hesitance of the ABCFM to openly express its disapproval of slavery affected its credibility and eventually caused schisms within the organization. These schisms had dramatic results in its operations in the years that followed. *Our Country's Sin* was a clear articulation of the resentment that many of the ABCFM missionaries felt about the evils of slavery.

During the time that Perkins was away from Urumia, he also corresponded with Lewis Tappan, a well-known anti-slavery reformer. To him, Perkins wrote:

> With my whole heart, I bid those God speed who are praying and toiling to remove this mighty evil, and avert these calamities, and I pledge them the only humble co-operation I can offer, my fervent and unceasing prayers. Their cause is the cause of God; and however weak and fallible may be the instruments engaged in it, the truth is mighty and it will prevail.

---

[114] Justin Perkins (1854), *Our Country's Sin*, p. 4.

[115] Ibid., pp. 59-60.

[116] McLoughlin (1973), *Indian Slaveholders and Presbyterian Missionaries: 1837-1861*.

Nor can I help believing that the day is not distant, when good people in America, much as they are now divided, will be of one heart and one mind on this momentous subject. It does appear to me that an evil, so appalling in magnitude and in guilt at as American slavery, incurring as it does the rebuke of the world, and provoking as it must the frowns of heaven, cannot, when fairly spread out to view, in the light the present day, much longer find advocates or apologists or neutrals among American Christians or American patriots.[117]

Interestingly, around this time, Perkins had also expressed hopes for the growth of Christianity in the East. He was hopeful that following the Crimean War between Turkey and Russia (1853-1856), and with the growing European influence on the Ottoman Empire, it would be possible to reach greater levels of growth not only within the Ottoman Empire but also possibly in Persia. Perkins' views on this matter were partially influenced by the Imperial Rescript of 1856. The Rescript was put into effect under British pressure on the Ottomans.[118] It gave increased legal and religious rights to Ottoman Christians, for example by allowing reconversion of Christians who had converted to other religions, back to Christianity, or the conversion of non-Ottoman citizens into Christianity.

References and Related Readings

Davidson, Roderick (1956). "The Hatt-i-Humayn of 1856 and the Climate of its Reception" in *Reform in the Ottoman Empire (1856-1876)*. Princeton: University Press.

McLoughlin, William G. (1973). "Indian Slaveholders and Presbyterian Missionaries, 1837-1861," *American Society of Church History*, pp. 535-551.

---

[117] Perkins (1887), *Life of Rev. Justin Perkins: Pioneer Missionary to Persia*, pp. 35-36.

[118] Davidson (1956), *The Hatt-i-Humayn of 1856 and the Climate of its Reception. Note that the Imperial Rescript of 1856 did not formally allow for the conversion of Ottoman Moslems into Christianity. It hence was applicable only to specific population sub-groups and not the general population in Ottoman lands.*

Perkins, Henry Martyn (1887). *Life of Rev. Justin Perkins, D.D.: Pioneering Missionary to Persia.* Chicago: Woman's Presbyterian Board of Missions of the Northwest.

Perkins, Justin (1853), *Our Country's Sin: A Sermon Preached to the Members and Families of the Nestorian Mission at Oroomiah, Persia on July 3, 1853.* New York: H.B. Knight

Taylor, Gordon (2009). "Deep Waters: Life and Death in the Perkins Family: 1834-1852," *Journal of Assyrian Academic Studies.*

The Persian Flower: A Memoir of Judith Grant Perkins. Boston: John P. Jewett and Company. Published anonymously in 1853.

Chapter 11

PERKINS' FINAL VISIT TO URUMIA

Upon the completion of his European visit in the summer of 1861, Perkins returned to America. The four years away from Urumia had allowed him to write a summarized version of *A Residence of Eight Years in Persia*. This new book was much shorter and more readable for the general public and non-scholars. Published in 1861, it was titled *Missionary Life in Persia*. It provided the highlights of Perkins' previous book and included new perspectives on missionary work in Urumia.

In the summer of 1862, Perkins began his return voyage to Urumia. His wife and son, however, did not accompany him. It was agreed that for the continued improvement of the health of his wife and the education of their son, it would be best for them to remain in America. However, the America that Perkins was leaving was about to drastically change in the next few years. The American Civil War had already begun and the abolition of slavery eventually changed the political and social landscape of America in the 1860s. This was something that Perkins had predicted in his earlier writings such as *Our Country's Sin*, as mentioned previously.

Perkins returned to Urumia, and remained there between 1862 and 1869. With the absence of his family, a void had been created in his life in Urumia. Despite this, he had returned to a mission station that was active and demanded his full attention. It had grown to approximately

20 American missionaries, many with their own families residing on Mission grounds. Perkins was physically a more fragile man, compared to his younger days when he had launched the Mission to the Nestorians. He was now viewed by the missionaries and their families as a father figure to whom everyone looked up. His days were filled with writing commentaries in Syriac on the Bible, translating hymns into Syriac, and other works for publication by the Mission's press.

One of Perkins' most important roles during this time period was mentoring the next generation of American missionaries who had come to Urumia. His living quarters were near other missionaries and their families. Because of his loving and caring manners, he was referred to as "Grandpa" by the missionaries' children, and "Father" by the native Assyrians.[119] Most missionaries could feel that he missed his family very much. One of the most touching facts was that on August 8th of every year, he celebrated his daughter's birthday and invited the missionary families to celebrate her life with him, despite Judith's passing away years earlier.

By the 1850s, some of the Nestorians had begun to feel a need for change in the Old Nestorian Church. This need was partially rooted in the early history of the Urumia mission station, and some of the conflicts with the Nestorian patriarch which had begun the 1840s. Grant's visits in the 1840s to the Nestorian settlements of the Hakkari mountains of Turkey took place at a time of significant instability in the Ottoman Empire. Differences between Grant and the Nestorian patriarch on how to handle the political and militarized forces of the Kurds and the Ottomans resulted in a fundamental dislike of Grant and the Americans. The patriarch believed that Grant had aggravated the tensions between the Nestorians and the Kurds, provoking some of the Kurdish tribes to rise against the Nestorians of the Turkish mountains.[120] A series of skirmishes quickly turned into religious warfare, and thousands of mountain Nestorians perished in 1842, 1843 and 1846. The relationship between the American missionaries and the patriarch, who was at the helm of the Old Nestorian Church, based in Turkey, gradually deteriorated over the years.

---

[119] Perkins (1887), *Life of Rev. Justin Perkins - Pioneer Missionary to Persia*, p. 67.

[120] This, however, is a matter of historical debate as will be explored in the chapters related to Asahel Grant.

In Persia, however, the relationship between the American missionaries and the Nestorians was much more positive. The Americans had done much good for the Nestorians of Urumia and had earned their trust and friendship. As such, in the Urumia plain, some of the followers of the Old Nestorian Church felt that the church was not adapting to the changes of modern times and was stuck in its old ways. Urumia's Nestorians felt that the Old Nestorian Church, with its headquarters far away in Turkey, was out of touch with the evolving needs of Urumia's Nestorian population.

While the missionary instructions given by the ABCFM to Perkins when launching the Mission to the Nestorians had been to not interfere in Nestorians' church governance matters, some of the Nestorians were now desiring change. Perkins considered it unwise for the Mission to be involved in facilitating such a change or participating in the breakup of the Old Nestorian Church. Such involvement would conflict with the clear instructions that the ABCFM had given him in the 1830s.

However, given that Perkins was no longer the head of the Urumia mission station and preoccupied with many other important matters, he did not participate in this decision. A younger missionary, by the name of John Haskell Shedd, who had become the head of the Urumia Mission, strongly advocated for change. Shedd had spent years preaching to the Nestorians (Assyrians) in the mountain villages of the Urumia region and felt that Persia's Assyrians needed change.[121] Shedd respectfully advanced his views, despite the opposing opinions of Perkins, the most senior missionary, to whom he looked up.

The members of the Old Nestorian Church who were not content with the Old Church eventually formed the Assyrian Evangelical Church in 1862 (also referred to as the "Syrian Evangelical Church," and "Evangelical Church" for short). The very name of the church, using the designation of "Assyrian" rather "Nestorian," signified the modernization aspirations of a congregation who clearly wished not to be addressed as "Nestorian." The newly formed church had three presbyteries in Persia and one in Turkey.[122] There were disagreements

---

[121] Note that as mentioned earlier in this book, the terms "Nestorian", "Assyrian" and "Syrian" were interchangeably used by the American missionaries. During the 1850s and beyond, the preferred way to address Nestorians was "Assyrian" or "Syrian," and hence these designations will be more frequently used in the remaining chapters.

[122] Shedd (1922), *The Measure of a Man*, p. 31.

among the missionaries about how much the Mission should be engaged in the formation and promotion of the Syrian Evangelical Church. This was an important question since the newly established church found its strongest following in the Urumia region, while the Old Nestorian Church was predominately active in the Ottoman territories.

From an administrative point of view, the formation of the Syrian Evangelical Church had great benefits for the Assyrians of Persia. One of the most important of these was the formation of the Legal Board. The Board allowed Assyrians to settle their legal differences under the umbrella of the Evangelical Church rather than to rely on Persian courts to rule on their cases. This was critical, in light of the fact that both the Assyrians and the missionaries felt that the Persian court system had the potential to put both the plaintiff and the defendant at a disadvantage due to mismanagement, corruption, and misconduct by Qajar government authorities. In the decades to come, the Legal Board of the Assyrian Evangelical Church became an advocate with the Persian government to improve the legal rights of Assyrians, and other Christian denominations of Persia, on a range of legal issues related to civil matters such as inheritance and marriage. It also intensively engaged missionaries who were members of its Legal Board in seeking Persian government intervention in unique, and at times disturbing, criminal cases.

In the formation of the Syrian Evangelical Church, Perkins demonstrated what it means to be an open-minded and democratic role model. He observed the forces calling for the formation of a new church. He articulated his opposing rationale and expressed his disagreement. Yet, he did not fight the will of the Syrians or question the intentions of his fellow missionaries. The manner of his response during the deliberations leading to the creation of the new church clearly demonstrated a genuine belief in democratic governance.

Given that a new generation of American missionaries was in place to thoughtfully navigate the future of the Mission, Perkins could instead focus on his other projects. One of the more critical priorities for him, before departing from the Urumia station and returning for good to America, was the construction of a church in Ardishai located to the south of Urumia. This structure still stands today.[123] According to his son: Henry Martyn Perkins: "Every Monday through the summer's heat, he mounted his big white horse, and rode after Sabbath services to Ardishai, a day's journey, over bad roads, and stood by the slowly ascending walls, and watched the placing of each brick and timber, till the great church was completed."[124] The Persian government as well as several European governments partially funded the construction of this church.

During 1869, Justin Perkins began to increasingly feel unwell. The supervision of the construction of the church in Ardishai proved to be demanding. Having been away from his family for years, he felt their absence a great deal. The combination of his physical ailments as an aging man, and his desire to reunite with his family made it necessary for him to commence his final return to America and leave Urumia for good. On the eve of his voyage back to America, he made a brief speech to the missionaries and Nestorian friends, an extract of which is below:

> My Nestorian Friends: I have sometimes been in circumstances
> when my heart was so full that my tongue could not speak.
> Such is the case to-day, and I shall try to say little. I came to
> your people young; I go out from you old. Twice before I have
> visited America since my first coming. Then I had the hope of
> returning to you again, and that hope was a comfort to me. *Now*
> I go for the last time, not expecting to return. We shall see each
> other's faces no more in this world. The parting makes this hour
> very sad. But it would be much more so, had I strength to labor
> more for your people, and were still obliged to leave. My
> strength is gone, and I could do little more for you were I to
> stay. There is another and yet greater mitigation. If we are the
> servants of Christ, our parting is not long. We may hope soon to
> meet in heaven.[125]

Perkins began his voyage back to America in June of 1869. He was accompanied by several missionary families from Urumia. His poor health made for a very difficult journey. Upon arriving in New York City he was not in sufficiently good health to travel further to his

---

[123] Also spelled "Ordushahi." For additional details, see: Shojadel (2020), *Typology of the Historical Assyrian Churches in Urmia.*
[124] Perkins (1887), *Life of Rev. Justin Perkins - Pioneer Missionary to Persia,* p. 69.
[125] Ibid., p. 96.

home in Chicopee, Massachusetts. He was hospitalized in Brooklyn for three weeks so that he would recover before leaving for his family. His ailments continued upon his arrival at home, and his physical condition gradually deteriorated.

Justin Perkins died on December 31, 1869. He is buried near his birthplace, in Rock Valley Cemetery in West Holyoke, Massachusetts. On his gravestone, the following words are appropriately engraved: "The first missionary to the Nestorians by whom he was loved as a father."

Perkins left the world when both America and Persia were experiencing great change. America had just emerged from a bloody Civil War, resulting in the abolition of slavery. There were also divisions that were about to affect the ABCFM. The Congregationalist and Presbyterian elements of the ABCFM had fundamental disagreements on priorities and vision. In December of 1870, the Board of Foreign Missions of the Presbyterian Church in the United States of America (PCUSA; headquartered in New York City) took on primary responsibility for the American missionaries in Urumia. The ABCFM, which had greater Congregationalist influences, took on primary responsibilities for activities in the Ottoman territories, and no longer operated in Persia. After December 1870, all American missionary activities in Persia were transferred to PCUSA.

To reflect this changed emphasis, the Mission's name was also changed from the "Mission to the Nestorians" to the "Mission to Persia." The change of name emphasized the newly expanded vision of the Presbyterians, beyond Urumia, into other parts of Persia. The Persian field was broken into the Eastern Persia Mission and the Western Persia Mission. In the coming years, new mission stations were established in Tehran (1872), Tabriz (1873), Hamadan (1881), Resht (1881), Qazvin (1906), Kermanshah (1910), and Mashad (1911). Although all these mission stations were established after Perkins' passing, had it not been for his pioneering work, none may have come to existence.

References and Related Readings

Perkins, Henry Martyn (1887). *Life of Rev. Justin Perkins, D.D.: Pioneering Missionary to Persia.* Chicago: Woman's Presbyterian Board of Missions of the Northwest.

Perkins, Justin (1861). *Missionary Life in Persia: Glimpses of a Quarter of a Century of Labors Among the Nestorian Christians.* Boston: American Tract Society.

Perkins, Justin (1857). *Nestorian Biography: Being Sketches of Pious Nestorians Who Have Died at Oroomiah, Persia.* Cambridge: Allen and Farnham.

Perkins, Justin (1843). *A Residence of Eight Years in Persia Among the Nestorian Christians.* Andover: Allen, Morrill & Wardell.

Shedd, Mary Lewis (1922). *The Measure of a Man: The Life of William Ambrose Shedd, Missionary to Persia.* New York: Gordon H. Doran Company.

Shojadel, Nadereh (2020). "Typology of the Historical Assyrian Churches in Urmia," *Journal of Critical Reviews,* Vol. 7, Iss. 19, pp. 9238-9250.

Chapter 12

ASAHEL GRANT

Asahel Grant was a missionary physician assigned by the ABCFM to the Nestorian Mission in 1834. He was the second American to take up residence in Persia, following in the footsteps of Perkins. They worked together in establishing the Urumia mission station. While his initial stay was in Urumia, his adventurous mind and missionary aspirations took him to the Kurdish mountains across the Turkish border, deep into Ottoman territory. There, he carried out an extensive study of Nestorian settlements in Turkey's remote and rugged mountains. He also witnessed the conflicts between the mountain Nestorians and their Kurdish neighbors, and the eventual atrocities experienced by the former.

Among Grant's many contributions were his medical services to almost every community he visited. He was the first American missionary with a medical role in Persia.[126] He is credited for healing and saving thousands of patients. Grant closely observed and carefully documented the unstable nature of the alliances and conflicts between the Kurds, Nestorians, and the Ottoman government. His observations provided one of the earliest and rarest perspectives by a Westerner, on issues related to Kurdish independence aspirations and the Ottoman Empire's handling of its minorities in its eastern regions at that time. What Grant witnessed in the 1840s was a preview of the violence that would eventually cross the Turco-Persian border several times in the decades ahead and in the years leading to the First World War.

Background

Grant was born on August 17, 1807, in Marshall, NY. He was the second son of William and Rachel Grant, who were both farmers. Early in life, he exhibited an interest in practicing medicine. As early as seven, he had accumulated miniature apothecary which he had purchased using his own savings.[127] This showed his early interest in becoming a physician. It was also indicative of his independence and self-discipline, from a very young age, as this was all procured without his parents' knowledge or help.

---

[126] Karimi (1971), *Implications of American Missionary Presences in 19th and 20th Century Iran.*
[127] Laurie (1853), *Dr. Grant and the Mountain Nestorians*, p. 15.

Grant's views of the world had likely been partially influenced in his youth by the industrial developments he had witnessed as a child. Marshall is a small town, half-way between Albany and Buffalo in upstate New York. While it was a small and rural town, it was only ten miles away from the Erie Canal. Construction on the Erie Canal had begun in 1817 when Grant was only ten years old. It was completed in 1825, at which point the canal connected Lake Erie to the Hudson River.[128] It was an engineering marvel, a monumental achievement for America, and a testament to human ingenuity.[129]

The Erie Canal was a massive human effort, not only because of its scale, but also because of its impact on the economic development of America as a country. It enabled the trade port of New York City to be connected to the interior states of America. Cargo from all over the world came by way of the Atlantic Ocean, passed through the port of New York, up the Hudson River, through the Erie Canal, and entered Lake Erie, where it could be transported to the interior states of America. The Erie Canal made it possible for America to expand westward and thereby grow economically. Barges containing supplies from all around the world passed through this canal. The sight of the global trade would have been obvious to any young child living so close to the canal. Grant would have witnessed the herculean construction effort of the canal. The spirit through which the builders of the canal constructed this structure is also noteworthy. Slave labor was intentionally not used for its construction. Paid labor, mostly consisting of immigrant workers, was used instead. The global nature and massive size of the canal construction project, so close to his home, must have created quite an impression on the young Asahel Grant.

During his teens, similar to Perkins, Grant worked on the family farm. He also spent much of his free time from a young age reading. Had it not been for a severe leg wound that was accidentally self-inflicted by an axe during his teens, he would have most likely become a farmer, similar to his parents. But the physical limits resulting from

---

[128] Bernstein (2006), *Wedding of the Waters: The Erie Canal and the Making of a Great Nation.*

[129] Although the Erie Canal was built over two centuries ago, during Grant's childhood, it is still operational and in use today. It is over 350 miles long and stretches the width of New York State.

this injury prevented him from farming, and he decided to direct his energies to the study and practice of medicine.

At the age of 16, Grant attended Hamilton College (located in upstate New York) to study chemistry. He also attended many medical lectures in Pittsfield, Massachusetts. Grant never received a formal college degree, as at that time, many doctors received their training directly through apprenticeship and hands-on learning, rather than formal class-based coursework.[130] At the age of 20, he married Electra S. Loomis, of Torrington, Connecticut. A year later, the couple settled in the village of Braintrim near the New York-Pennsylvania border. They had two boys together: Edwin and Hastings. Sadly, four years into the marriage, Electra suddenly passed away.

Deep in sorrow for his wife's passing, Grant resettled by moving into his parents' home, with his children. He then relocated again, moving to Utica, NY, where he developed a successful medical practice. During his years in Utica, he was known for attending to the needs of the poor and was considered as a "friend of the poor."[131] Grant did not seek wealth and lived a simple life. One of his main strengths was his simple manners which enabled him to get along with people from a wide range of backgrounds. In describing his manners and style of interaction with others, his close missionary colleague, Thomas Laurie wrote: "He showed great tact in approaching men, do as to disarm prejudice, and make a stranger feel at once that he was a friend."[132] This mode of interaction was to become an asset for Grant in the years ahead, as he had to traverse dangerous lands to reach vulnerable population groups in some of the most unstable parts of the world.

It was during his years in Utica that Grant developed an interest in missionary work. His original desire was to go to Singapore or China. But he was eventually inspired to go to Persia after attending an ABCFM meeting held in Utica in 1834. From thereon, his mind was set on becoming a missionary in Persia, and he also developed a great interest in visiting the mountain Nestorians.

---

[130] Taylor (2008), *Fever & Thirst: An American Doctor Among the Tribes of Kurdistan,* p. 6.
[131] Laurie (1853), *Dr Grant and the Mountain Nestorians,* p. 20.
[132] Ibid., p. 21.

The decision to pursue a missionary life was not an easy one since he had two young boys to look after and a profitable medical practice in Utica. He questioned if he would be a more useful person if he stayed in America with his two sons, or if he went abroad as a missionary to serve the Nestorians. His struggle to settle this type of question is commonly shared among many who pursue humanitarian and missionary endeavors. His resolution to this internal conflict, the most important part of which related to what would happen to his two children in his absence, was settled by his own words: "If God calls me to leave them for his sake, he will take care of them."

In October of 1834, the ABCFM formally offered Grant the assignment to Persia as a missionary physician. Since it was preferred by the ABCFM to dispatch male missionaries with a spouse, it was essential for Grant to find a spouse before his voyage to Persia. In describing the intention to marry his second wife, Thomas Laurie (p. 30) wrote: "Not the least important part of his preparation was still to be made, in the selection of a companion to aid and cheer him in his missionary toil." Laurie continued to explain that the ABCFM's view was that having a spouse join the male missionary would allow a mission station to relate better with the native female population of the mission field, thereby increasing their influence and reach.[133]

Judith S. Campbell had already been accepted by the ABCFM to serve as a missionary before meeting Grant in early 1835. At that time, she was only 21 years old — seven years younger than Grant. She had remarkable qualities. From a young age, she was interested in pursuing a missionary life and was an avid reader of *Missionary Herald*.[134] She was fluent in French and was able to read and write both Latin and Greek. In the years that followed, once settled in Urumia, her language skills became important assets as she used her knowledge of Greek grammar to confirm the correct translation of the New Testament from classical Syriac into modern Syriac.

The couple married in April of 1835 and sailed from Boston in May. Grant's two sons from his first marriage did not accompany them on the voyage. The boys were too young, and their care was therefore

---

[133] In Thomas Laurie's view, it also made the missionary's family a model for families in the native populations.
[134] The monthly publication of the ABCFM.

left with a trusted guardian. The couple arrived in Smyrna (modern-day Izmir, Turkey) in late June. They stayed there for a few days and then boarded a ship for Constantinople. In the final stretch of the voyage, they had to travel by land. Having arrived in Tabriz a year earlier, Perkins made a trip by land to meet up with the Grants mid-way through their journey. Perkins arrived in late August in the village of Balahor (Turkey) to meet the Grants for the first time, and to accompany them on the remainder of their journey to Persia.

References and Related Readings

Bernstein, Peter (2006). *Wedding of the Waters: The Erie Canal and the Making of a Great Nation.* New York: W.W. Norton & Company.

Karimi, Linda C. (1975). *Implications of American Missionary Presences in 19th and 20th Century Iran. Masters Dissertation.* Portland State University.

Lathrop, A.C. (1847). *Memoir of Asahel Grant, M.D.* New York: M.W. Dodd

Laurie, Thomas (1853). *Dr. Grant and the Mountain Nestorians.* Boston: Gould and Lincoln.

Taylor, Gordon (2008). *Fever & Thirst: An American Doctor Among the Tribes of Kurdistan*, 1835-1844. Chicago: Academy Chicago Publishers.

Chapter 13

GRANT'S ROLE IN THE LAUNCH OF THE
URUMIA MISSION

The company of Asahel Grant, Judith Grant, and Justin Perkins arrived in Tabriz on October 15, 1835. British diplomatic representatives welcomed the arrival of Perkins and the Grants in Tabriz. To provide them with additional protection in their travels in Persia, the embassy issued British passports for the Perkins and the Grants.

For Perkins to be accompanied by a fellow missionary physician was especially important in the initial interactions with the locals. Laurie reflected on this, suggesting that having a doctor such as Grant as a missionary helped in securing Persian government support for the eventual establishment of the Mission in Urumia:

> Mr. Perkins, as yet unacquainted with the language, had deemed it important to remove there alone; and now, as it was thought a physician would meet with a more favorable reception than a clergyman, and Dr. Grant, already called to prescribe for the Governor of Tabriz, had received from him a letter of introduction to the Governor or Oroomiah, he was sent to secure a house, and make arrangements for the commencement of the mission.[135]

---

[135] Laurie (1853), *Dr. Grant and the Mountain Nestorians,* p. 45.

Upon settling down in Urumia, Grant began to take on a considerable amount of medical work. He served Moslems, non-Moslems, nobility, the clergy, the rich, the poor, and everyone else who needed care. In his first year in Urumia, it is estimated that Asahel Grant prescribed for nearly one thousand patients and conducted more than fifty cataract surgeries. His collegial attitude towards Persian doctors, and his belief that he should train the local physicians to enable them to serve the masses, rather than to compete with them:

> And yet all was done so prudently that, though his services were entirely gratuitous, he gave no offence to the native physicians. There was no show to attract customers, and he was ready to aid the native practitioners with both medicine and instruction. He felt that a missionary-physician should seek to win their friendship, and prepare them for usefulness. It is vain to hope to supply the heathen with enlightened physicians. But he thought that, in a spirit of love, much might be done towards relieving the great mass of suffering he could not possibly attend to in person, by elevating those they had; and on this principle he always acted. A petty professional jealousy formed no part of the character of Dr. Grant.[136]

Linda Karimi believed that Grant's contribution to advancing new medical methods and practices in Urumia had a lasting effect on the practice of medicine in all of Persia:

> Grant provided a foundation for medical work that was to endure for the next one hundred years. Grant's attitude played a very important role in gaining the confidence of the people. His desire was to impart his knowledge as well as his medical abilities to the people. From the beginning he avoided competing with the native doctors. Instead, he gave samples of his medicines hoping that they would emulate his methods. Additionally, he lent his instruments to be used as patterns. As a surgeon he was much more advanced. One of the major medical problems in Iran throughout the 19th century was that of eye diseases trachoma and cataracts. The mission doctors were familiar with these and were able to give relief through surgery. Reviewing missionary records one notes that as many

---

[136] Ibid., p. 66.

as ten percent of the population were inflicted with this or similar eye ailments.[137]

Laurie asserts that the idea of deploying missionary physicians to Persia was pioneered by the arrival of Grant. Mission stations of other Christian denominations in Persia were not providing medical services at that time. Grant's special emphasis on serving the poor also affected how he served the rich. For wealthy individuals to receive his services, they were required by Grant to bring along a written statement from their priest, mullah, or rabbi stating that they have been charitable to the poor. This emphasis is consistent with how he served the poor in his years as a physician back in America, which reflected his genuine care for the weak and the vulnerable.

In addition to his medical practice, Grant conducted other services at the Urumia mission station. Early on, he took on an apprentice, who was Yohannan's younger brother. He instructed other medical students as well, and taught English. He also supervised the Boys' School, alongside Perkins, and headed the Sabbath School, both of which opened in January of 1836.

Mrs. Grant was also active in both the medical and educational tasks of the Mission. Well in advance of arriving in Persia, she had begun reading medical books to prepare herself for supporting Grant in his medical work. By 1836, she was speaking Turkish and was able to read ancient Syriac as well as read and write modern Syriac. These skills were instrumental in her services as a teacher and in her translation of Biblical texts from classical Syriac into modern Syriac. However, her most significant contributions were to female education, through the opening of a school for Nestorian girls.[138] She opened the school in March 1838 and was its very first teacher.[139]

---

[137] Karimi (1975), *Implications of American Missionary Presences in 19th and 20th Century Iran*, p. 32.

[138] Renamed the Fiske Seminary in 1888.

[139] To avoid prejudices, her first students were her own servants and their daughters.

Class in the Urumia Female Seminary (Fiske Seminary: c. 1890s)

A Fiske Seminary Graduate by the name of Khatun and Her Students in a
School in the Kurdish Mountains (c. 1905)

The Grants had three children together. Their first child was named Henry Martyn, born on June 2, 1836. Similar to Henry Martyn Perkins, he was named after the legendary Anglican priest, Henry Martyn. The Grants also had twin daughters, named Mary and Judith. Sadly, Grant was about to face significant challenges in his newly established home in Urumia. In early 1839, his wife began to suffer from high fever. She was also suffering from ophthalmia, an inflammation of the eye, which had resulted in the loss of vision in one eye. She died on January 14, 1839, at the age of 25.

At the time of her death, their son was two years old, and the twins were only five months old. Grant had also been feeling ill for some time, even before her passing. His poor health, combined with the emotional trauma of having lost his wife, required him to remove himself from Urumia for a short while. The Mission had consulted Dr. J.P. Riach (British embassy physician in Tabriz) as early as August of the previous year regarding Grant's physical health. The Mission had realized that the continued residence of Grant in Urumia might negatively affect his health and therefore recommended that he "seek a more favorable climate" (Laurie 1853; p. 97). Following his wife's passing, considering the addition of emotional pain to his physical ailments, the Mission voted in January to request the ABCFM to send a missionary physician from America to replace him. Dr. Austin Wright was the replacement that was eventually dispatched in response to this request.

Grant left the children with missionary families in Urumia and traveled to Tabriz in the hope of experiencing some form of relief. He visited Dr. Riach to seek his company and medical advice on his illness in hopes of feeling better. While in Tabriz, mourning his wife's passing, Grant had the opportunity to meet with Russian and British officials. They were supportive of his desire to visit the mountain Nestorians in the Ottoman territories. This helped reignite his long-held ambitions to visit the mountain Nestorians.

Even more unexpected and exciting was a letter that Grant received from Henry Homes, a missionary colleague in Constantinople. Homes was relaying to Grant instructions he had received from the ABCFM. The instructions were that Homes and Grant were to set up a mission station in Mesopotamia (modern-day northern Iraq) and Kurdistan, in what was then the eastern portions of the Ottoman

Empire. This had been a dream of Grant's since he was in America, and the news rejuvenated him.

The instructions from the ABCFM were for Homes (who was based in Constantinople) to meet up with Grant in Erzurum (Turkey), and the two would then head down to Mosul, where they would set up a mission station. The ABCFM's long-term plan was that Grant would eventually bring his family with him to live there. The ABCFM believed that setting up this station would allow access to the mountain Nestorians and the establishment of future outposts in the Kurdish mountains of Turkey.[140]

Energized by the news, Grant immediately returned to Urumia to make the necessary preparations. However, the weight of the decision to move forward was made heavier by the realization that he had three little children in Urumia that depended on him. He also had two other young children from his first marriage, back in America. Laurie characterized the family pressures that Grant felt as such:

> He was now utterly at a loss what to do. On the one hand, his children at home needed his presence. The guardian with whom he left them had died…. His own father, on whom the care of them then devolved, had died the year before. A younger brother, on whom he next depended, also died in 1837; and now his only surviving brother and Rev. Mr. Shaw had the temporary care of them. His children at Oroomiah, too, needed attention.[141]

Grant's desire to visit the Nestorians of the mountains, most of whom resided in eastern Turkey's Hakkari mountains, was strong even before he had left America. Having been in Urumia since the end of 1835, the desire to pursue this interest became overwhelming. In justifying the decision to visit the mountain Nestorians, Grant had in his earlier correspondences with the ABCFM provided several reasons to the Prudential Committee for why they should go. He felt that despite a national border separating Persia and the Ottoman Empire, the

---

[140] Grant's personal view was different from that of the ABCFM. Grant believed that a better approach was to directly reach the Kurdish mountains in the Hakkari region of Turkey through Persia, to immediately initiate the establishment of mission outposts (instead of first establishing a mission station in Mosul, which is to the south).

[141] Laurie (1853), *Dr. Grant and the Mountain Nestorians,* pp. 101-102.

mountain Nestorians are a unified population that deserves the Urumia mission station's attention.

Furthermore, since one of the primary objectives of the Urumia mission station was to translate the scriptures into modern Syriac and to provide literacy services, Grant argued that it was important for the Urumia missionaries to have greater familiarity with other dialects of Syriac spoken in the mountains, and not just the Urumia dialect. The dialect of Syriac spoken in Urumia (and hence much of the work being done by the Mission in developing a written form for the spoken Syriac dialect) might not have been applicable to the Syriac spoken among the mountain Nestorians. He therefore argued that an understanding of the dialect of the mountain Nestorians was essential, further justifying the urgency of his visit to the mountain Nestorians.

Perhaps the most compelling justification which Grant provided, with which the ABCFM fully agreed, was the fact that the Nestorian patriarch resided in the mountains of Turkey. To gain the patriarch's blessings for the ABCFM's services to the Nestorians, direct contact and conversation with the patriarch would be needed. Grant felt a great deal of competition and pressure from competing Christian denominations who were also attempting to make contact with the Nestorian patriarch, with the hope of influencing and perhaps converting the Nestorians. The two groups that stood out were Roman Catholics and British Anglicans. To Grant, reaching the Nestorian patriarch before others do had a sense of urgency to it. In April 1839, in a letter to the Prudential Committee of the ABCFM, he wrote:[142] "I am most deeply interested in the Nestorians, and know of no other people on earth with whom I would prefer to spend the remainder of my days."

It is important to realize that what Grant had in mind was a very dangerous undertaking in a historical context. Few civilians from the West had ever penetrated these mountains and come out alive. The most recent attempt was by a German archeologist by the name of Friedrich Eduard Schultz, working for the French government.[143] He was not just an archeologist, but also a talented philosopher, linguist

---

[142] Ibid., p. 94.

[143] The correct spelling of his last name was Schulz, but in the missionary writings it has been commonly misspelled as Schultz. For purposes of consistency, the American missionaries' spelling of the name is used here.

and Orientalist, with an adventurous temperament.[144] In 1829 Schultz had traveled to the same mountains that Grant was about to visit. He had visited the Nestorian patriarch at his residence in the village of Quchanes. On his return trip, Schultz and two of his Persian guards were murdered. Schultz was shot execution-style, in the back of the head. His murderer was a tribesman assigned as his guide, who was evidently ordered by a Kurdish tribal chief that Schultz had visited earlier in his journey.

His murder demonstrated the great dangers facing any Westerner desiring to visit the area. Schultz was erroneously suspected of being a spy. However, several facts related to Schultz' actions had been attributed to his killing, including his "injudicious show of wealth," having astronomical equipment with him, providing the locals with splendid gifts, and creating an impression that he was in possession of significant amounts of money (Laurie 1853, p. 93). Schultz was also an unusually tall man, which made him stand out as his physique attracted a great deal of attention from the locals. Most importantly, he had conducted excavation work, which involved a yellow mineral taken from an orpiment mine. The locals had suspected that Schultz might have discovered gold and were concerned that this would entice European governments to invade the area. In reality, the material Schultz had excavated was not gold, but in the locals' minds, by letting him leave the area alive, they could risk occupation by foreign powers.

Grant, on the other hand, had no intention of carrying himself into the mountains in the same manner as Schultz. He felt that his services as a physician would make him a welcome visitor rather than a source of irritation for the locals. To blend in, he would grow his beard long, wear local clothing, speak the local language, and other than for his supply of medicine, he would travel light. To improve his knowledge of the area, Grant sought the advice of an experienced British military officer by the name of Colonel Justin Sheil.[145] He provided Grant with an understanding of the terrain and the cultural norms of the mountains. Reflecting on the level of violence present in the region, it was obvious

---

[144] Potts (2017), *Achievement and Misfortune: On the Life and Death of Friedrich Eduard Schulz (1799-1829)*.

[145] In later years, Justin Sheil became minister at the British embassy in Tehran. His wife was an Orientalist and the author of *Glimpses of Life and Manners in Persia*, published in 1856.

to Sheil and others familiar with the area that tensions between the Hakkari Kurds and the mountain Nestorians had been ongoing for centuries. Sheil believed the dangers posed to a Westerner entering this region should not be ignored. The conflicts between the mountain Nestorians and the Kurds had risen in prior years, because of power struggles involving the central Ottoman government. With both groups being minorities living out-of-reach of the Ottoman army, the degree by which the Ottoman government recognized and supported each group varied from time to time. Ottoman relations with the two groups had great symbolic and real effects in the formation of jealousies between them, and the balance of power.

Grant left Urumia on April 1, 1839. His plan was to meet up with Homes in Erzurum. Homes would be coming from his mission station in Constantinople, and the two would meet in Erzurum and then head south to Mosul to set up an ABCFM mission station there. To get to Erzurum, Grant's travel path from Urumia was through the Salmas district to the north of Urumia. However, while in Salmas, he received word that the ABCFM mission station at Constantinople, which had jurisdiction over the ABCFM operations within the Ottoman Empire, feared that he would perish attempting to visit the mountains, and had therefore forbidden him to make the trip. The reason for the ABCFM's objection was the recent passing of Mrs. Grant. The ABCFM had not been aware of her passing at the time of their earlier correspondence with Grant, in which he was instructed to proceed to Erzurum to meet up with Homes. With their new knowledge about the passing of Grant's wife, the ABCFM feared that he would not be in the right state of mind to make such a demanding trip, which is why they had rescinded the original travel instructions.

Grant appealed this decision and wrote back to Urumia, pleading to enter the mountains. In his request to the Urumia mission station, he suggested that instead of the original plan of going to Erzurum and then to Mosul to set up a mission station there, he would like to approach the mountain Nestorians in the Hakkari mountains directly. To further strengthen his appeal, he included alongside his letter to Urumia an additional letter from Yahya Khan, the governor of the Salmas district in Persia. While an authority figure in that Persian district, Yahya Khan was also the Kurdish chieftain of one of the branches of a Hakkari tribe in Turkey, and therefore could have great influence across the Turkish border in ensuring the safety of Grant.[146]

One of the main concerns regarding the intended travel path of Grant was the growing political tensions between Persia and Turkey, which was almost reaching a breaking point. It had become impossible for Persian authorities to demand protection for Persian subjects in Turkey. The Urumia mission station voted on Grant's suggested change in travel path to enter the Hakkari mountains through Persia and recommended against it. Instead, they instructed him to proceed to Constantinople to see Homes, and then follow the instructions provided in the original correspondence from the ABCFM, by proceeding southward to Erzurum and then to Mosul to set up a mission station there. In essence, the instructions provided by Urumia were already different from the initial plan by the ABCFM, and in conflict with the second correspondence from the ABCFM which had asked Grant to completely abandon the plans. The instructions from Urumia allowed for some flexibility since Grant would be able to present himself to the mission station in Constantinople before making the journey to Mosul. Grant complied with the instructions provided by Urumia, and pressed forward.

As will be described in the coming chapters, Grant continued on, traveling north from Salmas. He first visited Erzurum, then traveled to Trebizond where he took a steamer ship to Constantinople to see Homes. However, Homes was preoccupied with mission work and was unable to join him immediately. Grant, therefore, returned to Erzurum and waited for Homes to join him. Homes eventually joined him, and the two proceeded south. However, before reaching Mosul, Homes had to abandon the plans due to obligations that required him to return to Constantinople. Grant continued south toward Mosul, where he arrived in September of 1839. He remained there for only three weeks and in the absence of Homes, abandoned the original plans of setting up an ABCFM mission station in Mosul. Instead, he headed north to make contact with the mountain Nestorians on his own.

In some ways, Grant's life path following the loss of his second wife resembles his experience upon losing his first wife. When his first

---

[146] Taylor (2008), *Fever & Thirst: An American Doctor Among the Tribes of Kurdistan,* p. 221.

wife had passed away, Grant was feeling deeply depressed. He had to remove himself and the children from their home. With his two children, he moved into his parents' home for a short while, and then relocated again to escape a setting in which he may have been constantly reminded about his first wife's loss. The loss of his second wife may have had a similar effect on him, evidenced by a similar sequence of responses, including an intense desire for him to remove himself from Urumia. It caused him to first travel to Tabriz as an escape, and then made him more committed to further travel to the Kurdish mountains in search of the mountain Nestorians. The emotional agony that he was experiencing may have been the primary source of the ABCFM's second communication with him, rescinding the original plans of traveling to Turkey.

References and Related Readings

Becker, Adam H. (2015). *Revival and Awakening: American Evangelical Missionaries in Iran and the Origins of Assyrian Nationalism.* Chicago: University of Chicago Press.

Grant, Asahel (1837). "An Appeal to Pious Physicians," in A.C. Lathrop's *Memoir of Asahel Grant,* Boston: M.W. Dodd, pp 203-216.

Karimi, Linda C. (1975). *Implications of American Missionary Presences in 19th and 20th Century Iran.* Masters Dissertation. Portland State University.

Laurie, Thomas (1853). *Dr. Grant and the Mountain Nestorians.* Boston: Gould and Lincoln.

Potts, Daniel T. (2017). "Achievement and Misfortune: On the Life and Death of Friedrich Eduard Schulz (1799-1829)," *Journal Asiatique,* 305(2), pp. 249-270

Taylor, Gordon (2008). *Fever & Thirst: An American Doctor Among the Tribes of Kurdistan,* 1835-1844. Chicago: Academy Chicago Publishers.

Chapter 14

GRANT'S FIRST VISIT TO THE
MOUNTAIN NESTORIANS

It is essential to consider the disapproval of the Constantinople and Urumia mission stations regarding Grant's original plans to approach the Hakkari region through Persia in the greater context of concerns that the ABCFM had regarding the rapidly deteriorating political conditions in the eastern portion of the Ottoman Empire. The various mountain tribes in this region had lived in relative autonomy for centuries. Prior to the events to be described shortly, which transpired in the middle of the nineteenth century, the common experience of living in such a physically challenging environment had created a shared human experience which partially countered the forces of prejudice. The commonalities rather than the differences among the Christians (Nestorians, Chaldeans, Armenians, Jacobites) and their Moslem (Kurdish) neighbors had created a sense of bonding among the seemingly different populations.

Up until the early parts of the nineteenth century, these groups, despite their periodic skirmishes, had a sense of bonding in the form of what Jwaideh characterizes as a form of "Tribal Sentiment."[147] These

---

[147] Jwaideh (2006), *The Kurdish National Movement: Its Origins and Development*, p. 33.

sentiments could often help reduce the level of religious or ethnic tensions between the tribes. They also increased the sense of independence that the people in this region felt, as a collective group that was distinct from the rest of the Ottoman population. Even though the region was officially part of the empire, Ottoman rule was not effectively in place due to its unique geography and difficulty of access by large armies.

However, by the middle of the nineteenth century, these tribal sentiments had started to dissipate as competition among the mountain tribes grew. The individual tribes' desires for independence from Ottoman rule also grew. The rough terrain and remoteness of the villages made it impractical for Ottoman rulers to have much power over the mountain tribes, keeping both the Kurdish and Nestorian tribes away from the reach of the Ottoman army. The Ottoman Empire had become too big and diverse to manage and was beginning to fall apart. Some of its provinces had already sought and gained independence. As early as 1807, the Ottomans had recognized that they no longer had ultimate power in all parts of the empire, and had to share power with local leaders, such as the Kurdish tribal chiefs and the Nestorian patriarch.[148] The Ottomans lost Greece in 1830. In later years, they were unable to suppress and independence movement in Egypt.

In the years leading to Grant's visit to the mountains, Kurdish hopes for independence had been further energized by the conditions facilitated through the Tanzimat reforms in the Ottoman Empire that began in 1839.[149] They were put in place under European pressure and were intended to modernize the Ottoman government, establish more democratic processes, and increase the rights of minorities. While the reforms were appealing from a modernization perspective, they also gave rise to voices for independence in various Ottoman provinces. The reforms were especially relevant to the aspirations of independence for minorities such as the Kurds, Armenians, and Nestorians who were well-armed.

---

[148] McDowall (2007), *A Modern History of the Kurds*, p. 41.
[149] Goldschmidt and Al-Marashi (2019), *A Concise History of the Middle East*.

Kurdish Fighters (c. 1920s)

Challenging Passes of the Kurdish Mountains (c. 1890s)

The rising tensions resulting from declining Ottoman authority in the region and growing independence aspirations would place any traveler, especially a Westerner, at great risk. This was one of the reasons that the ABCFM had doubts about Grant's visit through the Hakkari mountains. In addition to the political instability of the Kurdish mountains of Turkey, the ABCFM was concerned about the terrain that Grant intended to travel through. Even with modern mountaineering equipment and navigation tools, travelers with great mountaineering skills would find the terrain formidable. The steep slopes, rocky cliffs, and high altitudes, which for centuries had kept the Assyrians and Kurds in safety by blocking out intruders, would now be challenging Grant as he planned his own entry into these territories.

Following the instructions that the Urumia mission station had given him, Grant reached Erzurum, Turkey in April of 1839, traveling by foot and horseback. Erzurum at that time was a central in-land travel hub through which caravans of travelers passed through, half-way between Trebizond and Lake Van. Here, he spent some time with friends, including Dr. Riach from the British embassy in Tabriz. Upon their first arrival in Tabriz years earlier, Grant and his wife were welcomed by Dr. Riach, and as such he had a very special place in Grant's heart.

Grant continued with his journey and proceeded north to the Turkish coastal town of Trebizond. He then boarded a steamer ship and traveled to Constantinople to see Homes. Homes was based in Constantinople, in charge of the Mission's printing press. The ABCFM had envisioned them heading southbound to explore and identify the Nestorian settlements that may exist to the south and then proceed further south to set up a mission station in Mosul. The idea was that the Mosul station would eventually be used as a hub for launching outpost stations to serve the mountain Nestorians in the Kurdish mountains north of Mosul.

Much to the disappointment of Grant, Homes was preoccupied with mission activities in Constantinople and was unable to join Grant on such short notice. However, he suggested that Grant proceed back to Erzurum and wait for him so that the two can carry on with the original plan put forward by the ABCFM. Grant returned to Erzurum and waited for about two weeks for Homes to arrive, and once he did, the two men headed south toward Mosul.

On their way, Grant and Homes took some time to explore the area to the west of Turkey's Hakkari region in search of Nestorians. They were unable to find any Nestorian settlements. The difficulties of travel were also mounting. In one case, the two were lucky to escape with their lives from mob attacks in Diyarbakir. Having been on the road for over two months and having obligations to return to his mission duties in Constantinople, Homes could not join Grant for the remainder of the journey, as had been originally planned. He returned to Constantinople, and Grant proceeded to travel south toward Mosul by himself.

Grant arrived in Mosul in September of 1839. Mosul was a city of great diversity and historical significance, with a population of about 30,000. It was a melting pot of different religions, with a diverse population of people living in relative peace with one another. Mosul was populated by Moslems, Jews, Zoroastrians, Yazidis, and various Christian populations, including Armenians, Jacobites, Chaldeans, Catholics, and Nestorians.[150]

Mosul (from Wigram & Wigram; c. 1911)

---

[150] The Yazidis were of particular interest to Grant in demonstrating the diversity of Mosul through their adoption of a combination of elements of the other major religions present in Mosul.

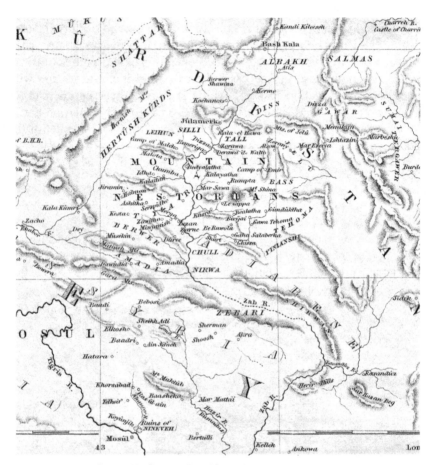

Regional Map Related to Asahel Grant's Visit to the Mountain Nestorians
(from Thomas Laurie's *Dr. Grant and the Mountain Nestorians*, 1853)

With the absence of Homes, the prospects of setting up a mission station in Mosul appeared less likely. Even before starting the journey, back in Urumia, Grant was of the firm belief that the ABCFM should be setting up mission stations directly in the Hakkari region, and Urumia could be used as the base for that. Grant believed his travel logistics would have been more efficient if entry to the Hakkari region was made directly through Persia, rather than the elongated path that the ABCFM had prescribed for him. He was faced with two options: return to Urumia empty-handed, or head north to attempt to make contact with the mountain Nestorians and the patriarch, on his own. In both cases, the original wishes of the ABCFM would not be executed. Reflecting on his seemingly rebellious decision to make an unapproved northbound journey to the mountains, Grant wrote to a fellow missionary, James Lyman Merrick: "I feel reluctant to enter upon so important an undertaking entirely unsupported by the Board or my missionary brethren, and I am aware that many will accuse me of madness for doing it."[151]

In early October of 1839, he left Mosul and headed north to visit the uncharted territories of the mountain Nestorians. On his way, he visited the ancient remains of Nineveh, as well as various Yazidi settlements.[152] By mid-October, he had arrived in the fortress city of Amadia, one of the most significant settlements in the area from logistical and military perspectives, located approximately one hundred miles north of Mosul.[153] He was the very first Westerner to have ever entered Amadia. Upon his entry, he found it to have a mix of Kurdish, Christian, and Jewish households. In describing Amadia, Grant wrote:

> Amadieh is pleasantly situated in an extensive opening or
> undulating plain between the mountains. The district is fertile in
> grain and fruit. The wheat is good and abundant, and the grapes
> are among the finest I have seen.... The climate is deemed
> insalubrious, and successive wars have made sad havoc among
> the unfortunate population, who greatly need a good and stable
> government. The town, or, more properly, the fortress of
> Amadieh, is situated on the level summit of a very precipitous
> mountain mass of rock, which rises, as I judged, nearly a
> thousand feet above the plain, and being entirely insulated and
> distant from the surrounding mountains, it is regarded as quite
> impregnable.[154]

---

[151] Laurie (1853), *Dr. Grant and the Mountain Nestorians,* p. 118.

[152] Nineveh was the ancient capital of the Assyrian Empire, and although reduced to ruins over the centuries, was and still is of great archeological significance due to its rich history, most of which predates Christianity.

[153] In Grant's own writings, he spells it "Amadieh."

[154] Grant (1841), *The Nestorians or the Lost Tribes,* p. 44.

Entrance to Amadia (from Wigram & Wigram 1911)

As evident from the passage, the high elevation of the town of Amadia and its seemingly dominant position overlooking the plain surrounding it were noted by Grant in his early visits to the area. These features made the city a valuable strategic asset for anyone in control of the region. In Amadia and surrounding villages, and throughout his continued trip northward toward the village of Lezan, Dr. Grant provided medical services to the villagers. In Lezan, he made two interesting observations about the Nestorians that he met there. The first was that Nestorian women were treated equally to men:

> The women appear to be neat, industrious, and frugal, and they are remarkably chaste, without the false affection of modesty too often seen in these countries. Two of the young married women in the

house came forward in the evening, and, in the presence of their husbands, joined in our social visit.[155]

This was an important observation. The equal footing of females and males, witnessed in these Nestorian homes, challenged conventions of male dominance widely assumed to have existed in the Middle East at that time. Such conventions were certainly not the case among his Nestorian hosts in Lezan.

His second observation was regarding the similarities that he had noticed between the church practices of these Nestorians and what was known at that time, through ancient inscriptions and accounts of the Nestorians of China, centuries earlier: "A thin piece of board was struck rapidly with a mallet, to call the villagers to church at the rising of the sun."[156] Grant believed that these similarities were evidence of a long historical connection between the mountain Nestorians and the Nestorians who lived in China centuries earlier.

A Mountain Nestorian Home (c. 1890s)

---

[155] Grant (1841), *The Nestorians or the Lost Tribes,* p. 58.
[156] Ibid., p. 60.

He continued his voyage northward into Kurdish territory. Here, the Nestorian population lived under the nominal jurisdiction of the Kurdish chiefs, who in turn had allegiance to the Ottoman governor ("pasha") of Erzurum. He arrived at the village of Chumba in late October of 1839. The Nestorian patriarch ("Mar Shimon"), having heard of Grant's arrival, sent several men to escort him. The patriarch's house was located further north in the mountain areas of Diss, and Grant was greeted by him with warmth and affection. Remarking on the patriarch's appearance, Grant's first impression was that the patriarch looked much older than he really was:

> The patriarch is thirty-eight years of age, above the middle
> stature, well proportioned, with a pleasant expressive, and rather
> intelligent countenance; while his large flowing robes, his
> Koordish turban, and his long grey beard, give him a patriarchal
> and venerable aspect, which is heightened by a uniformly
> dignified demeanour. Were it not for the youthful fire in his
> eye, and his vigour and activity, I should have thought him
> nearer fifty than thirty-eight.[157]

Mar Shimon Abraham (Patriarch of Assyrian Christians between 1820 and 1861)

---

[157] Ibid., p. 80.

Regarding the patriarch's residence and household, Grant characterizes his home as "plain." The patriarch lived with his two brothers and a younger sister and six servants. His younger sister, Helena, who was in her early twenties, managed many of the patriarch's domestic affairs. At that time, she was the only Nestorian female among the entire population of mountain Nestorians who was literate. This fact highlighted the feeling of urgency that Grant had for setting up schools in this region. The stay with the patriarch was essential for helping Grant gain a better understanding of the Nestorians of the mountains and their needs. During this five-week visit with the patriarch, he was able to tour the various mountain villages in the region.

The patriarch's residence was within half a mile of the residence of one of the main Kurdish chiefs of the Hakkari region named Suleiman Bey.[158] The patriarch had very good relations with Suleiman Bey, and in many ways, considered him family.[159] The fact that a Kurdish chieftain was in such close company with the Nestorian patriarch relates to the tribal sentiments that were strong in the early parts of the nineteenth century between Christians and Kurds in the Hakkari mountains. According to Jwaideh, this was one incident that the Nestorian and Kurdish tribes in the mountains found greater bonding due to their commonalities rather than their religious differences: "In the Hakari emir's absence, the Nestorian patriarch administered the principality, sitting in judgment on Christians and Muslims alike, and even receiving the sultan's envoys."[160] The closeness that Grant had observed between the patriarch and the Kurdish chieftain during this

---

[158] "Bey" being an honorary title, meaning Sir or Chief.

[159] Suleiman Bey (also spelled Sulayman Bey) was the younger nephew of another Hakkari chief by the name of Nurullah (also spelled Nurulah and Nurallah), to be discussed shortly. The latter enjoyed a greater degree of political power in the Hakkari region. However, the Nestorian patriarch felt more friendly toward Suleiman, and this had resulted in some jealousies by Nurullah. Nurullah and Suleiman had also been in a power struggle in earlier years. Some of their differences lingered, resulting in the formation, abandonment, and redirection of alliances with the Ottoman government. The complex and shifting dynamics between these two men and other tribal leaders created an unstable and confusing political setting for the Nestorians as well as visiting Westerners such as Grant, to be elaborated on further in this and the following chapters.

[160] Jwaideh (2006), *The Kurdish National Movement: Its Origins and Development,* p. 33; Note the difference in the spelling of Hakkari used by Jwaideh.

visit was among the last cases of tribal sentiment ever to be seen in the region between the Nestorians and the Kurds.

Having not heard from the Prudential Committee of the ABCFM, Grant decided to return to Urumia. To him, the fact that he had made contact with the Nestorian patriarch was a clear indication of success, as it was a significant accomplishment on behalf of the Urumia mission station. Upon leaving, the patriarch and his sister Helena provided Grant with gifts, which included a pair of scarlet shalwar (trousers) trimmed with silk and a seven-hundred year old copy of the New Testament. Helena also provided Grant with food and supplies for one week and a pair of warm mittens she had made for him.

Grant decided to return to Urumia by going through Julamerk, to the south-west of the Diss region. It was the place of one of the many residences of Nurullah Bey (also referred to as the 'emir' in Grant's correspondences). He was a powerful Kurdish chieftain of the Hakkari region, and at times in a power struggle with Suleiman Bey. He was also widely suspected for having authorized the murder of the German explorer Schultz, mentioned in the previous chapter.[161] More importantly, Nurullah Bey had a desire to increase his influence in the Hakkari region by overpowering his nephew, Suleiman Bey. He also had ambitions for pushing out Ottoman rulers from the region in favor of an independent Kurdish state.

Grant's reason for choosing to make his return trip to Urumia through this route was to have an opportunity to meet this powerful Kurdish leader. He believed that he would be able to secure a line of communication between Urumia and the mountain Nestorians with Kurdish approval and mediated through Nurullah. However, upon arriving in Julamerk, he was told that emir Nurullah had traveled to Bash Kala, located several days of travel to the north, near Lake Van. This is where the emir's primary residence, in the form of a large castle, was located. He was ill and desperately needed the attention and medical expertise of Grant, and was suffering from a violent cold, inflammation, and high fever. Grant began traveling northbound toward Bash Kala.

---

[161] Potts (2017), *Achievement and Misfortune: On the Life and Death of Friedrich Eduard Schulz (1799-1829)*, p. 259.

Upon arriving at the emir's castle, Grant immediately attended to the emir. Grant prescribed the emir medicine and bled him.[162] The doctor was given lodging at the foot of the emir's castle, where the town of Bash Kala was located. During the early hours of the morning, the emir's attendants called on Grant, since the emir was still not feeling well. He examined the emir once again and told him that he needs to be patient until the medication takes effect, and offered him some additional medication. Interestingly, the emir did not fully trust him and asked some of his aids to take the medicine that Grant was offering him, to make sure it was not poison. By the morning, the emir was feeling much better. His improved health increased his trust in Grant, who wrote:

> He rapidly recovered, and said he owed his life to my care. I became his greatest favourite. I must sit by his side, and dip my hand in the same dish with himself. I must remain with him, or speedily return and take up my abode in his country, where he assured me I should have everything as I pleased.[163]

The fact that this powerful Kurdish tribal chief was ill, and that Grant had come to his rescue, was an opportunity for Grant to demonstrate his goodwill. In the mind of Nurullah, the alternative possibility was for him to view Grant with suspicion, potentially as an assassin sent out to kill him for having ordered the murder of Schultz.[164] By Grant demonstrating his care for Nurullah, he was able to earn his trust and secure a verbal promise of support for future American missionary endeavors in the Hakkari region. As will be seen later, this sense of trust was to be short-lived.

---

[162] Bleeding was a common medical practice in the nineteenth century, believed to reduce the intensity of disease. It could be achieved through surface cuts and the attachment of leeches on the skin.

[163] Grant (1841), *The Nestorians or the Lost Tribes,* p. 90.

[164] Note that as suggested by Potts, the identity of the individual who ordered the murder of Schultz was never determined. However, Nurullah was the most likely suspect, who may have provided the instructions to kill Schultz, through Suleiman, who resided in Julamerk where Schultz had visited prior to his return trip.

References and Related Readings

Acikyildiz, Birgul (2014). *The Yezidis: The History of a Community, Culture and Religion.* London: I.B. Tauris.

Goldschmidt, Arthur, and Ibrahim Al-Marashi (2019). *A Concise History of the Middle East.* New York: Routledge.

Grant, Asahel (1841), *The Nestorians, or, The Lost Tribes.* London: John Murray.

Jwaideh, Wadie (2006). *The Kurdish National Movement: Its Origins and Development.* Syracuse: Syracuse University Press.

McDowall, David (2007). *A Modern History of the Kurds.* New York: I.B. Tauris & Company.

Potts, Daniel T. (2017). "Achievement and Misfortune: On the Life and Death of Friedrich Eduard Schulz (1799-1829)," *Journal Asiatique*, Vol. 305, No. 2, pp. 249-270.

Chapter 15

"THE LOST TRIBES OF ISRAEL"

Having visited the Nestorian patriarch and having made contact with
emir Nurullah, Grant joined a caravan of travelers headed for Salmas
(Persia). His eventual destination was Urumia. He arrived in Urumia in
early December of 1839, after having been away for nearly eight
months. He had left his three children in the care of other American
missionaries in Urumia. Within one month of returning to his home in
Urumia, tragedy struck. One of his twin daughters, Mary, died of
influenza on January 13, 1840. Her twin sister Judith passed away due
to measles twelve days later.

The sorrow from the loss of the twins added to the grief of having
lost his wife a year earlier. Henry Martyn was the only surviving child
from Grant's marriage to Judith Grant. The need for finding a stable
environment for his son became more pressing. While Grant was
mourning the twins' loss, during the early months of 1840, two of the
patriarch's brothers visited Urumia. They asked for support from the
mission station, and invited Grant to return to the mountains in the
spring. Grant accepted the invitation and decided to take Henry Martyn
along with him, first to visit the patriarch, and then back to America,
where Henry Martyn could remain in the care of family members and
be close to his half-brothers.

Return to America through the Kurdish Mountains

Grant and his son, who was four at that time, left Urumia in early May of 1840. Along with them was Mar Yohannan, the Nestorian bishop of northern Urumia plain and Mar Yoosuf, the Nestorian bishop of Salmas, who volunteered to join them as they were concerned about the wellbeing and safety of Grant and his son. Considering the dangerous terrain ahead, to take a small child along was undoubtedly an extreme act. As Thomas Laurie described the travel conditions:

> The road along the Zab was still obstructed by the remains of avalanches. Into one of these his horse fell, and threw him and his little son into the snow, but providentially without injury. Once or twice afterwards they had similar falls, though he dismounted whenever danger was apparent.[165]

The Zab River and Surrounding Terrain (c. 1890s)

---

[165] Laurie (1853), *Dr. Grant and the Mountain Nestorians*, p. 159.

He spent ten days with the patriarch in Julamerk. The patriarch was himself a guest of Suleiman Bey in the chief's castle in Julamerk. As mentioned earlier, Suleiman Bey and the patriarch were close and mutually supported each other's family members.[166] Grant's son attracted the affection of Suleiman, the patriarch, and both their families. One indication of the notion of tribal sentiment between the Nestorians and the Kurds was evident in how the families of Suleiman Bey and the patriarch collectively made preparations for their departure:

> His [Suleiman Bey's] mother prepared food for us to eat on the road, spreading honey over the bread with her own hands, and rolling it up with great care. She then brought forward a bag of raisins and nuts, into which she put a small loaf of sugar, and gave it to my son, who had become a great favourite with her and with the whole household, especially with the little Koordish children. He was now able to speak three languages, Turkish and Syriac as well as English. The patriarch's sister had also sent a quantity of bread, in which was rolled up a large supply of *holwa*, or honey, butter, and flour simmered together so to form a kind of rich cake…. The bey had already given my son a small sum of money … His mother, at the same time, suspended a small gold coin, with some beads, to my son's neck as a memento of her affection.[167]

Grant proceeded to Bash Kala where he hoped to find Nurullah. However, Nurullah was nowhere to be found. He had gone north to Erzurum to meet with the local Ottoman governor ("Pasha") of Erzurum. There, emir Nurullah negotiated with the governor by giving up his initial desires for pushing the Ottomans out of the area, and instead became an official of the Ottoman government. In effect, Nurullah betrayed his own cause for independence from the Ottomans. His earlier rhetoric about mobilizing the Kurds and the Nestorians to

---

[166] In a future account (Laurie 1853, p. 180), we find that on a separate occasion, the patriarch took care of Suleiman's mother in his own home: "The Mother of Suleiman Bey was there, under the care of Mar Shimon, during the absence of her son in Gawar." Note the connection to Jwaideh's concept of "Tribal Sentiment," in which Kurds and Nestorians prior to the first half of the nineteenth century were on good terms — unlike anything that was about to unfold in the second half of the century.

[167] Grant (1841), *The Nestorians, or, the Lost Tribes,* p. 96.

push out the Ottomans from the region were seemingly abandoned. Instead, Nurullah negotiated a deal with the governor of Erzurum who had oversight of the Hakkari region. The deal would provide Nurullah with greater powers as a representative of the Ottoman government. It would indisputably make him the most powerful chieftain of the Kurds in the Hakkari region. Grant was able to find Nurullah in the city of Van, and spent a total of ten days in various meetings with him. Reflecting on the emir's expanded role, Grant wrote:

> Changes have occurred which have modified his power, and hereafter the traveller through his heretofore lawless country will have less to fear. It is now placed under Turkish jurisdiction. The chief has bartered his independence for an appointment from the pasha of Erzeroom; and he was returning, an officer of the Porte, to govern his spirited clans, whom he had found too restless to control by his single arm. [168]

It is clear from this passage that at that point in time, Grant viewed the emir's acceptance of a government role as a change for the better. In his mind, this would bring more order to the region and make travel and missionary work safer. Grant had not anticipated the greater desires of Nurullah to eventually use this increased authority as a means for oppressing the Nestorians, as will be seen shortly.

Interestingly, instead of creating more tensions between Nurullah and Suleiman due to Nurullah's decision to work with, rather than to fight against the Ottoman government, the relations between the two seemed to have improved. Nurullah's decision must have inclined Suleiman to also oblige with the change. Furthermore, this drastic change of position regarding the pursuit of independence resulted in both Nurullah and Suleiman viewing and treating the patriarch and his Nestorian subjects differently in the months that followed. Some of the poor treatment, hostility, and violence that the Kurdish tribes would eventually direct at the Nestorians and the patriarch were due to the close relationship that they felt the patriarch was developing with the Americans and the British. Nurullah and Suleiman shared in their concerns about the support that the Nestorians were likely to receive

---

[168] Ibid., pp. 104-105. Note the varied spelling of Erzeroom; "Porte" means the central Ottoman government.

from foreign powers, in the mountains that were for centuries primarily considered as Kurdish territories.[169]

Having visited emir Nurullah in Van, Grant proceeded to Erzurum, where he met Dr. Riach, Consul Brant, and Colonel Sheil. He also met for the very first time with Dr. Austin Wright, a fellow American missionary physician assigned by the ABCFM to replace Grant as the lead missionary physician in Urumia. At around the same time, in early June, two British representatives from the Church of England, William Ainsworth and Isa Rassam, visited Julamerk. There, they spent time with the patriarch, and initiated conversations about bringing the Nestorians under the support of the Church of England.[170] By doing so, Ainsworth and Rassam began a period of intense competition between the Church of England and the ABCFM for the approval of the patriarch.

In late June of 1840, Grant and his son left Erzurum for Constantinople. There, they took a steamer ship to Smyrna (modern-day Izmir, Turkey). They boarded another steamer in late July, taking them from Smyrna to Boston. After seventy days, they arrived in Boston in early October. One could only imagine how confusing and disorienting Henry Martyn's presence must have felt for his two older half-brothers, Edwin and Hastings. Grant used his time in America to find homes for the three boys. According to Laurie, the children were not put under one roof. A "pleasant home" was found for Henry Martyn. Edwin and Hastings were placed in what Grant had hoped would be permanent homes among Christian families in Utica.

Linking the Nestorians to the Lost Tribes of Israel

The return to America gave Grant an opportunity to pull together his personal notes and recollections from his journeys into the mountains and craft the manuscript for his book, *"The Nestorians, or, The Lost Tribes."* In this book, he attempted to identify connections between the Ten Lost Tribes of Israel, mentioned in Biblical writings, and the

---

[169] Joseph (1961), *Nestorians and their Muslim Neighbors,* p. 53.

[170] Ainsworth and Rassam's expedition was co-supported by the Society for Promotion of Christian Knowledge (which was and still is an Anglican mission) and the British Geographical Society.

Nestorians he had come across in the mountains of eastern Turkey. According to the Old Testament (2 Kings 17:6), around 700 BC, the Assyrian empire captured ten of the twelve Israelite tribes and deported them to Assyria.[171] The whereabouts of these tribes had long been a source of controversy and disagreement among Biblical scholars, historians, and archeologists. Any modern-day evidence of their existence would have rendered empirical validation to the Biblical story of the ten tribes. Given that the 1800s were a period of Christian revival, the prospects of the Nestorians being related to the Lost Tribes would have naturally excited the world of Christianity and would have been considered a major discovery for humanity.

Grant was one of the few Westerners who had extensively spent time with the mountain Nestorians. He felt especially equipped to comment on the relationships he had observed in the rituals and practices of the Nestorians and what had been depicted in the Biblical descriptions of the Lost Tribes of Israel. The time available to him for writing the book was limited by his own pressing desire to return to the mountain Nestorians as soon as possible. Given that the primary reason for his visit to America was to bring his son home and find improved living arrangements for his two other sons, he had no intentions to remain in America for a long period of time.

In the approximately six-month time period that he was in America, Grant was overwhelmed with a range of personal and missionary tasks. In addition to the writing of the book and attending to his three sons' needs, Grant was engaged in advocating for the missionary cause and attending various missionary gatherings. As a result, the available time he had with his children, especially Edwin and Hastings, his sons from his first marriage who had not seen their father for several years, was brief. Grant's recollection of this period indicates a sense of regret for not having been able to spend more time with them. In later years, in his correspondences with them, Grant recalled this time period and his relationship with his two sons as being remote and detached: "We saw each other so little, that it was tantalizing rather than satisfactory. I was such a stranger that you hardly knew me; and

---

[171] Benite (2013), *The Ten Lost Tribes: A World History.*

then my visit was so hurried that you must have felt, when we parted, that I was still almost a stranger."[172]

His desire to return to the mountain Nestorians was very strong, and he had very limited time to write the book. He finished writing the book in as short a time as humanly possible. He, himself acknowledged the rush to write:

> They were written partly amid the incessant toils of a missionary life, and partly during my homeward voyage. The constant pressure of other cares, and imperative duties, during my transient stay in my native land, has left no opportunity of rewriting the manuscript, and for correcting inaccuracies of style incident to an inexperienced writer, under circumstances so obviously unfavourable to careful composition.[173]

His book was published in April of 1841. It was well-received in both America and England. Despite the emergence of other travel books related to this area, Grant's book was the only one that solely focused on the mountain Nestorians. It made an explicit claim of a Biblical link between the Nestorians and the Lost Tribes, based on his personal observations. It sold well, and the royalties generated income to support his children's expenses in America. The very notion that the Lost Tribes of Israel had been discovered had a great degree of appeal to the Christian world, and for this reason, the book was a popular one for its time.

However, it is important to recognize that the main theory that Grant had advanced in this book, linking the Nestorians to the Ten Lost Tribes was almost immediately disputed. Among the critics was his closest missionary colleague, Perkins, who wrote:

> Dr. Asahel Grant, one of my respected fellow-laborers, has published a work in which he endeavors to prove that the Nestorians are descendants of the lost ten tribes. His theory has been examined by Dr. Robinson and rejected, many of the arguments being found to prove too much, by adducing, a peculiar to the Ancient Israelites and the Modern Nestorians, customs and practices which, from time immemorial, have been oriental, rather than *national*.[174]

---

[172] Laurie (1853), *Dr. Grant and the Mountain Nestorians,* p. 393.
[173] Grant (1841), *Nestorians, or, the Lost Tribes,* p. 2.
[174] Perkins (1843), *A Residence of Eight Years in Persia,* p. 2.

One notable point about this assessment by Perkins is the frankness and honesty with which he spoke about a fellow missionary who he considered a colleague and a good friend. His open criticism reveals a sense of openness in their relationship. Nevertheless, Perkins' rejection of Grant's theory had been supported by renowned Orientalists as well. The many similarities between the Nestorians and the descriptions of the Lost Tribes, which Grant had noted in his book, were commonly observed among other tribes in the region. Therefore, it could not be definitively establishing that a connection between the Nestorians and the Ten Lost Tribes existed simply based on these similarities. However, the theory about such a connection lingered for decades, more as a myth than a scientifically proven fact.

In April 1841, Grant boarded a steamer ship to England, where he was able to secure the copyrights for his book. On his voyage back to the East he was not accompanied by any of his three children. They were left in the hands of guardians in America. He arrived in Trebizond in early June, then proceeded to Erzurum, and then to Van, where he arrived later that month.

References and Related Readings

Ainsworth, William F. (1842). *Travels and Researches in Asia Minor, Mesopotamia, Chaldea, and Armenia.* London: John W. Parker.

Benite, Zvi (2013). *The Ten Lost Tribes: A World History.* Oxford: Oxford University Press.

Grant, Asahel (1841). *The Nestorians, or, The Lost Tribes.* London: John Murray.

Joseph, John (1961). *Nestorians and their Muslim Neighbors.* Princeton: Princeton University Press.

Jwaideh, Wadie (2006). *The Kurdish National Movement: Its Origins and Development.* Syracuse: Syracuse University Press.

Laurie, Thomas (1853). *Dr. Grant and the Mountain Nestorians.* Boston: Gould and Lincoln.

Perkins, Justin (1843). *A Residence of Eight Years in Persia Among the Nestorian Christians.* Andover: Allen, Morrill & Wardell.

Chapter 16

GRANT'S SCHOOLHOUSE

Instead of returning to Urumia where his mission station was, Grant decided to remain in Turkey for a while and continue his exploration of the mountain Nestorian settlements. At that time, the area was inflicted with famine, and there was a shortage of bread. Many people lived on boiled vegetables and yogurt. He proceeded to Bash Kala where he arrived in early July, hoping to meet up with the patriarch. However, the patriarch was not at Bash Kala at that time, and Grant proceeded to tour the various Nestorian villages of the area, which included: Zerany, Mar Ezeiya, various villages in the Jelu and Bass regions, Lezan, and Ashitha. During these visits he provided medical care to the villagers, including one of the most needed procedures, which was the removal of cataracts.

Rising Tensions between the Kurds and the Nestorians

The Kurdish desire for independence from Ottoman rule was at first with the hopes of incorporating the Nestorian Christians in the independence effort and to seek their aid in pushing out the Ottomans from the region. However, as will be seen in this and the following chapters, with the arrival of Grant, and two competing British representatives from the Church of England, a great deal of confusion among the Nestorians resulted. As such, the nature of the alliances between the Nestorian and Kurdish tribes in countering the Ottomans became unstable. The resulting confusion turned the Kurdish itch for independence into an irritation, and eventually into devastating armed attacks on the mountain Nestorians. The increased tensions with the Nestorians and the weakening of central Ottoman government authority had given the Kurds new hopes for developing their own national identity through the establishment of an independent Kurdish state without a Nestorian presence. Tribal sentiments that may have existed in earlier years between the Kurds and the Nestorians were seemingly disappearing quickly.

Grant's return to the area revealed signs of unrest. During the time that he was away in America, the alliances in the Hakkari region had shifted due to Nurullah giving his allegiance to the governor of Erzurum. Nurullah felt that, with the Ottoman government backing him, he should now have sole control of the region and did not desire to share any authority with the Nestorian patriarch.[175]

The position of the Nestorians in Kurdish areas was that of a minority within a minority. The Nestorians pledged allegiance to the Kurdish tribal chiefs, who in turn pledged allegiance to the Ottoman government. Yet, in the Hakkari region, given that there were large numbers of Nestorian villages, with significant numbers of armed men of their own, the relationship between the Kurds and the Nestorians was more along the lines of co-governance. The Nestorian patriarch had in the past co-governed his own subjects alongside the Kurdish chiefs. However, Nurullah wanted the patriarch to step down from his civil leadership responsibilities and delegate much of these responsibilities to subordinate Nestorian civil tribal heads ("maleks"), of which there were three in the Hakkari region, as well as to Nurullah himself.

---

[175] Taylor (2008, p. 118) argues that part of the motivation of Nurullah may have been because he had witnessed the recent Ottoman occupation of Amadia, and Ottoman history dating back to the 1830s indicating that in places such as Baghdad, Mosul, and Mecca, where rebellious efforts for independence had appeared, the Ottoman forces at the end prevailed and suppressed the rebels. To avoid this, Nurullah may have had a motivation to not repeat such outcomes by keeping good relations with the Ottomans through the governor of Erzurum.

Nestorian Church Congregation in the Bass Region (c. 1890s)

Nurullah felt that the reduced political power of the patriarch would be essential to Nurullah's own desire for dominance of the Hakkari region.[176] Interestingly, many Nestorians agreed with Nurullah's suggestion of a reduced role for the patriarch. However, Suleiman Bey opposed Nurullah on this matter and sided with the patriarch. There were already indications of violence between Nestorians and Kurds. The Nestorians in some villages were making plans to attack Kurdish villages and vice versa.

The tensions between the Nestorians and the Kurds became more intense in August of 1841, when the patriarch attempted to organize an army of Nestorians in anticipation of an attack by a combined army consisting of Kurdish and Ottoman army forces. The rising tensions

---

[176] The Nestorians were under the nominal jurisdiction of Nurullah, who in turn owed nominal allegiance to the Ottoman governor of Erzurum. The governance agreement in Hakkari at that time was that as long as the Nestorians agree to provide armed contingents to the Kurds in times of trouble, they would be given a voice on civil matters, through the patriarch in Hakkari tribe councils. See Joseph (1961), p. 50.

between the Kurds and the Nestorians were confirmed by Grant's letter to Asustin Wright (who by that time had settled down in Urumia as the Mission's lead physician): "Were it not for their need of me, I should be tempted to come to Oroomiah; for to remain with the Patriarch might be to enlist as a military surgeon, an honor to which I do not aspire." [177]

Grant soon realized that he had entered an unstable and potentially deadly region of the world, which was about to experience large-scale tribal warfare. Recognizing the danger, in his letter to Wright he continued to confirm the fear: "The situation of the Nestorians is likely to become a trying one, if the Turks, as is probable, unite with the Kurds against them." His observations gave him the impression that due to the rising tensions between the patriarch and the Ottoman government, the Nestorians were losing their freedoms and becoming subjugated. He wrote to the ABCFM, to clarify his position, expressing how important it is for the patriarch to make peace with the Turks. [178]

Return to Mosul and Urumia

Recognizing the dangers and his inability to serve in an increasingly violent environment, Grant decided to leave the area and head south to Mosul. There, he met with Abel Hinsdale, a fellow ABCFM missionary who was experiencing health issues. It was only until November of 1841 that he was sufficiently recovered that the two men could head north from Mosul to tour the Nestorian villages between Mosul and Amadia. They visited settlements and villages belonging to Nestorians, Chaldeans, Jews, and Yazidis. The descriptions of their experiences and records of their interactions with the Yazidis provide a unique perspective on a religious minority that had been, and still is, poorly understood by the world. Grant and Hinsdale also visited Sheikh Adi, a scared village of the Yazidis.

Grant had suspected that the pasha (local Ottoman governor) of Erzurum would unite with the pasha of Mosul and the Kurds to attack the Nestorians. He expressed this in a letter written in January of 1842 to William Stocking, a fellow American missionary living in Urumia. As it turned out, Grant's instincts were indeed correct. While Grant was

---

[177] Laurie (1853), *Dr. Grant and the Mountain Nestorians,* p. 190.
[178] *Missionary Herald* (1842), pp. 310-320.

in Mosul and away from the Hakkari mountains, Nurullah attacked the village of Quchanes where the patriarch resided, and burned down his house. The patriarch was able to escape in advance of the attack and took refuge at another Nestorian village. Although within a few months, the patriarch came to peace with Nurullah, the attack resulted in the patriarch appearing as weak among his followers. As a condition for peace, he also had to give up some of his civil authority. It seems that Nurullah was finally able to get some of what he had demanded the prior year, in terms of a reduced role for the patriarch, through the use of violence.

In early June of 1842, Grant traveled from Mosul to Urumia, joining a caravan headed to Persia. Having been away for two years, he finally returned to Urumia and was welcomed by his fellow American missionaries. However, Perkins was not present in Urumia as he had traveled back to America. The day after Grant's arrival in Urumia, "the mission assembled, and resolved unanimously to send one of their number with him into the mountains. Mr. Stocking, who had been much interested in the enterprise from the first, was chosen, and two of the best native helpers appointed to accompany them."[179] It seems that Grant's passion for the mountains was still unyielding.

Back to the Mountain Nestorians

With the blessing of the Urumia mission station to dispatch two missionaries to the mountain Nestorians, Stocking and Grant headed north from Urumia in mid-summer of 1842. Their first stop was the Salmas district. There, they met with several Kurdish tribal chiefs of Turkey who had gathered in Persian territory, in anticipation of tensions ahead. They met with Yahya Khan, governor of Salmas and a tribal chief in Hakkari. Yahya Khan, as noted in Chapter 13, had written to the Urumia mission in 1839, supporting Grant's travel into the Kurdish mountains of Turkey and provided his personal assurances about the safety of Grant.

Grant viewed Yahya Khan as a man of great integrity and a friend. On this occasion, Yahya Khan warned Grant about the expected hostilities between the Kurds and Ottoman government forces, and told him that he had given his allegiance to the Shah of Iran. Being the

---

[179] Laurie (1853), *Dr. Grant and the Mountain Nestorians,* p. 127.

chieftain of a tribe with presence in both Persian and Ottoman lands, it was important for Yahya Khan to have made this point. The Qajar government of Persia benefited a great deal from such allegiances by Kurdish tribes who operated in the frontier between the two countries. At that time, tensions between Qajar Persia and the Ottoman Empire were high, and there appeared to be an interest among the Persians to agitate the Ottomans by supporting the Kurds in the border region.

Kurdish Realignments

The goal of the Kurdish alliance, to which Grant and Stocking were a witness, was the liberation of Amadia from Ottoman occupation. Amadia, was a small historic city, at an elevation of approximately 5,000 feet above sea level. At that time, it was occupied by Ottoman forces, under the leadership of the governor of Mosul, Muhammad Pasha. Yahya Khan was to help Ismael Pasha, who was the displaced Kurdish chieftain of Amadia, in returning Amadia to the Kurds. Present at the meeting was another Kurdish chief, Bedir Khan Bey, from the district of Buhtan in Turkey.[180]

The union of the Kurdish chiefs in Salmas was, therefore, with the intent to organize an attack on Ottoman government forces that had occupied Amadia. Interestingly, emir Nurullah, who had recently pledged allegiance to the Ottomans, seemed to have had flipped yet again, this time against the Ottoman government. He, too, was present at this meeting in Salmas and was very welcoming to Grant. Laurie, reflecting on this point and Nurullah's reaction to an idea proposed by Grant to set up a school for the mountain Nestorians, wrote:

> In such circumstances, Dr. Grant was cheered to find the emir
> still regards him as his physician and friend, and urged him to
> accompany him to Julamerk, whence he promised to send him
> in a few days to Tyary. Suleiman Bey earnestly seconded the
> request, and proposed to go there with him in person. Dr.
> Grant's plans and objectives were now fully explained to the
> emir, in the presence of the [Yahya] Khan, who confirmed each
> statement from his own observation of missionary labors at
> Oroomiah; and in his presence Nurullah Bey promised to protect

---

[180] Also spelled Badr Khan, Bedr Khan, and Badir Khan by other writers.

Dr. Grant and his associates, and permit them to erect buildings
for themselves and their schools, as they should be needed.[181]

There are several points about this passage and the general context
of the conversation that are important to consider. First, is the social
setting for the conversation, in which Nurullah had provided verbal
approval for Grant's idea of setting up a school in his district for the
Nestorians. It is unclear if Nurullah's approval was genuine support or
if it was in compliance with Oriental norms of courtesy and politeness
in social settings. These norms, especially in social gatherings, yield a
more positive tone to conversations than truly intended. It is possible
that Grant was misinterpreting Nurullah's positive tone about his plans
to build a schoolhouse and was overestimating Nurullah's degree of
approval.

Secondly, it is essential to view the Kurdish plans against the
Ottomans, which Grant was observing in light of the greater picture of
nationalism and independence aspirations by minorities in the Ottoman
Empire at that time. To ensure that he had the sufficient number of
forces needed to face the Ottomans occupying Amadia, Ismael Pasha
had asked for the support of emir Nurullah and Bedir Khan. Ismael also
wanted the Nestorians of the Kurdish mountains to join them in this
campaign and had asked for support from the patriarch in mobilizing
his forces.

A Mountain Nestorian Fighter (c. 1890s)

---

[181] Laurie (1853), *Dr. Grant and the Mountain Nestorians,* p. 228.

While some Nestorian tribes joined the effort, the patriarch was hesitant about such a campaign. He seemed to view this as an effort by the Kurds to gain full control of the mountains. In the patriarch's mind, Ottoman rule would be less chaotic and more supportive of the Nestorian population, compared to having the Kurds in full control of the region.

Given his hesitations about joining the Kurds, the patriarch decided to secretly disclose the intent of the Kurdish leaders to Muhammad Pasha (the Ottoman governor of Mosul who had led the occupation of Amadia). This constituted a significant disclosure to an enemy, of what was to be a secret alliance between the Kurds and the Nestorians. In return, Muhammad Pasha secretly corresponded back with the patriarch and promised him the support of Ottoman forces and the safety of the Nestorians if the patriarch chose to not cooperate with the Kurdish campaign against the Ottomans. All of these communications were to take place in secret. However, they were eventually discovered and revealed to the Kurds, with devastating retributions inflicted on the patriarch and his people, as will be discussed shortly.

Building the Mission School in Ashitha

One of the primary objectives of Grant was to commence the educational work of the ABCFM for the mountain Nestorians, which meant that a schoolhouse with the necessary facilities had to be constructed. The village of Ashitha was chosen for the school. It was a central village with a population of about 3,000 people, an abundance of water streams, and a beautiful mountainous location overlooking the valleys around it. Grant sought the approval of emir Nurullah, who by this time had become the most powerful Kurdish chieftain in the Hakkari region. The verbal reassurance of the emir regarding the building of a mission school, which he had provided during their earlier meeting in Salmas, was viewed as critical to Grant, even more so than getting Ottoman government approval.[182] In fact, Grant never sought

---

[182] Grant did not seek the approval of the Ottoman government since the Ottomans had little direct control in this region, and Nurullah was their nominal representative in Hakkari. See Taylor (2008; p. 313) for the justifications Grant provided to the American embassy in Constantinople in 1843 for not seeking Ottoman approval.

the latter and only relied on the words of Nurullah in determining whether or not to proceed with the construction of the schoolhouse.

From Salmas, Grant and Stocking headed northeast to the village of Oolah where they arrived in July of 1842. However, Stocking began to feel ill and had to abandon the journey altogether and returned to Urumia. Also, both of the native assistants who had accompanied Grant and Stocking up to this point decided to withdraw from the journey and desired not to go any further, fearing the dangers ahead. They were concerned about the growing number of robberies on both sides of the Turco-Persian border.

However, Mar Yoosuf, who had previously accompanied Grant and his son on his earlier trip from Urumia to the mountain Nestorians, decided to accompany him for the remainder of the journey. On their way, they were momentarily joined by Austin Wright (the Urumia mission lead physician) and Edward Breath (the Urumia mission printer), who were on the same road but headed in the opposite direction. Although the encounter was brief, Wright and Breath spoke in some detail with Grant about his plans and expressed their acknowledgment and support for his intentions. Wright and Breath then rode off on their horses, heading south to Urumia.

By late July of 1842, Grant had reached the Van area, with the protection of two Kurdish guards provided by Yahya Khan. As he advanced into the Van area, he noticed that the Kurds near Van were working alongside the Ottoman soldiers and had begun a retribution campaign against the Nestorians. The road was full of terrorized and displaced people:

> It was one of those scenes not to be forgotten by the observer, though no language can describe it to another. The road was literally thronged with the frightened fugitives, — men, women and children, crowded on each other, terror visible in every feature. The little ones, packed on the loaded animals or slung in large sacks fastened together across the backs of the cattle, were crying as they went. Women, on foot, urged, with the cries and blows, the slow-footed beasts loaded with their baggage, leaving husbands and brothers to drive the flocks.[183]

---

[183] Laurie (1853), *Dr. Grant and the Mountain Nestorians*, pp. 234-235.

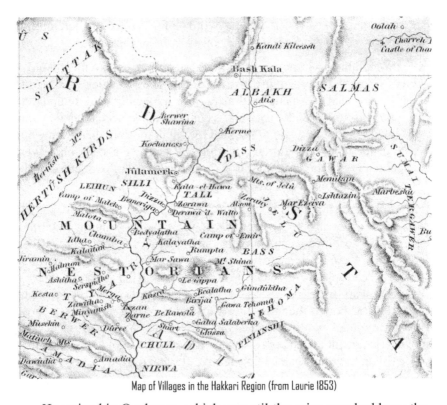

Map of Villages in the Hakkari Region (from Laurie 1853)

He arrived in Quchanes, which up until the prior year had been the patriarch's home village until his house was burned down by Nurullah. He then ascended to the village of Berchulla, which was the location of the summer residence of emir Nurullah. He was received by the locals there and given temporary lodging. Among the people present were Ismael Pasha and Suleiman Bey, who were both on their way to see the patriarch to encourage him again to rise against the Ottomans. They asked Grant if he would like to join them. Grant had no interest in being involved in such matters, and given that emir Nurullah was feeling ill, he had the perfect excuse to not join them in their visit to the patriarch. Instead, he stayed back to attend to the emir's medical needs:

> At the emir's suggestion, he now exchanged his Frank dress for
> their own costume, and soon was seated, 'a la Kurd,' dipping his

hand with him in the dish, to good purpose, if not with all the finished grace of an oriental.[184]

While Grant was able to benefit from the trust and friendship of Nurullah, it is important to realize that just days earlier, he had entered Ottoman territory, witnessing Nestorian villagers who had been attacked by the Kurdish forces. The friendly nature of Nurullah's relationship with Grant suggests that this issue was not brought up by Grant to question or confront the most powerful Kurdish leader of the Hakkari region.[185]

In late July, the emir left for Julamerk. Grant stayed back and spent time with Suleiman Bey's mother, who had been very kind and friendly to him and his son during their earlier visit to the area. She asked about his son whom she adored, and protested as to why Grant had left the adorable Henry Martyn alone in America. More importantly, she hinted to Grant about the jealous and territorial tendencies of Nurullah. Grant had also noticed this on other occasions. In the months to come, the jealousies that the two had noticed in Nurullah will reach beyond personal matters and engulf the entire region in a blood bath.

The Rise of Kurdish Tensions with the Ottomans

Grant headed to Jualmerk and spent some time visiting the Nestorian villages in that area. By early August of 1842, he had caught up with the emir and was in the Tehoma mountain area, further south, accompanying the emir. The emir had set up camp there, and his army was organizing for a march southwest against Amadia, where the Ottomans had taken over the town. To avoid being dragged into the conflict, Grant left the camp to head north to the Jelu and Bass regions

---

[184] Ibid., p. 238.

[185] The friendly and neutral tone with which Grant conducted himself with the Kurdish chiefs, in light of the atrocities inflicted on the Nestorians, is one of the critiques made about Grant's presence in this tense environment. His passive approach may have come across to the Kurds as an expression of approval or indifference, while to the Nestorians it must have been frustrating to see him not put forth persuasive arguments to these tribal chiefs to stop their violent acts. On the other hand, it is important to realize that with the degree of determination that Nurullah and the other tribal leaders had in carrying out their plans, it would have been unlikely that any words from Grant could have persuaded them to act differently.

for several days. Upon his return to the camp, he realized that the emir was beginning to receive visits from various Kurdish chiefs.

Interestingly, the emir's favorable treatment of Grant meant that he was often given the closest and most honorable spot next to the emir in many of the ceremonial and political visits of the Kurdish chiefs. The visitors were seeking to align themselves with the emir in his campaign against the Ottomans occupying Amadia. The emir was still hoping to gain the support of the Nestorians in this campaign. Laurie quoted Grant as such: "The monotony of the camp was relieved by the occasional arrival of recruits, who were sent on immediately to Amadia; and it is painful to record that some Nestorians from Tehoma were rewarded with cheap articles of dress for several ears of Turks they brought to the emir."[186]

As evident from the above passage, while the Nestorian patriarch had not given the full support of his people in fighting the Ottomans, some Nestorian tribes were cooperating on their own with the Kurdish forces in their campaign against the Ottomans. To avoid being dragged into the military campaign, Grant asked if he could leave for Tyary. However, the emir would not let him go until he had a conversation with Grant about his plans for the schoolhouse building. The mission schoolhouse that Grant had planned to construct in Ashitha was becoming a source of concern and anxiety for the emir, despite his earlier approval. The emir suspected that it would serve as a military fortress for the Nestorians, rather than a schoolhouse:

> Not, however, till the emir had urged him to give up his plan of building there, and come and live nearer to himself. When he [Dr. Grant] pleaded that this would involve much inconvenience to his associates, and derangement of plans he [the emir] then requests him [Dr. Grant] to defer building till he should see him again, to which the doctor readily assented.[187]

Grant left some supply of medicine and instructions for the emir and departed in mid-August of 1842, heading north to the Tyary mountain region. He caught up with the patriarch. The patriarch was on his way to see Suleiman Bey and Ismael Pasha. He seemed to have had a change in heart and was considering having the Nestorians join the

---

[186] Laurie (1853), *Dr. Grant and the Mountain Nestorians*, p. 244.
[187] Ibid., p. 244.

Kurds in their fight against the Turks. Laurie asserts that Grant preferred the Turks over the Kurds, believing that the Kurds had greater ill intentions towards the mountain Nestorians:

> He [Dr. Grant] regarded it [the fight between the Kurds and the Turks] as a strife between them [Nurullah and his nephew Suleiman] and the latter [the Turks] for supremacy over the Nestorians; and, of the two, he preferred the success of the Turks as the more responsible.[188]

Oddly enough, despite the patriarch's stated intention to join the Kurds in fighting the Turkish forces, as mentioned earlier, he had secretly been in communication with the Ottoman governor of Mosul (Muhammad Pasha). The governor had secretly assured the patriarch that if the Nestorians under the patriarch's control did not join the Kurds, the Ottoman forces would make sure the Kurds do not harm them:

> Probably, also, he [the patriarch] had the secret hope that, in that case, Christian powers would do more for their protection. Had he [the patriarch] done otherwise, he might have made peace with the emir, and thus had but one enemy to combat; but having received friendly letters from the Pasha of Mosul, he [the patriarch] thought gratitude for present neutrality would make them firm friends in the future. To this the doctor could only listen in silence. He says of it: 'The pacific nature of his plan was at least commendable; and, on the principle of following peace with all men, I afterwards recommended him to be reconciled with the emir, and thus, if possible, avert disaster. I also tried to persuade the emir to peace with him; but, further than this, I could not interfere, and had nothing to do with their political relations.'[189]

It is clear that Grant was caught between the Kurds and the Nestorians, who were considering becoming allies against the Ottomans. Yet they were uncertain in their own hearts about the strength of their alliance, and their own commitment towards each other in the proposed campaign against the Ottoman occupation of Amadia. The revelation of the patriarch's communications with the governor of Mosul will come to haunt him, as it deeply aggravated the

---

[188] Ibid., p. 255.
[189] Ibid., p. 255-256.

intolerant nerves of emir Nurullah and the other Kurdish chiefs allied with him.

At the same time, the Kurds in the Tyary region began to assemble for battle, in favor of the emir's proposal to attack the Ottoman forces in Amadia. The patriarch chose to continue with his position of neutrality, which frustrated the Kurds.[190] Signs of tensions between the Nestorians and the Kurds were beginning to become more evident to Grant. For example, in the village of Ashitha, representatives from various Kurdish tribes had assembled to discuss a plan of attack against the Turks. However, they refused to leave the village. The village's Nestorians began to prepare to go to battle against these occupying Kurds, in order to expel them from the village. It was only after the outbreak of minor scuffles that the occupiers gradually began to drift out of the village on their own.

Despite emir Nurullah's earlier expressions of concern about the schoolhouse and the growing tensions between the Kurds and the Nestorians, the construction of the schoolhouse in Ashitha began. It became a source of employment and economic opportunities for the locals, mostly the Nestorians. The selected location for the schoolhouse was a piece of land that, because of the poor quality of its soil, could not be used for farming. It had been previously owned by a village notable who had lived there for such a long time that it was referred to by the locals as "the castle."[191] The land was priced attractively because it had no agricultural potential, and Grant was able to purchase it for the equivalent of six American dollars.

In August of 1842, the Ashitha school began to operate on a small scale, with only thirty students. One priest was assigned as the teacher. To further strengthen the administration of the newly opened school, Hinsdale traveled from Mosul to join Grant in October and stayed with

---

[190] In fact, the patriarch had originally assembled an army of 3,000 Nestorian soldiers to join the Kurds, but having secretly received instructions from the Ottoman governor of Mosul to not participate in the offensive, he recalled these forces, claiming that they would not be able to fight due to a religious fast, further frustrating the Kurdish chieftains.

[191] A reference which did not help in easing the nerves of Nurullah, given his suspicions about the potential use of the schoolhouse for Nestorians' military purposes.

him for approximately one month. Hinsdale had brought along eight mule loads of books and supplies for the school.[192]

At approximately the same time that the school in Ashitha had begun operating, the Kurdish campaign against the Turks who had occupied Amadia came to a disappointing end for the Kurds. Amadia was a fortress city with an elevated position overlooking a plain. It was nearly impossible to penetrate for most armies. This was a lesson that the Kurdish forces ended up learning the hard way. More importantly, the Kurdish chiefs attributed their defeat to the patriarch's unwillingness to mobilize the Nestorians in support of the campaign.

As such, the tensions between the Kurds and the Nestorians were reaching a boiling point. The patriarch informed Grant that the Kurds had become suspicious of the schoolhouse and thought that it was being built by Grant for military use by the Nestorians. He also told Grant that the emir had just returned from visiting Bedir Khan Bey (the Kurdish chieftain of Buhtan region to the west of the Hakkari region) and was told that Bedir Khan has plans for "the complete subjugation of the Nestorians."[193]

The hostile posture of Bedir Khan toward the patriarch and the Nestorians was uniquely concerning. He was inarguably the most powerful Kurdish chieftain anywhere in the Ottoman Empire at that time. McDowall describes him as one who "remains for many Kurds the most illustrious of an illustrious dynasty. He was brave, charming, pious and ambitious, but he was reckless, too."[194] He came to power in Buhtan in 1820 at the age of 18. Being young and inexperienced, in his early years, he was submissive to Ottoman rule. As a young leader, he forced large numbers of Yazidis to convert to Islam under the threat of a sword's blade. He made those who converted into his loyal followers, in some cases more loyal than his own family members. In his conquests, he had developed a good understanding of the importance of using religious fervor to mobilize armies.

---

[192] Joseph (1961), *Nestorians and their Muslim Neighbors*, p. 58.

[193] Laurie (1853), *Dr. Grant and the Mountain Nestorians*, p. 271; It is possible that by then, the secret communications between the patriarch and the Ottoman governor of Mosul had been revealed to Badir Khan.

[194] McDowall (2007), *A Modern History of the Kurds*, p. 45.

In 1839, Bedir Khan had been given an official rank in the Ottoman army. His Kurdish forces were to be integrated with the Ottoman forces. His troops were to join in the battle against the rebels seeking independence in the Ottoman province of Egypt. These rebels were under the command of Ibrahim Pasha, who had turned against the Ottoman government, and was seeking Egypt's independence. The Ottoman army and its allies lost the battle. Despite being part of the losing side of the battle, the loss alongside the Ottoman forces gave Bedir Khan an inside perspective of the weaknesses the Ottoman forces had in suppressing militarized independence movements.

The defeat gave him insights on how the Kurdish forces under his own command can challenge the Ottomans in the near future, with the ultimate aim of establishing an independent Kurdish state.[195] However, for Bedir Khan, a truly independent Kurdish state would not include Christian subjects. As subsequent events would demonstrate, the presence of the Nestorians and Armenians in the mountains would challenge the uniformity of the Kurdish state that he was envisioning. He feared that their presence might ignite their own desires for separate Nestorian or Armenian states, within the Kurdish mountains. In such a case, the presence of Nestorians and Armenians would be an inconvenience that could only be addressed through elimination, which he preferred to carry out sooner rather than later.

The Emir's Anxieties about the Schoolhouse

Grant traveled to Julamerk to visit emir Nurullah, and found that Suleiman Bey was also there. The emir repeated to Grant his continued concerns about the building of the schoolhouse, which he now referred to as "the castle." He asked Grant how many rooms it had, to which Grant replied four, adding that it was built with mud that can be torn down by hand (emphasizing that it has no defensive or fortress-like features). The emir said that he believed him, and then faced his audience of fellow Kurdish chiefs, and said: "There, did I not tell you he was a true man?" The emir then asked Grant about the "large holes in the sides of your house" which he had suspected would be loopholes

---

[195] However, as subsequent events will show, for Badir Khan, the presence of the Nestorians (and Armenians) in the Kurdish mountains would challenge the purity of a Kurdish state he was envisioning.

for guns.[196] He then asked Grant to stop further construction of the schoolhouse building and instead move the school to the village where the emir himself lived. Grant replied that he needed the school to be established in a location where there are Christians that can use its services, which is why Ashitha was the chosen location.[197]

While Nurullah's response seems to suggest he was somewhat satisfied with Grant's response, in reality, he was agitated and deeply disappointed. Grant's insensitivity towards the emir's anxieties about the schoolhouse building was a true miscalculation.[198] In order to muster support for his efforts to contain Grant's assistance to the Nestorians, Nurullah communicated a complaint, without Grant's knowledge, to the Ottoman governor of Erzurum. In it, he stated that Grant was constructing a fortress for the Nestorians, and that he (Nurullah) would be willing to expel Grant but that he would only do so if authorized by the Ottoman government.[199]

Similarly, the Ottoman governor of Mosul, who was recently in battle with Nurullah, sided with him on this matter. He too was concerned about the possibility of the presence of Americans in the area. Similar to Nurullah, he provided a fabricated and vastly exaggerated account to the central Ottoman government, stating that Grant was constructing a facility containing over two hundred rooms on top of a mountain.[200]

It is important to recognize that Grant's insistence on the location and structure of the schoolhouse was clearly a source of continued aggravation for Nurullah and the other Kurdish chiefs. They seemed to

---

[196] Laurie (1853), *Dr. Grant and the Mountain Nestorians*, p. 275.

[197] Grant seemed to have missed a clear signal from Nurullah on this occasion. Grant's expression of an intent to continue construction of the schoolhouse in Ashitha is indicative of his inability to pay attention to the sensitivity of the circumstances facing the Nestorians at that time, and the clear objection by a powerful Kurdish chieftain.

[198] Taylor (2008; p. 183) suggests that part of the reason why Grant was so adamant about building the schoolhouse was the competition he perceived from the Roman Church in setting up schools for the mountain Nestorians. As such Grant wanted to move forward with his plan as quickly as possible and was less attentive to the signals of disapproval that he should have recognized from the tone and words of Nurullah and others around him.

[199] Laurie (1853), *Dr. Grant and the Mountain Nestorians*, p. 287.

[200] Joseph (1961), *Nestorians and their Muslim Neighbors*, p. 59.

be genuinely concerned that it could be used as a military compound by the Nestorians, who were direct recipients of American aid.[201] Furthermore, the fact that a foreign power, in this case, America, was providing direct aid to a Christian minority in what Bedir Khan hoped would become an independent Kurdish state was troubling to him, Nurullah Bey, and Suleiman Bey.

References and Related Readings

Gunter, Michael M. (2011). *Historical Dictionary of the Kurds.* Lanham, MD: The Scarecrow Press, Inc.

Joseph, John (1961). *Nestorians and their Muslim Neighbors.* Princeton: Princeton University Press.

Kinneir, John M. (1818). *Journey Through Asia Minor, Armenia, and Koordistan, in the Years 1813 and 1814.* London: John Murray.

Laurie, Thomas (1853). *Dr. Grant and the Mountain Nestorians.* Boston: Gould and Lincoln.

McDowall, David (2007). *A Modern History of the Kurds.* New York: I.B. Tauris & Co.

Salt, Jeremy (2002). "Trouble Wherever They Went: American Missionaries in Anatolia and Ottoman Syria in the Nineteenth Century," *The Muslim World,* Vol. 92, 287-313.

Taylor, Gordon (2008). *Fever & Thirst: An American Doctor Among the Tribes of Kurdistan,* 1835-1844. Chicago: Academy Chicago Publishers.

---

[201] In fact, in later years, the Kurdish forces modified the schoolhouse for use as a military fortress, as will be discussed in the following chapters.

Chapter 17

GEORGE BADGER AND THE RISING
NESTORIAN-KURDISH TENSIONS

The failed campaign on Amadia against the occupying Ottoman forces had increased Kurdish apprehension toward the Nestorians who had not supported the Kurds in this campaign. The Kurds were further irritated by the construction of the schoolhouse in Ashitha, as it had increased their suspicions about American support for political and economic gains by the Nestorians. The warning that Nurullah had given the patriarch about Bedir Khan's intent to eliminate the Nestorians was a sign of yet another realignment and political power-grab among the Kurdish tribal chiefs in the region.

By December of 1842, realizing how quickly the region was destabilizing, Grant headed south for Mosul. The urgency of him getting to Mosul was amplified since Hinsdale, who had earlier returned to Mosul, was again in poor health and in desperate need of Grant's medical care. Grant arrived in Mosul in mid-December, finding Hinsdale in very poor health and with a high fever. Despite Grant's best efforts, he arrived too late and could not save Hinsdale, who died on December 26, 1842.

The passing of his missionary colleague was not the only source of agony for Grant. There was now also a price on Grant's head. The Ottoman governor of Mosul had written a letter to the tribal chief of Nirwa to ask for an assassin to kill Grant on his way to Mosul.

Evidently, the letter was delayed, which had bought Grant time, as he was rushing back to attend to Hinsdale's illness. Lucky for Grant, he had already arrived in Mosul before the assassination plot on the road could be organized, and the governor called off the assassination.[202] The governor of Mosul wanted Grant dead because given the crimes and mass murders that the governor had carried out (and intended to do more of in the coming months), he did not want inquisitive Westerners like Grant to be present in Mosul.

George Badger

An Anglican missionary by the name of George Badger was also in Mosul at that time and gravely ill, under the care of Grant. By February 1843, Badger's health had improved. As soon as he felt better, despite it being the cold winter season and most of the roads being impassable due to snow, he ran off north in search of the Nestorian patriarch. Badger eventually became a source of great tension with Grant and the American missionaries because of his attempts to disrupt the relationship between the ABCFM missionaries and the patriarch. Badger's goal was to advance the Anglican Church's cause with the patriarch, hoping to create converts among the Nestorians. He felt a sense of cutthroat competition with the American missionaries to influence the Nestorians of the mountains.

In essence, Badger was following up on a visit that two fellow representatives of the Church of England, William Ainsworth and Isa Rassam, had made to the patriarch three years earlier. Back then, the two men had suggested to the patriarch to cease cooperation with the American missionaries, and instead bring his followers closer to the Church of England. This was a proposition which the patriarch seemed open to, but had not followed up on. In his meetings with the patriarch, Badger reiterated some of the conversations that had already taken place in 1840 between the patriarch, Ainsworth, and Rassam. Badger told him that the Americans were not real Protestants, and that if the Americans were allowed to set up schools for the mountain Nestorians,

---

[202] Laurie (1853), *Dr. Grant and the Mountain Nestorians,* p. 281.

then the Anglicans would no longer be interested in providing support for the Nestorians.[203]

Badger's actions were consistent with the British attitude at that time toward the Ottoman Empire, whereby various provinces and regions were encouraged by the British to seek independence. The British were also intimately involved in reform programs in Turkey to improve the conditions of minorities and reduce the grip of the central Ottoman government.[204] Among the reform programs which were pressured by the British onto the Ottomans were the Tanzimat reforms, which increased the independence aspirations of minorities in outlying Ottoman provinces. In later years, the Imperial Rescript of 1856, allowing non-Moslems to join the army, to seek justice in mixed (i.e., Moslem and Christian) tribunals, and to exercise greater degrees of religious freedom (beyond the limits set by the Pact of Umar centuries earlier). These reforms were put into effect, under British pressure.[205]

While the reforms had a great appeal from a modernization perspective, they were not welcomed by the masses of Turkey's Moslem population. Instead, they were, for the most part, viewed as foreign intervention in the country's internal affairs. Badger's actions in attempting to affect the Nestorians' position with respect to the Ottomans and Kurds falls perfectly in line with this narrative. His role seemed to have been to advance the British policy of the time to weaken the Ottoman government's central authority.

Between February and April of 1842, two messengers from emir Nurullah came to see the Nestorian patriarch, with Badger present as well. The messengers asked the patriarch to set up a meeting place with the emir to work out their differences and come to peace. However, the patriarch refused. It is believed that his refusal was because Badger, who was present when the messengers had arrived, encouraged the patriarch to ignore the emir's request. Instead, he had suggested to the patriarch that the British government would directly protect and support the Nestorians and there was no need for an alliance with the Kurds through the emir. It was clear that Badger was putting a great deal of pressure on the patriarch and was attempting to exert influence on him

---

[203] Ibid., pp. 284-285.
[204] Goldschmidt and Al-Marashi (2019), *A Concise History of the Middle East.*
[205] Davidson (1956), *The Hatt-i-Humayn of 1856 and the Climate of its Reception.*

to lean on the Anglicans and British support, rather than on the Americans.

To prove to the Ottoman government that the Nestorians did not desire to side with the Kurds, the patriarch dispatched a fighting force from Ashitha to fight a bandit named Zeiner Bey. Zeiner Bey was allied with Bedir Khan and his forces were lined up and ready to fight against the Ottoman governor of Mosul. The patriarch's deployment of Nestorian forces to fight a Kurdish ally of Bedir Khan further irritated the Kurdish chiefs. It was evident to them that the Nestorians under the command of the patriarch were no longer allied with the Kurds in the fight against the Ottoman government. In the months to follow, the position of the Nestorians triggered Kurdish revenge.

In the meantime, the emir continued expressing his concerns to Grant about the schoolhouse in Ashitha. Perhaps he truly viewed it as a military compound that could threaten the Kurds, because of its strategic position overlooking a valley. It may also have been that the schoolhouse was simply an excuse for the emir to take a hostile stance against Grant and the Nestorian Christians, which Grant had come to help. These views were not mutually exclusive, and both may have driven the emir's suspicions about the schoolhouse.

Grant's Return to the Mountain Nestorians

By April of 1843, the weather had warmed up sufficiently that it was finally possible to travel north from Mosul. The snow had melted and roads were passable. Grant was now accompanied by Thomas Laurie, a fellow American missionary in his northbound journey from Mosul to the mountains.[206] They first took a boat up the Tigris River. On their way, they visited one of the excavation sites of Paul-Émile Botta, the renowned French archeologist who also served as the French Consul in Mosul. Botta hosted them with great hospitality and showed the two Americans an ancient Assyrian seal he had recently excavated. Grant and Laurie had a very positive impression of Botta.

A few days later, Grant and Laurie arrived in Amadia, which had earlier been a battleground between the Kurdish and Ottoman forces.

---

[206] Thomas Laurie eventually wrote the biography of Asahel Grant, titled *Dr. Grant and the Mountain Nestorians*, published in 1853.

Signs of war and destruction were becoming apparent as they approached the city. Cannon balls and mines deployed by the Turkish forces were to be seen everywhere, and the town was destroyed. They proceeded further north to the village of Lezan and settled in a house that Grant had previously rented as a winter residence while the schoolhouse was being constructed in Ashitha.

After a brief period of rest, they proceeded to visit the village of Ashitha. The schoolhouse building, which was still under construction, had only one of its four rooms finished. The design was for it to house three missionary families, have a chapel, a schoolroom, and a stable. Laurie was able to visually inspect the schoolhouse, and elaborated on the peaceful nature of its design: "As our mode of building would not warrant the erection of a second story, it necessarily occupied a large surface; but, with a roof within the reach of every boy, and windows almost level with the ground outside, it was hardly a castle in any sense of the term."[207]

In May of that year, Laurie returned to Mosul so that he would be able to make arrangements to welcome new American missionaries sent by the ABCFM. The new missionaries were already on their way to Mosul. But when he reached Mosul, he found out that the governor of Mosul had denied entry to these missionaries. His refusal to allow foreigners to enter Mosul was in line with the climate of censorship that he was seeking to create there. It is the reason that he had previously hired assassins to kill Grant. Given that the governor was planning more killings in and around Mosul, he preferred not to have any Western observers present in the weeks and months to come.

While Laurie was on his way to Mosul, Grant proceeded and met with the patriarch. By then, Badger had already met and spoken with the patriarch and was no longer in the area. Grant recommended to the patriarch to "follow peace with all men," conveying a sense of neutrality and a clearly different position than the one advocated by Badger.[208] Grant proceeded to then meet with emir Nurullah in the village of Chumba, as the patriarch and Nurullah could not come to peace. The condition of peace that the emir had presented was the same as it had been in his earlier demands — that the patriarch should give

---

[207] Laurie (1853), *Dr. Grant and the Mountain Nestorians*, p. 308.
[208] Ibid., p. 314.

up all his civil authority, and move back from Ashitha to Quchanes, where he previously resided. The emir wanted the patriarch to serve his role solely as the head of the Nestorian Church, and abandon politics altogether.

As such, the emir's request was for the patriarch to remove himself from some of the roles that were officially granted to the patriarch, under the Tanzimat reforms and what is referred to as the millet system of governance. During the nineteenth century, within the Ottoman Empire, a "millet" was defined as a specific minority religious group which could be considered by the Ottoman government as a single legally protected population.[209] This concept is closely related to the way religious minorities were treated since the early days of the rise of Islam.

As Islam expanded its geographic range, non-Moslem populations residing in Islamic lands were given protection by their Islamic rulers. The administration of legal matters related to civil law within the millet members (i.e., not involving Moslems or those of other millets) were guided by the millet's own internal judicial processes, informed by the religious and social norms that were predominant within the millet. This required little or no input from the Ottoman government and, as such, facilitated a great deal of autonomy in the administration of justice and the collection of taxes within each millet.[210] The benefit of the millet system to the Ottoman rulers was that in light of the empire's large size, its vast geographic range, the diversity of its minorities, and the challenges in tax collection, this system allowed for efficient and harmonious administration by the central Ottoman government.

The emir's request for the patriarch to abandon his political role significantly reduced the patriarch's authority. However, according to Laurie, some of the patriarch's followers desired the patriarch to make this compromise, and many were upset that he would not budge.[211] Anticipating an attack, the patriarch asked his followers to begin preparing to go to war. However, his leadership had diminished and the Nestorians seemed to pay little attention to his call to mobilize. The

---

[209] Goldschmidt and Al-Marashi (2019), *A Concise History of the Middle East.*

[210] It is important to note however that legal cases involving a millet member and a Moslem would have to be tried in Ottoman courts and could not be settled by the millet's own judicial system.

[211] Laurie (1853), *Dr. Grant and the Mountain Nestorians,* p. 344.

Nestorians therefore made little if any preparations for the hostilities that were about to come their way. Shortly thereafter, the fighting began.

References and Related Readings

Badger, George P. (1852). *The Nestorians and their Rituals*. London: Joseph Masters.

Becker, Adam H. (2015). *Revival and Awakening: American Evangelical Missionaries in Iran and the Origins of Assyrian Nationalism*. Chicago: University of Chicago Press.

Davidson, Roderick (1956). "The Hatt-i-Humayn of 1856 and the Climate of its Reception" in *Reform in the Ottoman Empire (1856-1876)*. Princeton: University Press.

Goldschmidt, Arthur, and Ibrahim Al-Marashi (2019). *A Concise History of the Middle East*. New York: Routledge.

Lathrop, A.C. (1847). *Memoir of Asahel Grant, M.D.* New York: M.W. Dodd

Laurie, Thomas (1853). *Dr. Grant and the Mountain Nestorians*. Boston: Gould and Lincoln.

Miller, Duane M. (2017). "Anglican Mission in the Middle East up to 1910," in *The Oxford History of Anglicanism*, Rowan Strong (ed.), Oxford: Oxford University Press. pp. 276-295.

Chapter 18

THE SUBJUGATION OF THE NESTORIANS

At the initial outbreak of violence, the patriarch asked the Ottoman governor of Mosul for help, as he had been promised by the governor of such protection. In earlier secret communications, the governor had promised that he would defend the Nestorians if the Kurds attacked. This was clearly an empty promise, as evident by the destruction of the Nestorian villages, which was already underway. In fact, Bedir Khan seemed to have made his own dealings with the governor of Mosul, so as to be able to freely attack the Nestorians with no expected retaliation from Ottoman forces. The desire for Bedir Khan to attack the Nestorians was partially fueled by his discovery of the patriarch's earlier secret dealings with the governor of Mosul.

However, Bedir Khan also saw this as an opportunity for himself to rise above the other Kurdish chiefs, and to become a leader for a much greater cause: that of Kurdish independence. These aspirations were strengthened by his knowledge of the differences that existed between Nurullah and his nephew Suleiman. Bedir Khan agreed with Nurullah that having the patriarch as the leader of the Nestorians was not consistent with Kurdish independence plans. The fact that the patriarch was on better terms with Suleiman fueled Nurullah's jealousies, which Bedir Khan felt he could capitalize on. Therefore, Bedir Khan decided to take a hands-on approach in suppressing the Nestorians, and by doing so, demonstrated his strength as the definitive leader for all

Kurds, including those in the Hakkari region, where Nurullah had been considered the most powerful until that time.

However, in this power-grab, Bedir Khan went even further, to enlist the informal approval of the Ottoman governors of the region, including the governors of Erzurum and Mosul.[212] This was intriguing since only a short while ago, his forces, alongside those of the other Kurdish chiefs, were fighting the Ottoman forces in Amadia. Yet, as future events demonstrate, this short-term partnership was simply a ploy in a long-term Ottoman strategy to have the Kurds eliminate the Nestorians. The grand Ottoman strategy was to first use the Kurds as a proxy force to eliminate the Nestorians which, due to the mountainous terrain, was militarily difficult for the Ottoman forces to do alone. As the second step, once the Nestorians were eliminated by the Kurds, the sympathy of the Western Christian world (Britain, France, and Germany) would give an excuse to the Ottomans to eliminate the Kurds, as punishment for what they had done to Ottoman Christians.

Laurie explained the Ottoman choice of using Kurdish forces to attack the Nestorians, as such: "Men of similar habits, accustomed to their mode of warfare, must do the work. For this the conquests of Reschid Pasha had prepared the way; and, though the Kurds were not loyal to the Porte, they were zealous for their faith, and eager to wipe off many a long score of blood."[213] Giving the Kurdish chiefs the informal go-ahead would allow the Ottomans to have them carry out this task, given that the Kurdish forces were highly effective in the mountains, where they had lived, fought, and survived for centuries. More importantly, by having the Kurds eliminate the Nestorians, in the eyes of the world, the Ottomans would be able to deny responsibility for the massacres that were about to take place.

The Ottoman calculation had correctly predicted that in the longer-term, European powers, especially Britain and France, would be made aware of the massacres of the Nestorians, and they would demand the Turks to punish those Kurdish tribes which had inflicted the carnage. The Turks would then be able to eliminate not one, but two minority groups with potential independence aspirations (the Nestorians and the Kurds), by first manipulating the Kurds to become the eliminators of

---

[212] McDowall (2007), *A Modern History of the Kurds*, p. 47.

[213] Laurie (1853), *Dr. Grant and the Mountain Nestorians*, p. 334.

the Nestorians. Bedir Khan and the other Kurdish chiefs had not envisioned the complexity of the two-stage Ottoman strategy, which included their own subjugation as its second stage. The Ottoman strategy was indeed one of divide-and-conquer. It would enable them to enforce their authority further into the mountains by eliminating the Nestorians and weakening the Kurds.

Sensing the growing tensions, and despite the hostilities and the dangers of travel, Grant decided to visit Bedir Khan himself, and left Ashitha in early June of 1843. Within two hours on the road, he began to notice signs of violence and destruction. In the Berwer district he passed by a ruined village, with burned houses. At night, he stopped by the Nestorian village of Dey. The village chief had just returned from the village of Zacho and reported that Zeiner Bey had robbed that area. The village chief also mentioned that Bedir Khan was mobilizing Kurdish forces in the Tyary region, in preparation for attacking the Nestorians.

Despite the mounting evidence of increased violence, Grant decided to proceed further into the territory of Bedir Khan. By mid-June, he had reached the stronghold of Bedir Khan, which he had never visited before. Laurie described his approach as such:

> At the summit of the pass an uneven upland lay before the traveler, and soon two castles and the village of Derguleh appeared, crowning a high bluff, whose base is washed by the torrent. This was the stronghold of Badir Khan Bey, eighteen miles from Jezira. The castles were square, turreted buildings, whose clean white walls contrasted pleasantly with the rough crags around. On the north needle-shaped rocks shot up above the rest, and on one of the least accessible stood the treasure-house of the Bey.[214]

Ismael Pasha and Nurullah were also present in Bedir Khan Bey's castle and had set up their tents at the foot of the castle. Emir Nurullah saw Grant at the entrance to the castle and was surprised as to why he was there. Grant told the emir that it was purely for the purposes of rendering medical care that he was visiting Bedir Khan. Although it was not his own castle, the emir welcomed him to Bedir Khan's castle and said: "Do not interfere with our plans" as he was concerned that

---

[214] Ibid., p. 333.

Grant would attempt to find terms of peace on behalf of the Nestorians and destroy the grand plans to subjugate them.[215]

Grant stayed at the castle for several days. He spent part of his time with the emir. During this time, he also discovered that Ismael Pasha who was also there, was thankful that his wives were released by the governor of Mosul. They had been kept there for sixteen months and were released when Bedir Khan negotiated their freedom by promising to the governor of Mosul that Zeiner Bey will stop his robberies in that area. The alliances had clearly shifted, and now the relations between the Kurdish leaders and the Ottoman governor of Mosul, whom they previously considered as an arch-enemy, had become friendly.

Commencement of Large-Scale Violence

The Kurdish chiefs openly spoke in the presence of Grant about their planned destruction of the Nestorians. They felt reassured that he followed a non-interference policy and would not affect the nature of the relations between them and the Nestorians. Nurullah and Bedir Khan gave assurances to Grant that his life and property, including the schoolhouse, would not be harmed. The fact that the chiefs were discussing their plans so openly in his presence must have felt awkward for Grant. It also conveys a sense of neutrality in his interactions with them, which, while not condoning their planned acts of violence, must not have come across as opposed to them either. Grant's ability to not interfere and simply take on the role of an observer is somewhat surprising, given that in his writings, he expressed so much love and affection toward the Nestorians of the mountains.

A military force of the Kurds had begun to organize a campaign against the Nestorians in the Diss region. Grant had a desire to leave, feeling conflicted about being present among leaders who were planning a massacre. However, Bedir Khan did not allow him to leave and instead asked him to attend to the health of one of his senior military officers. Finally, having attended to the medical needs of this

---

[215] Jwaideh (2006, p.64) points out that in an interview in 1846 which Bedir Khan had held with two American missionaries, Austin Wright and Edward Breath, he had admitted that his decision to attack the Nestorians had the blessing of the Ottoman government.

officer for several days, Grant managed to leave the camp of Bedir Khan. A guide was sent by Bedir Khan to help him navigate his return. Through the guide, Bedir Khan also offered Grant a purse of gold, which Grant respectfully declined while sending an appreciation note back to Bedir Khan.[216]

Grant arrived in Ashitha at the end of June of 1843 and was greeted by the patriarch. The patriarch was anxious for any news of upcoming dangers. Grant reported everything that the Kurdish chiefs had said in his presence about their plans to attack the Nestorians. The limited defensive abilities of the Nestorians were further constrained by the wide dispersion of their villages across the mountain ranges, as they had not made any defensive arrangements. Furthermore, the distances between the villages in the mountains limited their ability to communicate, coordinate, and unite. Leaving one's village to aid another under attack could compromise the defenses of one's own village. As such, the Nestorian villages were easy targets for attackers who overwhelmed the villages one-by-one as they moved through the region. McDowall estimates the Kurdish army deployed to attack the Nestorians was massive, ranging from 70,000 to 100,000 men.[217]

The power and leadership of the patriarch in mobilizing his people was clearly missing. The division among the Nestorians from earlier years, as to how to deal with the Kurds was a primary contributing factor. Grant left Ashitha in early July, heading south to Mosul, and arrived there in mid-July. However, on his way, more news of attacks on the Nestorians began to reach him:

> The news at first was disbelieved, but too truly confirmed, as
> messenger after messenger arrived from the scene of action.
> The tribe of Diss, the home of the patriarchal family, was laid to
> waste. The blood of nearly eight hundred, of both sexes, had
> stained her valleys, and mingled with her mountain torrents.
> The leading men had been assassinated at a council to which
> they were invited to settle terms of peace, and then the whole
> tribe was overwhelmed. Neither sex nor age was spared. The
> survivors were hurried into slavery, except a small band, that

---

[216] The gift of gold coins that Bedir Khan offered Grant is indicative of the closeness he felt toward Grant, which may have been aided by the neutrality and passive attitude of Grant in not confronting Bedir Khan regarding his deadly plans for the Nestorians.
[217] McDowall (2007), *A Modern History of the Kurds,* p. 47.

still defended a mountain fastness against the united hordes of
Hakkary and Buhtan.[218]

The patriarch's mother was killed and her dead body was thrown
into a river. The patriarch's oldest brother (Zadok) was also killed, as
well as his son, who would have by Nestorian tradition become the next
patriarch. Bedir Khan was now advancing even further to attack Tyary,
a predominately Nestorian section of the Hakkari region. Bedir Khan's
forces united with the forces of another Kurdish chief, and together
they destroyed Diss. All the captives were sent to Buhtan, where Bedir
Khan was the controlling tribal chief:

> Troops were sent out thence in every direction, to destroy the
> surrounding villages. The war was little more now than a
> succession of massacres. The Kurds passed from place to place,
> slaying the people and burning the houses at their leisure,
> generally without even the shadow of resistance. The panic-
> struck Nestorians seemed alike incapable of flight or defence
> and awaited in agonizing suspense their turn to suffer.[219]

Bedir Khan sent the patriarch's other brother (Benjamin) from
Chumba to Ashitha, to ask the patriarch to surrender, or otherwise be
killed. The Patriarch intended to flee to Persia but the path was blocked
by Kurdish forces. He therefore fled south to Mosul. Grant had already
arrived there in July and the patriarch arrived two weeks after him.
Laurie recites Grant's own words:

> He [the Patriarch] said he had no definite plans, and at once
> accepted my invitation to make our house his home at least till
> he should see the pasha. But presently we met Messrs. Rassam
> and Badger; and the former told me, 'It was arranged between
> him and the pasha that the Patriarch should be his [Mr.
> Badger's] guest. Moreover, he had instructions from the English
> government concerning him [the patriarch], and it was important
> he should be under the protection of the British flag.[220]

It was clear that Badger had interfered again in the relationship
between the patriarch and Grant, and that British support was the
enabler for this. Also evident in this passage is the continued

---

[218] Laurie (1853), *Dr. Grant and the Mountain Nestorians*, p. 349.
[219] Ibid., p. 354.
[220] Ibid., p. 357.

competition between the Anglicans and the ABCFM for the attention of the Nestorians.

While the outcome for the Nestorians was devastating, the Kurds prospered. The notorious bandit, Zeiner Bey, was assigned as the Ottoman governor of Tyary. He also took over the schoolhouse constructed by Grant. He made drastic changes to it, and turned it into a military fortress. The windows were converted into loop-holes to allow muskets to shoot at advancing forces. The mud walls were covered with limestone for extra protection, and the walls were raised and the corners of the walls were changed into observation posts. A large water reservoir was also constructed on the grounds.

Of the nearly one hundred houses in Ashitha, only four were left unburned, and the remainder were all destroyed. Graphic accounts of atrocities are evident in the writings of renowned British archeologist Austen Layard, who visited the area. He recalled:

> Emerging from the gardens, we found ourselves at the foot of an almost perpendicular detritus of loose stones, terminated, about one thousand feet above us, by a wall of lofty rocks. Up this ascent we toiled for above an hour; sometimes clinging to small shrubs, whose roots scarcely reached the scanty soil below; at others, crawling on our hands and knees; crossing the gulleys to secure a footing carried down by the stones which were put in motion as we advanced. We soon saw evidences of the slaughter. At first a solitary skull rolling down with the rubbish; then heaps of blanched bones; further up, fragments of rotting garments. As we advanced, these remains became more frequent, — skeletons, almost entire, still hung to the dwarf shrubs. I was soon compelled to renounce an attempt to count them. As we approached the wall of rock, the declivity became covered with bones, mingled with the long platted tresses of the women, shreds of discolored linen, and well-worn shoes. There were skulls of all ages, from the child unborn to the toothless old man. We could not avoid treading on the bones as we advanced, and rolling them with the loose stones into the valley below.[221]

Discussing the tortures experienced by the captives, Thomas Laurie wrote about his visits to the area the following year. His observations

---

[221] Layard (1854), *A Popular Account of Discoveries at Nineveh*, p. 134.

and eye-witness accounts are disturbing and demonstrate the extent of violence inflicted on the population:

> In 1844 we saw those who had lost the use of their arms by the inhuman twisting of the cords that bound them behind their backs. Some lost the use of their legs by similar cruelties. Others had their breasts burned with red-hot irons, or were suspended by hooks thrust into the muscles of their arms and legs, till they revealed every hoard they know of, and even after there was no more to reveal.[222]

Final Months in Mosul

Having settled in Mosul, Grant continued to provide humanitarian services to help the Nestorians who had fled to Mosul. He rented a house to provide shelter for orphaned children and widows with children. He also made arrangements to feed, clothe, and provide schooling for them. In early April of 1844, Grant complained of feeling unwell. Sick as he was, he wrote to Edwin in America. These were his last words

> I am happy to hear that so many feel a lively interest in your welfare. But, while truly grateful for this, I cannot forget the stronger ties that bind us together. Nor could you, my son, doubt for a moment the warm love I feel, did you know the yearnings of my heart towards you, and how greatly I long to see you. That strong desire I now hope will be gratified; and I trust the gratification will not be so transient as in my former visit. We then saw each other so little, that it was tantalizing rather than satisfactory. I was such a stranger that you hardly knew me; and then my visit was so hurried that you must have felt, when we parted, that I was still almost a stranger.[223]

Asahel Grant died on Wednesday, April 24, 1844 of typhus fever. He is buried in the Syrian Orthodox Church of Mar Toma (St. Thomas) in Mosul.

---

[222] Laurie (1853), *Dr. Grant and the Mountain Nestorians,* pp. 363-364.
[223] Ibid., p. 393.

The Mountain Nestorians after Grant's Passing

A second major attack on the Mountain Nestorians by the Kurds occurred in 1846. In this attack, those Nestorian villages that had not sided with the patriarch and instead sided with Bedir Khan were also destroyed. This time, the village of Ashitha, which had been left untouched in the original attacks due to Bedir Khan's promises to Grant, was also destroyed. Accurate estimates of the total number of casualties between 1842 and 1846 are impossible to obtain, due to the absence of neutral observers, journalists, or Western army officers to produce reliable casualty counts.

In describing the extent of the casualties, Laurie mentioned that "Many Kurds were killed, as well as Nestorians."[224] Clearly, the Nestorians were also armed, and fought back. Therefore, to conclude that all the casualties were among the Nestorians would be inaccurate. Joseph estimated that about 10,000 lives had perished (one-fifth the Nestorian population of the region).[225] Those who survived either escaped to Mosul or Urumia, or were enslaved.[226] Joseph also considered the massacres as being "the first major conflict between native Christians and Muslims in modern times" and that the atrocities inflicted on the Nestorian population could only be outmatched with the ravages that they had experienced during the Mongol reign of Tamerlane.

The Nestorian massacres were of great concern to the Europeans, who considered the protection of the Christian minorities of the Ottoman Empire of great importance. Britain and France demanded justice and with their encouragement, the Ottomans attacked Bedir Khan. One of the first engagements between the Ottoman forces and those of Bedir Khan took place in the Urumia region, in which forces allied with Bedir Khan prevailed. However, by then, Bedir Khan had established alliances among the Kurdish tribes in Hakkari, Van, Muks and Bitlis.[227]

---

[224] Laurie (1853), *Dr. Grant and the Mountain Nestorians*, p. 364.
[225] Joseph (1961), *Nestorians and their Muslim Neighbors*, p. 64.
[226] Jwaideh (2006), *The Kurdish National Movement*, p. 72.
[227] Ibid.

Bedir Khan was able to push back the early Ottoman attacks and declared an independent Kurdish state. He even went so far as to mint his own coins and set up a factory for the production of rifles and ammunition. Having his own currency and being able to produce his own armament were symbolically meaningful accomplishments for demonstrating the establishment of a truly independent state. However, a second Turkish attack in 1847 eventually subdued him. He was encircled for eight months in his fortress at Urukh and eventually had to surrender.

Badir Khan was then sent to exile, alongside his entire family, to the island of Crete, which at that point in time was under Ottoman rule. Emir Nurullah was also arrested by the Turks but not put to death. He later died in Persia. Suleiman was sent to exile to Trebizond but died on his way there. Most of the other Kurdish leaders who had assisted in the massacres were executed, exiled, or imprisoned. The excessive use of violence exhibited by the Kurds helped them achieve short term territorial gains, but the violence also caused a loss of sympathy by the West for their cause. The fall of Bedir Khan was to be the first chapter in the Kurdish desire for independence, as more chapters would open in the coming decades, all directly affecting the American missionaries in Urumia.

Village of Dizza in Gawar District (c. 1895)

Despite the massacres and Grant's passing, the American Board of Commissioners for Foreign Missions continued its activities in the Kurdish mountains. As detailed by Perkins these activities were centered in the village of Memikan (to the south of the village of Dizza) in the Gawar region.[228] This Mission's activities primarily included schools and preaching. There were also outstations from this mission station, staffed by Nestorians educated at the Urumia mission schools. The Gawar station was staffed by American missionaries, including Edwin Crane and Martha Harris Rhea, both of whom died there of natural causes. An ABCFM mission station was established in Mosul in 1850 and continued to operate for approximately a decade.

Reflections on Grant and His Visits to the Mountains

Grant was the second missionary to enter Persia. He commenced the Mission's medical services. After a relatively short stay in Urumia, he ventured into the Kurdish mountains of Turkey in search of the mountain Nestorians. His journeys in this region of the world, where tribal violence combined with a rough terrain made for dangerous travel conditions, were daring and pioneering. He was one of the first Westerners ever to set foot in this region of the world. His inquisitive mind and methodical recording of what he had seen gave us a glimpse of a world unknown to many then, and unobservable by us today.

In assessing the actions and labors of Grant, Orientalists and those with whom he interacted have evaluated him in many different lights, often with contrasting assessments. What is indisputable is that as a missionary physician, Grant's skills were superb. In Urumia, he began the mission station's medical practices, was generous in sharing his knowledge with local doctors, and was an effective healer for the thousands of patients that came to him. As a missionary who defied the instructions given by the ABCFM, and on his own ventured into the dangerous territories of the Kurdish mountains of Turkey, he was indeed a risk-taker. His hunger for visiting the unexplored mountains where the mountain Nestorians were known to live, had clearly overpowered his desires to comply with the strict instructions of his superiors.

---

[228] Perkins (1861), *Missionary Life in Persia*, pp. 137-144.

Despite the undeniable facts above, there are different perspectives when it comes to the nature of Grant's influence on the relationship between the mountain Nestorians and their Kurdish neighbors. On the one hand, once the Kurdish hostilities toward the Nestorians began, Grant was passive and non-vocal in his interactions with the Kurdish chiefs. The fact that as a missionary physician he was a trusted man among these Kurdish leaders could have potentially given him some luxury in attempting to persuade the Kurds to not take on a hostile stance toward the Nestorians.

However, it can be argued that to assume that a traveling physician would have had any influence on powerful warlike chiefs would be simplistic and unrealistic. Individuals such as Bedir Khan and Nurullah had for years envisioned the formation of an independent Kurdish state, and relied on religion as a mobilizing force. For them, the suggestions and words of a foreign physician could not have reversed years of passion, anticipation, and tribal aspirations. Therefore, while in glancing over Grant's interactions with them, one may be disturbed by his seemingly passive attitude when the massacres of the Nestorians were being discussed by the Kurdish chiefs, given the context and environment that he was in, the prudent thing would have been to not be vocal. Anything else would have most likely rendered him a dead man at the hands of well-armed men with much killing experience.

Another possible critique of Grant relates to his persistence in building the schoolhouse in Ashitha. The schoolhouse seemed to have become a constant source of irritation for Nurullah. The increased irritation among Nurullah's circle seems to have been associated with the suspicion that the Nestorians were being supported by the American missionaries, and that this may in the longer term result in the strengthening of the Nestorians. This perspective may be quite reasonable, since the idea of a foreign power supporting minorities, especially Christians, within Ottoman territories was not a new concept. The efforts by the Roman Church to convert Nestorians into Catholics had in the past resulted in the formation of the Chaldean Christian community. Furthermore, Ainsworth's visit to the patriarch in 1840 was an expression of an Anglican appeal to the Nestorians, under the supportive wings of the British Empire. This was reinforced by Badger's visit to the Patriarch in 1843, in which alliance with the

Church of England was proposed, again under the protection of the British government.

Therefore, it would have been quite reasonable for the Kurds to have developed suspicions about the imperialistic motives behind the construction of the schoolhouse, even though it was not a British, but rather an American initiative. When Nurullah suggested to Grant that he could instead build the schoolhouse in Nurullah's own village, Grant refused the proposal on the grounds that not as many Christians resided in that area. It is possible that had Grant been more flexible in his choice of location for the schoolhouse, which Nurullah suspected of being a fortress due to its towering position overlooking a strategic valley, the suspicions of Nurullah would have been calmed somewhat.

However, based on other facts that are known about Nurullah, such as his jealously toward Suleiman and his temperamental tendencies, the likelihood of his nerves being calmed by a simple change of location for a schoolhouse was most likely slim. Nurullah was executing a power grab in the Hakkari region and any excuse to increase his power relative to others would have been justifiable to him. The schoolhouse itself was most certainly not the sole cause for the violence Nurullah and his allies inflicted on the thousands of massacred Nestorians in the mountains.

Another criticism of Grant which has been forwarded is that he misdirected the patriarch in terms of how the patriarch should react to Nurullah's demands. Grant took a neutral stance and suggested to him that he should pursue peaceful relations with both the Kurds and the Turks. Complying with Nurullah's demand that the patriarch should give up his political powers was something the patriarch was not willing to accept. Jwaideh suggests that considering the complexity of the situation that the patriarch was trapped in, Grant seemed to be unable to see why the patriarch was not in favor of Nurullah's demands to relinquish some of his authority. In describing the position of Grant and his colleagues, Jwaideh suggests the following regarding the American missionaries' approach:

> Being convinced of the superiority of their beliefs and the righteousness of their intentions, they embarked on their missionary work with little or no awareness that their activities might be misrepresented, misunderstood, or resented by those among whom they labored. They should have anticipated and

avoided difficulties with the patriarch. A man in the patriarch's position could not be expected to abandon the tenets and practices of the ancient church he headed and to yield his spiritual and temporal authority without a struggle.[229]

The same criticism however can be applied to Badger, the Anglican missionary who attempted to influence the patriarch's position with respect to the Kurds. Badger was in direct competition with Grant for the patriarch's attention and approval. The suggestions provided to the patriarch, by both Grant and Badger, may have produced a strategically confused state in terms of what the patriarch eventually did. By secretly communicating with the governor of Mosul, the patriarch was attempting to steer away from partnering with the Kurds in their attack on the Ottoman forces occupying Amadia. Had the secrecy of this communication not been revealed, it is possible that the nature of the relationship between the Kurds and the Nestorians would have been less violent.

It is also difficult to isolate the effect of the patriarch's own indecisiveness and his high hopes for receiving help from the British or Americans through their missionary efforts. In the end, both Grant and Badger, though in direct competition with one another, may have equally amplified the confusion for the patriarch and his followers. The loss of loyalty toward the patriarch among some of the Nestorian tribes caused a division that was harmful to the unity of the mountain Nestorians. Evidence of this can be found in the fact that although in the patriarch had encouraged his followers to not take part in the 1842 Kurdish attacks on the Ottomans in Amadia, three Nestorian tribes chose to participate and fought the Ottomans, alongside the Kurdish forces.

There were clear disagreements among the Nestorians, which neither Badger nor Grant could be fully responsible for. These were indicative of a deeper divide eventually contributed to a split in the Nestorian Church two decades later and resulted in the formation of the Syrian Evangelical Church in Urumia. In contrast to the divisions experienced among the Nestorians, the Kurdish tribes were united during this time.

---

[229] Jwaideh (2006), *The Kurdish National Movement*, p. 71.

The alliances formed between the Kurdish chieftains of Hakkari, Buhtan, and elsewhere allowed the Kurds to mobilize and unite, thereby becoming a more formidable force in the region. The unity would fuel Kurdish independence aspirations, which eventually affected not only the Ottoman Empire, but also Persia and the Urumia mission station during the last two decades of the nineteenth century and the years leading to and including the First World War.

References and Related Readings

Bird, Isabella L. (1891). *Journeys in Persia and Kurdistan.* London: John Murray.

Jwaideh, Wadie (2006). *The Kurdish National Movement: Its Origins and Development.* Syracuse: Syracuse University Press.

Laurie, Thomas (1853). *Dr. Grant and the Mountain Nestorians.* Boston: Gould and Lincoln.

Layard, Austen H. (1867). *Nineveh and its Remains.* London: John Murray.

Layard, Austen H. (1854). *A Popular Account of Discoveries at Nineveh.* London: John Murray.

McDowall, David (2007). *A Modern History of the Kurds.* New York: I.B. Tauris & Company.

Said, Edward W. (1994). *Culture and Imperialism.* New York: Vintage Books.

Salt, Jeremy (2002). "Trouble Wherever They Went: American Missionaries in Anatolia and Ottoman Syria in the Nineteenth Century," *The Muslim World*, Vol. 92, 287-313.

Chapter 19

A TRANSITIONARY TIME

The 1850s through the 1870s was a time period that witnessed several important transitions related to America's missionary presence in Persia. The question as to which American missionary society would lead the American efforts in Persia received a great deal of attention during this period and was settled in 1870. The question had stemmed from the scrutiny that the American Board of Commissioners for Foreign Missions (ABCFM) had received in earlier years in America, some as early as the 1850s, regarding its reluctance to articulate a clear position on the issue of slavery. With the American Civil War (1861-1865) and the abolition of slavery in America, the dividing lines became more evident. There was a transfer of the Persian mission responsibilities from the ABCFM to the Presbyterian Board of Foreign Missions (PBFM).

Changes were also taking place in Urumia, as it related to the Old Nestorian Church. A large portion of the membership of the Church in the Urumia region were dissatisfied with the Old Church's inability to modernize and its lack of desire to address the changing needs of its congregations in Persia. The Syrian Evangelical Church was formed to address these evolving needs. The formation of this church, which, to a large extent, was aided by the American missionaries, created a division among Nestorians, who now had two competing churches to choose from.

There were also changes that both the Persians and the Ottomans were experiencing in terms of their interactions with foreign powers. Both countries had multiple encounters with European powers, in the form of skirmishes and all-out wars. Significant amounts of territory were lost in several cases. The Europeans also grew in their influence in guiding the national politics within Persia and Turkey. In Turkey, modernization efforts were implemented to increase the rights of minorities. A constitutional government was established in 1876 (lasting only two years). In addition, aspirations for independence by ethnic and religious minorities grew, causing a weakening of the central authority of the Ottoman government. In Persia, Naser al-Din Shah's careless engagement with the Russians and the British and his economic concessions began a period of rapid economic decline. The internal politics and conflicts of both nations, and the location of the Urumia mission station being close to the border between the two countries, greatly affected the American missionaries during the second half of the nineteenth century.

The Presbyterian Board of Foreign Missions

During the middle of the nineteenth century, the position of the ABCFM with respect to slavery was questioned by some of its powerful donors in America. The question was triggered by the fact that since 1816, the ABCFM had missionaries deployed to work with the Cherokee and Choctaws Indians in the southern states. The members of the two Indian tribes were themselves allowed to own slaves, and many did. The fact that the ABCFM missionaries were working with slave owners was a source of concern among ABCFM's abolitionist supporters.

At the same time, the ABCFM needed the financial backing of all its supporters, regardless of their views on abolition. As a result, the Prudential Committee of ABCFM chose not to express a clear position on slavery and did not explicitly state its opposition to the practice of owning slaves. This position, as explained by Robert Lewit: "conformed to the Congregational ideals of democratic faith in which the individual Christian, guided by the Scriptures, establishes the rule of worship."[230] The passive approach of the ABCFM caused church congregations with abolitionist views to withdraw their financial support from the ABCFM, and instead support competing missionary societies in America.

The isolation that the ABCFM experienced due to its ambivalence on the important matter of slavery caused a schism within the ABCFM itself. The "New School" Presbyterians who supported the abolition of slavery and the Presbyterian Church in the United States of America (PCUSA) formed their own missionary society: Presbyterian Board of Foreign Missions (PBFM).[231] In December of 1870, many of the mission fields were divided between the ABCFM and the PBFM. In the case of Persia, the PBFM took primary responsibility. As such, after December of 1870, the American missionaries stationed in Persia labored under the Presbyterian Board and no longer reported to the ABCFM.

A Weakened Persia and Failing Reforms in Turkey

In Persia, the poor leadership of Naser al-Din Shah had detrimental effects on the country during the second half of the nineteenth century. He was preceded by earlier Qajar kings whose actions had resulted in some of Persia's greatest territorial losses. Conflicts between Persia and Russia in the early years of the 19th century had resulted in the 1813 signing of the Treaty of Gulistan during the reign of Mohammad Shah Qajar. Through this treaty, Persia gave up territories north of the Aras (Araxes) River, including Dagestan, Baku, Shirvan, and Ganja, as well as many other economically and strategically important towns. Russia also gained exclusive military rights of the Caspian Sea.[232]

Similarly, the Treaty of Turkmenchay, also signed during Mohammad Shah's reign in 1827, gave Russia some of Persia's other northern territories and cities such as Erivan, Nakhchevan, and Talesh. It also granted Russian subjects living in Persia exemption from Persian

---

[230] Lewit (1963), "Indian Missions and Antislavery Sentiment: A Conflict of Evangelical and Humanitarian Ideals."

[231] Also referred to as the Presbyterian Board, for short, in much of the missionary writings.

[232] Farrokh (2011), *Iran at War*.

law. Military tensions between the two countries continued, and in 1828, only three years before Smith and Dwight visited the Urumia plain, the city of Urumia was occupied by Russian troops for several months. Mismanagement of the country's finances, governmental corruption, and weakness in dealing with the British and the Russians facilitated Persia's decline. Concessions given to the British and Russians during the second half of the nineteenth century accelerated the economic decline.[233]

The weakening of Persia's military and the country's poor economic standing contributed to its inability to exhibit strength in facing European powers. This resulted in a gradual decline in the Persian population's sentiments towards Europe. Toward the end of the nineteenth century the negative feeling that the Persians had developed about European powers carried over to their feelings about their own Christian minorities. This was due to the fact that Europeans were viewed by Persians as Christian powers. The anti-European views in parts of Persia where large Christian populations lived, gradually became confused with anti-Christian prejudices.

As argued by John Joseph, some of the rise in anti-Christian sentiments was due to the fact that in the former regions of Persia, which Russia had taken over in earlier wars, the tables had turned against the Moslems.[234] Christians were no longer the minority under Moslem rule, and they were given a favored status by the Russians in those acquired regions. The Persians' feelings were that in territories lost to Russia, Moslems had become the oppressed class. This further engulfed anti-Christian feelings within Persia, especially toward the end of the nineteenth century. These negative sentiments were more evident in those parts of Persia that were at risk of being taken over by the Russians, such as northwestern Persia where large numbers of Assyrian and Armenian Christians lived.

Significant changes within the Ottoman Empire also took place during the second half of the nineteenth century. The Crimean War of 1853-56 had a weakening effect on the Ottomans.[235] It was triggered by

---

[233] See Farrokh (2011), *Iran at War*, for additional details related to Persia's military losses during the nineteenth century.

[234] Joseph (1961), *Nestorians and their Muslim Neighbors*, p. 46.

[235] Armajani and Ricks (1986), *Middle East: Past and Present.*

Russia's concerns over the rights of Christians in Palestine (which at that time was part of the Ottoman Empire). The war ended with the Paris Treaty of 1856, which forced Western-style reforms onto the Ottomans. One of these reform elements was the Imperial Rescript of 1856, which was advanced under British pressure, with the goal of improving religious freedoms within the Ottoman Empire.[236] The Rescript helped accelerate the momentum of the Tanzimat Reforms, which had begun in the 1830s.

One side effect of the forced reforms in the Ottoman Empire was discontent among its Moslem population with the changes being forced onto the population. For example, Western notions of religious freedom and independence were new and in many ways in conflict with centuries-old traditions and norms. Another side effect was the rise of independence aspirations among the minorities in various Ottoman territories. This is because instead of the old system of having princes rule the various territories, governmental authority was partially transferred to tribal chieftains in certain regions, which resulted in significant decentralization of power. For example, in Kurdistan, there were different chieftains for Buhtan, Hakkari, Bahdinan, Baba, and Soran and nearly 200 Kurdish tribes were in existence.[237] Centralized authority and control, especially in remotely located parts of the empire became difficult to achieve, partially due to the reforms.

In 1876, a new sultan named Abdul Hamid II came to power in Turkey. He resisted European influence, to a large extent stopping the reforms, and initially received much popular support for doing so. He established the Constitution of 1876, ending the Tanzimat period, and attempted to centralize the government.[238] This was welcomed by the general population as it countered Western pressures. However, by the time he began his work, the Tanzimat reforms had already inspired independence aspirations throughout many Ottoman provinces. Political forces favoring independence in these provinces were fully in motion, despite Abdul Hamid's desires to centralize power.

---

[236] Davidson (1956), "The Hatt-i-Humayn of 1856 and the Climate of its Reception."
[237] Jwadieh (2006), *The Kurdish National Movement,* p. 75.
[238] Goldschmidt and Al-Marashi (2019), *A Concise History of the Middle East.*

As Abdul Hamid II rose to power, in 1876, a constitution was drafted by members of the New Ottomans. This was a group of Turkish intellectuals who were discontent with the Tanzimat reforms' effects on the independence and integrity of the empire. They considered Islam to be the appropriate basis for the judicial system of the empire. The 1876 constitution was formally put into effect, with great public excitement, but was only in effect for two years.[239] Abdul Hamid II used the 1876 constitution as a ploy to claim ultimate power for himself. By 1878 he had abolished the constitution and the parliament, and conveniently proclaimed himself monarch with full judicial authority.[240]

Abdul Hamid II is responsible for much of the massacres of the Armenians, Assyrians, and Jews in the Ottoman Empire between 1876 and 1909. He held strong Pan-Islamist views, which he believed would replace "Ottomanism" which had been advocated during the Tanzimat reforms.[241] He openly exercised prejudice against minorities. He believed that Islam would be the primary uniting force in the Ottoman Empire, and can be used to repulse European influence. This line of thinking contributed to growing violence between the Kurdish and Christian tribes in eastern Turkey in the late nineteenth century and the opening years of the twentieth century. It also contributed to decades of border skirmishes and Ottoman occupation of Persia's border areas, including the Urumia plain, empowered by Ottoman alliance with Kurdish tribal forces in the region.

Despite the weakened states of Persia and Turkey, and their own conflicts with one another, they shared several similar world views, including a dislike for European influence. The Russians and the British had come into direct military conflict with both countries during the nineteenth century. Furthermore, in both countries, Islam had a growing influence on national politics. The words of the Islamic clergy could at times outweigh those of government officials, the Shah, the

---

[239] See Goldschmidt and Al-Marashi (2019), *A Concise History of the Middle East,* pp. 159-160 for additional details of the dynamics surrounding the 1876 constitution.

[240] He remained in power as a monarch until 1909, at which point another group (with a similar name and common aspirations as the New Ottomans) called the Young Turks formed another constitutional effort, put him out of power, and reinstated the 1876 constitution.

[241] Ottomanism attempted to encourage minorities within the Ottoman Empire to view themselves as a united and connected nation of Ottoman subjects.

Sultan, and foreign powers. A clear example of this was the tobacco concession granted to the British by Naser al-Din Shah.

The concession resulted in wide-scale public unrest in Persia. Following a decree by the clergy in Persia, banning all Moslems from the consumption of tobacco, the Persian government had to revert from the concession.[242] This demonstrated the immense power that Islam had on guiding the political direction of Persia. There were similar dynamics at play in Turkey, as Abdul Hamid II relied on Islam and jihad as a means for mobilizing Turks and Kurds in fighting European forces. Such mobilization was clearly evident during the Russo-Turkish War of 1877-78. Despite the fact that the Turks were Sunni and the Persians were Shi'ites, and despite the centuries of hostilities between Shi'ites and Sunnis, the common ground of a Pan-Islamic view of the world helped in the formation of unexpected political alliances in both countries during the second half of the nineteenth century and in the years leading to the First World War.

The Mission to Persia and the Formation of the Syrian Evangelical Church

With the December 1870 separation of missionary efforts between PBFM and ABCFM, the latter became a primarily Congregationalist organization. The two missionary organizations divided the field: the ABCFM took lead responsibility for American missionary activities in the Ottoman Empire, and the PBFM focused on Persia. Compared to the ABCFM's original vision, the Presbyterian Board had a much broader vision for Persia. In their view, missionary efforts should no longer be limited only to the Nestorians of the Urumia region. The Presbyterians believed that such efforts could also have significant potential elsewhere in Persia, especially in major population centers such as Tehran, Isfahan, Shiraz, Hamadan, and Tabriz. The expansion would enable them to serve population groups beyond just the Nestorians of Persia. Therefore, the name of the mission was changed from "Mission to the Nestorians" to the "Mission to Persia," and the resources and mandates were expanded to match the greater scope that the new name implied.

---

[242] Browne (1910), *The Persian Revolution of 1905-1909.*

Similar changes were taking place at a micro-level in Urumia. Since the 1860s, mixed feelings had developed among the American missionaries in Urumia regarding how to support the Nestorian population's evangelical needs. Concerns existed regarding the ability of the Old Nestorian Church, headquartered deep in the Turkish mountains, to address the changes being experienced by the Nestorians of Urumia. The involvement of the Mission in facilitating this change was a drastic shift from the missionary instructions which Perkins had been given decades earlier when he first embarked on setting up a mission station in Persia. Back then, interference in how the Nestorians practiced their faith was not an option. Now it was, and a new chapter in America's missionary role in Persia was opened.

References and Related Readings

Barton, James L. (1908). *Daybreak in Turkey.* Boston: The Pilgrim Press.

Bassett, James (1890). *Persia: Eastern Mission.* Philadelphia: Presbyterian Board of Publication and Sabbath-School Work.

Elton, Daniel. L. (2012). *The History of Iran.* Santa Barbara, CA: Greenwood.

Farrokh, Kaveh (2011). *Iran at War.* London: Osprey Publishing.

Fraser, David (1910). *Persia and Turkey in Revolt.* Edinburgh: William Blackwood and Sons.

Goldschmidt, Arthur, and Ibrahim Al-Marashi (2019). *A Concise History of the Middle East.* Routledge.

Joseph, John (1961). *Nestorians and their Muslim Neighbors.* Princeton: Princeton University Press.

Jwaideh, Wadie (2006). *The Kurdish National Movement: Its Origins and Development.* Syracuse: Syracuse University Press.

Keddie, Nikki R. (2012). *Qajar Iran and the Rise of Reza Khan.* Costa Mesa, CA: Mazda Publishers.

Lewit, Robert T. (1963). "Indian Missions and Antislavery Sentiment: A Conflict of Evangelical and Humanitarian Ideals", *The Mississippi Valley Historical Review*, Vol. 50, No., pp. 39-55.

McLoughlin, William G. (1973). "Indian Slaveholders and Presbyterian Missionaries, 1837-1861," *American Society of Church History*, pp. 535-551.

Mirzai, Behnaz A. (2017). *A History of Slavery and Emancipation in Iran, 1800-1929.* Austin: University of Texas Press.

Pickett, Otis W. (2013), Interracial Ecclesiastical Interaction in Presbyterian Mission Churches from South Carolina to Mississippi, 1818-1877. Doctoral Dissertation: University of Mississippi.

Speer, Robert (1898). *Missions and Politics in Asia.* New York: Fleming H. Revell Company.

Chapter 20

JOSEPH PLUMB COCHRAN

Joseph Plumb Cochran was the child of American missionaries serving in the Urumia mission station. He represented a new generation of American missionaries, born in Persia to American missionary parents, and influenced in their upbringing by both American and Persian customs and cultural norms. As an American born in Persia, the duality gave Cochran the ability to gain a deep and personal understanding of both countries' customs and value systems, which helped him mediate the cultural gaps that often characterize Oriental and Western relations.

In addition to his mother-tongue, English, he was fluent in Persian, Syriac, and Turkish. He was often able to mediate relations between opposing sides in ways that any modern diplomat would envy. It is no surprise that he was instrumental in negotiations with Kurdish forces attacking Urumia in 1880, resulting in the saving of thousands of civilian lives, and possibly the integrity of Persia's national boundaries. It was also during this time that America's formal diplomatic relations with Persia were established, in the form of an official American legation in Tehran. Cochran's knowledge of the cultures and languages of the region made him a peacemaker in the politically unstable regions surrounding Urumia. As Robert Speer stated:

> Born in the country, speaking the three languages of the people as fluently and beautifully as the people themselves, with an intimate and sympathetic knowledge of all the races, their conditions, their customs, their social and political relations, and with a skill at race diagnosis which brought him into touch with their inner life, their modes and currents of thought and motives of action, their ideals, their prejudices, the secret springs of their racial, social and religious consciousness, — possessing a mind of exceptional powers of observation and receptivity, and with a thorough practical training, he began his work at the age of twenty-three.[243]

At that age, having gone through medical training in America, he returned to Urumia as a missionary physician. His contributions to Persia in the form of medical work and innovations in public health were monumental. In Urumia, he was respected by the diverse groups

---

[243] Speer (1911), *The Hakim Sahib*, p. 295.

populating the region, and was commonly addressed as "Hakim Sahib" ("Hakim" meaning doctor, and "Sahib" meaning master, a term often used at that time in Persia to respectfully address foreigners).[244]

One of Cochran's most significant contributions was the opening of the first medical college in Persia in 1880, modeled after hospitals in America. To recognize the American contribution, which arrived in the form of private donations from American citizens, the hospital was named after the Westminster Church in Buffalo, which had provided the bulk of the funding for its construction. By the time he was 26 years old, Cochran had taken on a leadership role in the Urumia mission. At that time, he was the lead physician, overseer of the Mission compound, temporary president of the Boys' School, and the lead liaison missionary for Persian government affairs.

The combination of his medical and leadership skills and his cultural awareness made Cochran a trustworthy individual to whom many confided in. Some of the most influential individuals in the region sought medical advice from him, and in some cases, gave him the opportunity to negotiate paths towards peace. The most notable case was his ability to negotiate in 1880 with the Kurdish rebel, Sheikh Obeidullah, to delay his attack on Urumia. By doing so, he was able to save thousands of civilian lives, preventing the total collapse of Urumia under a Kurdish attack. The events of 1880 and Cochran's critical role in mediating between the opposing sides helped American politicians in Washington recognize the pressing need for the establishment of formal diplomatic relationships with Persia. It eventually resulted in the establishment of the American legation in Tehran in 1883.

Birthplace and Legacy

Cochran was born in the village of Seir, on January 14, 1855. His father, Joseph Gallup Cochran, was the head of the Urumia mission, and had done extensive evangelical work, focusing on the Nestorians in the villages in the Urumia plain and beyond. His mother, Deborah Plumb Cochran, was a highly influential member of the Urumia mission and a visionary in how medical care should be delivered by the

---

[244] Robert Speer's biography of Joseph Plumb Cochran is titled "The Hakim Sahib," and is a commonly used source on the life and accomplishments of Cochran.

Mission to the locals. In her older years, she came to be known as "Madame Cochran" by the missionaries and "Khanem Gurta" (great lady) by the locals.

Cochran was referred to as "Josie" at home. His birth to American parents stationed in Persia was at a transitionary point in time in terms of the mindset of missionary work. In Urumia, Persian-born American missionaries who, like Cochran, had grown up alongside the local population, were the future of the Mission. They were far better embedded in the culture and value system of the locals compared to their own American-born parents. Among the other American missionary children born in Urumia with similar impact were Frederick Coan, a childhood friend of Cochran, and William Shedd, who was ten years his junior.

Early on in life, Cochran exhibited behaviors that in many ways resembled the childhood interests of Asahel Grant. He showed a passion for medical work and loved to role-play being a physician as a child. He was also especially well-behaved. Perkins, in his final years at Urumia, briefly interacted with him, and referred to him as a "young nobleman."[245]

The first ten years of Cochran's life were spent in Urumia, most of which was spent at Seir in his family home. In 1865, the entire family traveled to America and was on furlough for two years in Buffalo, NY, and they returned to Urumia in 1867. Much to their sorrow, in 1869, his brother Theodore ("Thedie") passed away due to typhus fever. A year later, in 1870, Cochran, alongside his younger sister Emma and his mother returned to Buffalo to join his other sister (Mary), who was already in America for medical treatment related to a spinal injury from a horseback riding accident years earlier. In August of 1871, Mrs. Cochran returned with the two girls but left Joseph in Buffalo so that he would be able to advance his education in America.

On their path of return to Urumia, his mother and the two girls met up with his father in Constantinople. They continued their return to Urumia, passing through Trebizond. However, along their return path to Urumia, near the same village where Perkins' daughter, Judith Grant Perkins, had passed away, Mr. Cochran began to feel ill. The family continued on their journey back to Urumia, where they arrived in

---

[245] Speer (1911), *The Hakim Sahib*, p. 41.

October of 1871. However, his father's illness had set in, and he passed away in November due to typhoid fever at the age of 52.

Joseph Plumb Cochran's Motivations and Interests

It is difficult to assess the emotional state of Cochran, who was in Buffalo by himself at the time of his father's passing. Away from his family and the land in which he had grown up, the emotional impact was overbearing. Only a few correspondences from that time are cited in the missionary literature that would reflect on the distress that the 16-year-old felt. However, the passing of his father, which had followed the passing of his brother years earlier, and the medical challenges that his sister had been facing, may have sparked in his mind the desire to consider a medical career. At that time, he was completing his high school studies at Buffalo Central High School.

In addition to the internal struggles that would have affected Cochran, additional pressures from those in Persia and the native Assyrians who had high regards for him and his father were clearly at work. The correspondences from this time indicate explicit expectations of him to eventually return to Urumia to fill the void left by his father's passing. In her correspondences to him, his mother wrote:

> Deacon T. prayed, that you, Joseph, might return to fill, and more than fill, your father's place.... The eyes of all are on you as much as ever were a people's on the son of their deceased King. May they not be disappointed... Those who revere the memory of your father, Joseph, look forward to your filling his place. Their enthusiasm is truly wonderful to me, and often it seems to me a bow of promise that you will eventually be welcomed back to this locality.[246]

Since his brother had passed away, Cochran was his mother's only surviving son. The pressure for him to return to Urumia in a missionary capacity was further reinforced by the fact that among his father's last words was the expression of his wish for his son to "ever be brought under all missionary influence possible."

---

[246] Ibid., p. 37.

His Education

While thousands of miles away from his family in Urumia, Cochran was surrounded by a supportive community in Buffalo. He had joined the Westminster Church, where he was liked and respected by its congregation, who helped him through his sorrow. During his teens in Buffalo, Joseph stayed in the home of Stephen Mallory Clement (Sr.) and grew up with his son, Stephen Merrell Clement, Jr., who became Cochran's closest and best friend for life. As a student, one of his teachers in Buffalo's Central High School described Cochran as a young man who "was the most perfect gentleman I have ever known among my pupils. Instinctive gentlemanliness was emphasized by a singular gentleness towards, and thoughtfulness for others. I have never, even under most trying circumstances, know him to be impatient or thoughtless of others' feelings."[247] In many ways this description matches the observations made by Perkins nearly a decade earlier on the qualities of "Josie" as a young child.

The Clement family, with whom Cochran lived while he was finishing high school, had high regard for the American missionary efforts in Urumia. They also had the financial resources to support the Mission in critical times, especially in later years when Cochran took on leadership roles in Urumia. Clement Sr. was the president of a major regional bank in New York State. His wealth enabled him to provide financial support for Cochran's college education.

Cochran graduated from Buffalo Central High School in 1870 and proceeded to attend Yale University. At Yale, he studied science and medicine. He continued his studies at Buffalo Medical College and Bellevue Medical College in Brooklyn, NY. In the spring of 1877, at the age of 22, he completed his medical degree. In addition to medicine, Cochran studied pharmacy and dentistry.[248]

On June 10, 1878, the Board of Foreign Missions of the Presbyterian Church in the United States of America formally appointed Cochran as a missionary physician for Urumia. Similar to many other male missionaries assigned to serve in foreign lands, and as was the case for Perkins and Grant, Cochran was expected to marry

---

[247] Ibid., p. 367.

[248] Although he was unable to complete the entire dentistry training due to limited time.

before his foreign deployment. Shortly after his missionary assignment was announced, he married Katharine Hale of the Hale family of Buffalo, who knew him from his youthful days visiting Buffalo and regularly corresponded with him during the years he had returned to Urumia in his early teens. Katharine had gotten to know him while she was visiting her uncle in Buffalo. She was a graduate of Vassar College, a women's Christian college in upstate New York.

References and Related Readings

Bird, Mary R.S. (1908). *Persian Women and their Creed.* London: Church Missionary Society.

Jwaideh, Wadie (2006). *The Kurdish National Movement: Its Origins and Development.* Syracuse: Syracuse University Press.

Karimi, Linda C. (1975). *Implications of American Missionary Presences in 19th and 20th Century Iran.* Masters Dissertation. Portland State University.

Speer, Robert (1911). *The Hakim Sahib.* New York, Fleming H. Revell Company.

Wilson, Samuel G. (1896). *Persia: Western Mission.* Philadelphia: Presbyterian Board of Publication and Sabbath-School Work.

Chapter 21

COCHRAN RETURNS TO URUMIA AS A MISSIONARY PHYSICIAN

Cochran's return to Urumia was a celebratory event for those related to the mission station who had anticipated his return for years. Upon his arrival in December of 1878, he and his wife were welcomed with great cheers and admiration by the missionaries and the city's Assyrians. Groups of Assyrians, missionary families, and associates came to celebrate the couple's arrival. Having been away from Urumia for well over a decade, he soon realized that he had to brush up on his Syriac, Turkish, and Persian.[249]

Within the first four months after arriving in Urumia, Cochran had seen nearly two thousand patients and was training five medical students. Frederick Coan, a fellow missionary who accompanied Cochran on a tour of the Kurdish mountains, described the public's great need for him as such: "Long before we reached the village of Mawana, word had preceded us, and everyone turned out to do honor to the great Hakim Sahib. It was so all through that tour. Kurds and Christians alike vied with each other in doing him honor. It was not only his great medical skill, but the man himself the people approached with a feeling of awe and deepest reverence and affection."[250]

---

[249] Speer (1911), *The Hakim Sahib*, p. 54.
[250] Coan (1939), *Yesterdays in Persia and Kurdistan*, p. 66.

The Effects of the Russo-Turkish War and Famine

Cochran's joyous return had been preceded by events across the Ottoman border, which were bound to affect the region a great deal in the coming years. The Russo-Turkish war of 1877-1878 changed the dynamics of minority relations in eastern Turkey, with subsequent effects in Persia. In this war, Ottoman forces were dominated by Russia and lost considerable amounts of territory. The Russian troops advanced as far as the gates of Constantinople and were held back through intervention by other European nations. The treaty that ended this conflict required of Turkey to provide special protections for its Armenian population. It thereby opened up a broader question about the rights of other minorities, such as the Kurds and the Assyrians, to seek independence from the Ottoman Empire.

The Russo-Turkish war resulted in a chain reaction that eventually affected Urumia directly. The war had weakened Turkey's military capabilities. It had allowed the Kurds residing in eastern portions of the Ottoman Empire, bordering Persia, to begin considering the possibility of establishing an independent Kurdish state. The Russo-Turkish war also raised the level of religious and ethnic tensions in the mountainous regions of eastern Turkey and western Persia. Given that the Russians were Christians and the Turks were Moslems, to some, the war implied a confrontation between Christianity and Islam. While the Kurds benefited from Russia's influence in weakening the central Ottoman government, the Russian victory also increased the level of religious fanaticism exhibited by the Kurds and the Ottoman government against the region's Christian populations. In the years that followed, as documented in Cochran's correspondences and other archival records, there were growing hostilities between Christians and Moslems in the Turkish mountains and on the Urumia plain.

There were also natural causes that contributed to the ensuing difficulties. In the late 1870s, the Urumia region and surrounding areas were hampered by a lack of rainfall. This resulted in a significant drop in agricultural output and food shortages. At the same time, due to the Russo-Turkish wars, the little grain that was produced was being sent to the frontlines to feed the troops. By the fall of 1879, the shortage turned into famine in Urumia. Although the harvest began to return to normal production levels by 1880, the year 1879 was one of great suffering in Urumia and the surrounding areas. It is important to recognize the extent of human suffering and how it challenged Cochran and other American missionaries in attempting to equitably aid the local population. Correspondences from Cochran's wife indicate great suffering and the need for the missionaries to exercise discipline and consistency in how their limited resources were to be used to aid the locals in distress:

> We are going to have fearful times with the famine this winter, I am afraid. Already it is beginning. Monday a mob of starving people rushed into the bazaars, carrying off anything they could lay their hands on. They also broke into the storehouses of wheat belonging to some wealthy Khans. The Prince is absent, and there is no one to exercise any authority.[251]

In the same letter, she continued to elaborate on the difficulties of serving the needy with the limited resources of the Mission: "Beggars come to us every day, but how can we feed and clothe all Urumia? The native pastors are sending out a petition to the churches of America for aid, and their petition will be endorsed by all our gentlemen."

The Wheat Market in Urumia (c. 1905)

---

[251] Letter dated November 2, 1879 cited in Speer (1911), pp. 67-68.

In a follow-up letter in January of 1880, she elaborated on the efforts of the American mission to help the locals by keeping industrial production active: "We try as far as possible to make the people work for the money. We buy cotton and wool, and let them work it into thread and cloth, and then buy it from them."[252] Given the difficult circumstances, the population of Urumia looked to the Mission as a source of aid. This required the Mission to exercise care in how it prioritized aid through the formation of a Native Charity Board in charge of such decisions.

John Haskell Shedd, the missionary at the head of the Urumia mission station at that time, estimated the total number of Christian families in Urumia to be 5,000. He summarized the approach for prioritization of aid, such that the highest priority was given to the members of the Syrian Evangelical Church, then to all other Christians (e.g., other Assyrians, Armenians, Catholics, etc.), and finally to Jews and Moslems. The Mission attempted to find and create employment for the local population by using the Mission's grounds and facilities as space where clothes could be manufactured. Locals would also be employed in the construction of schoolhouses and chapels, thereby increasing the level of employment. The Mission also had a soup kitchen in Urumia, which fed approximately sixty individuals every day through the issuance of food stamps.

The Westminster Hospital of Urumia

By 1880 the harvest had returned to nearly normal levels. However, economic hardship and the famine had inflicted much hardship on the people of Urumia and the surrounding regions. The desperate needs of the locals for medical services inspired Cochran to envision the construction of Persia's first contemporary hospital and medical college. He presented a formal request to the Presbyterian Board for funds to support the construction of the hospital:

> We have purchased a site for our college, and the buildings are
> going up. The plot contains fifteen acres of land, part orchard,
> part field, with five acres now enclosed by a strong wall. It is
> over a mile from the city gate on a slope facing the river, and is

---

[252] Ibid., p. 68.

in full view of the mountains. Here are the best conditions as to air, water, and retirement for a good school, and the same conditions for a hospital. There is ample room, and the Mission Station has set apart the necessary ground. The idea of a hospital has greatly pleased all classes, and probably has saved us from governmental interference thus far. If we could assure all inquiries that a hospital will surely be built it would be a better safeguard than a firman from the Shah.[253]

His proposal was strongly endorsed by the Mission, and financial support for the construction of the hospital building came from a range of sources, including the Clement family of Buffalo and the congregation of Buffalo's Westminster Presbyterian Church.[254] It is no surprise that the hospital's official name, due to the generosity of the Westminster Church congregation, was to become the Westminster Hospital of Urumia.

In describing the massive undertaking needed to construct the hospital and other missionary facilities, John Haskell Shedd, the head of the Urumia mission station at that time, wrote:

Several times efforts have been made to hinder, but now for more than seven months we have been steadily at work. 600,000 large sundried brick. 200,000 burnt brick, 25,000 loads of stone and 2,000 loads of gypsum, all brought to the spot on donkeys are some of the material put into the buildings. There is a wall four feet thick at the bottom and fourteen feet high, more than a third of a mile in length, surrounding the grounds. The main building is 107 ft. X 47 ft. with basement and two stories. Our dwelling house is commodious and makes a delightful home, and there are stables and outhouses. All these have been erected and are now in use.[255]

Construction was finally completed by the end of 1882. Upon completion, the hospital could hold as many as 40 patients and was equipped with essential features such as an operating room and a "drug room" where medications were prepared for the patients.

---

[253] Ibid., p. 62.

[254] He estimated the hospital building cost to be between $1,500 to $2,000, and its operating expenses would come from a combination of charity and fees charged to patients who could afford payment.

[255] Shedd (1912), *The Life of John Haskell Shedd,* Chapter 14; correspondence dated Dec. 10, 1879.

Westminster Hospital of Urumia (c. 1880s)

In the following years, the hospital grew in size and developed a unique approach to patient care. Due to the ingenuity and caring mindset of Cochran's mother, there was great emphasis in making the patients feel at home. Plants were placed in all windows. As Cochran's sister, Emma, reflected on the collaborative approach of Cochran and his mother: "The hospital was ever a revelation to the people. Mother made the home part of it so perfect with flowers and pictures, and her own bright, cheery presence, and Joe the physicians', and one could hardly say that one could have worked without the other those first years, in making the institution what it was." In her memoir, Emma Cochran-Ponafidine, who later joined her brother to assist him in his medical work in Urumia, recalled the humble beginnings with which the Westminster Hospital functioned:

> As I look back to the results achieved there in spite of the primitive means at hand, I wonder at the faith and courage of my brother. An ordinary table for operations, a smovar for heating water, no trained assistants, no other physician to consult with, his own druggist, a servant to give anesthetics – these were the conditions under which the young Doctor had taken up his great responsibility. Up to the time of her death, Mother was, in the hospital, just what she had always been in the home. Her motherly ways, her cheery smile, the neatness and cleanliness of the place, the growing plants that filled

rooms and corridors, all made an appeal to the patients. Some of those sick folk had come from squalid homes in the mountains, some from Turkey across the border, but all took back new visions of life.[256]

The Westminster Hospital was eventually expanded through the construction of the Howard Annex in 1890.[257] One of the unique features of this annex was a room specifically for Cochran's mother, so that she could be constantly present as a mother-like caretaker for all patients. The mother and son partnership in making the hospital a welcoming environment for the patients was working. Her constant presence at the hospital and her care for those in medical distress are among the reasons she was often referred to as "Khanem Gurta," meaning "great lady" by the locals.

The 15-acre lot of land that the Mission had purchased provided the setting for significant growth of Mission facilities in the decades that followed the initial construction of the hospital. It was a major and fruitful investment. The property eventually became the home for the Boys' School. Residences for the school teachers, hospital assistants, and the missionaries were also constructed here.

The buildings were constructed using sun-dried bricks and had flat mud roofs. At its maturity, the compound, which contained the hospital, the school, and the residences, came to be known as the "College" (which the locals pronounced "Kola") as it resembled the layout and appearance of a typical college campus, housed the medical college and was often referred to as such by the missionaries themselves. It was surrounded by tall walls. The compound was divided into four subsections, one for the school buildings, one for the hospital, and the other two for residences. The four sections of the compound were divided by wide avenues with towering trees.[258]

---

[256] Ponafidine (1932), *My Life in the Moslem East*, p. 49.

[257] The funding was provided by Mrs. Ellen Howard of Buffalo. She was the widow of George Howard, an affluent businessman and a trustee of the Westminster Presbyterian Church of Buffalo, who had passed away in 1886.

[258] Cochran's home is still standing and is part of what is now the campus of Urumia University. His former home has been retained for its historical significance as an acknowledgement of his legacy.

Interior View of Part of the College Compound (c. 1890s)

The College Compound Driveway (c. 1911)

The Boys' School in its New Location on the College Compound (c. 1888)

References and Related Readings

Bassett, James (1890). *Persia: Eastern Mission.* Philadelphia: Presbyterian Board of Publication and Sabbath-School Work.

Benjamin, Samuel G. W. (1896). *The Story of Persia.* New York: G.P. Putnam's Sons.

Benjamin, Samuel G. W. (1887). *Persia and the Persians.* London: John Murray.

Coan, Frederick G. (1939). *Yesterdays in Persia and Kurdistan.* Claremont, CA: Saunders Studio Press.

Karimi, Linda C. (1975). *Implications of American Missionary Presences in 19th and 20th Century Iran.* Masters Dissertation. Portland State University.

Ponafidine, Emma C. (1932). *My Life in the Moslem East.* Indianapolis: The Bobbs-Merrill Company.

Shedd, William A. (1912). *The Life of John Haskell Shedd.* Unpublished manuscript.

Speer, Robert (1911). *The Hakim Sahib, the Foreign Doctor: A Biography of Joseph Plumb Cochran.* New York, Fleming H. Revell Company.

Wilson, Samuel G. (1896). *Persia: Western Mission.* Philadelphia: Presbyterian Board of Publication and Sabbath-School Work.

Chapter 22

THE SHEIKH OBEIDULLAH ATTACK

Since his return to Urumia in 1878, Cochran had treated thousands of individuals from various backgrounds. His medical skills, combined with his knowledge of the languages and cultural norms of the area made him a trusted individual. This was uniquely important in a region where deeply rooted prejudices between different groups had long been embedded in the people's history. Among Cochran's patients was the Kurdish leader Sheikh Obeidullah, one of the most influential Kurdish leaders in the mountainous regions of eastern Turkey and northwestern Persia.[259] His rise to power took place at a time when the Ottoman government was weaker in its enforcement efforts in its eastern regions and had become more reliant on Kurdish forces to bring law and order to the highlands. As a religious figure of great authority, Obeidullah was highly respected in the Kurdish mountains and had a mass following in Turkey and Persia.

From the perspective of the history of Kurdish nationalism, Sheikh Obeidullah is widely considered a legend. After Bedir Khan's attempts in the 1840s to create an independent Kurdish state, the next Kurdish leader to attempt to establish an independent Kurdish state was Obeidullah. He was an intellectually gifted visionary, capable of both

---

[259] The "Sheikh" designation means Islamic scholar or leader. Also spelled Shaykh Ubayd Allah and similar variations by other authors.

kindness and butchery. Obeidullah was the Islamic spiritual head of the Nihri Sayyids, and therefore a spiritual leader to many of the Kurds in Turkey and Persia.

In his early days, he was considered an ally by the Ottoman government. During the Russo-Turkish war of 1877-78, he had served as a commander fighting alongside Ottoman forces against Russia. Being the spiritual leader of the Nihri Sayyids, to mobilize forces against the Russian army, a Christian force, he had declared *jihad* (holy war) in 1877. Since Turkey's Armenian population was also Christian and had sided with the Russians, a prime target for Obeidullah's military campaigns was Turkey's Armenian settlements.

The Russo-Turkish war ended with the Treaty of Berlin. This created the pretext for the weakening of the Ottoman Empire, and gave Britain, another Christian nation, authority in guiding reforms in Turkey. Under Article 61 of the Treaty of Berlin, one of the reforms required was specifically focused on the protection of the Armenians of Turkey. It explicitly stated:

> The Sublime Porte undertakes to carry out, without further
> delay, the improvements and reforms demanded by local
> requirements in the provinces inhabited by Armenians, and to
> guarantee their security against the Circassians and Kurds. It
> will periodically make known the steps taken to this effect to the
> powers, who will superintend their application.[260]

Article 61 created the context for conversations regarding the possibility for the creation of an independent Armenian state. While Sheikh Obeidullah would not have been happy with the notion of an independent Armenia carved out of Ottoman territory, the conversation helped justify the formation of other states around ethnic and religious lines, including one for the Kurds. Obeidullah was therefore hopeful for European support for Kurdish independence. In addition to the idealistic appeal for independence, given that in aiding the Turks fight the Russo-Turkish war, the Kurdish forces of Obeidullah had been provided with weapons (which were not returned to the Ottomans afterward), the ability of the Sheikh to militarily advance his cause was significantly enhanced. Thanks to the Ottomans, Obeidullah's military

---

[260] Hurewitz (1956), *Diplomacy in the Near and Middle East: A Documentary Record 1535–1956, Vol. I*, p. 190.

arsenal included new weapons and a factory for the production of ammunition.[261]

Cochran had good relations with Sheikh Obeidullah. His writings indicate that there was a great deal of mutual respect between the two men. For example, reflecting on his visit with the Sheikh in 1880, Cochran wrote: "We hope and believe that our visit to this great man's country has done good, both for now and for the future. We had opportunity given us to speak very freely on religious subjects."[262] In this passage, Cochran refers to Sheikh Obeidullah as being a "great man." Furthermore, the mutual respect and connection between the two men is reinforced by Cochran's accounts of the Sheikh's intellectual depth, as the two men openly debated one another on religious matters and deep theological questions.

Sheikh Obeidullah's intellectual acumen and his respect for outsiders had also been noted by other visitors to the area at that time.[263] Lord George Curzon, in describing him, stated that he: "acquired a great reputation for personal sanctity … and gradually came to be looked upon as the head of Kurdish nationality."[264] Samuel G. Wilson, who was the head of the Presbyterian mission station in Tabriz, stated that "Next to the Sultan and the scherif of Mecca, he was the holiest person among the Sunnis. Thousands were ready to follow him, not only as a chief, but as the vicar of God."[265]

In describing the Obeidullah's castle in Nochea, located only a few miles from the Persian border, an 1883 article published in the New

---

[261] Note the striking similarities in the life experiences of Sheikh Obeidullah and Bedir Khan Bey. Both men were at one point in time collaborators working as military commanders alongside the Ottomans to subdue others (Egyptian separatists in the case of Bedir Khan and Russian forces and Armenians in the case of Obeidullah). Both men developed an understanding of Ottoman military weaknesses during these collaborations, by participating in battles in which the Ottomans had lost. Both had independence aspirations requiring them to construct their own ammunition production capabilities. They were both considered religious leaders, and their religious fervor was at the heart of their call for the armed mobilization of their followers.

[262] Speer (1911), *The Hakim Sahib*, p. 75.

[263] Jwaideh (2006), *The Kurdish National Movement*, p. 77.

[264] Curzon (1892), *Persia and the Persian Question, Vol. I.* p. 553.

[265] Wilson (1895), *Persian Life and Customs*, p. 110.

York Daily Tribune elaborated on the unique public services his immense European-style compound rendered to the community of Kurds:

> Obeidullah's castle was a centre of good things to all the Kourds of the border. Besides the private apartments of the Sheikh, and the mosque where he was want to import religious instruction, and besides a regularly organized orphan asylum where no applicant was ever denied admittance to the Sheikh's bounty, the castle contained a long series of rooms facing upon the great quadrangle, where Kourds of any tribe or rank might dwell for any reasonable length of time, fed from the Sheikh's kitchen, and without question as to why they came, why they stayed or why they left.[266]

His innovative thinking in constructing such a castle cannot be overstated. It was built following a European style of architecture and conveyed a message of modernity to the Kurds visiting it. More importantly, it was intended as a central gathering point for the Kurds to come together and enjoy each other's company in a welcoming environment. It was intended to counter the effects of the topography of the region, which had pushed Kurds into their individual remote highland settlements, with limited opportunity for regular contact among the various Kurdish settlements.

Sheikh Obeidullah's Castle in Nochea (c. 1880s)

---

[266] "Obeidullah's Fall," *New York Daily Tribune*, February 25, 1883, p. 3.

The castle allowed for frequent conversations among the Kurdish communities of the highlands, and more opportunities for collaboration rather than competition. Being Obeidullah's castle, it also reasserted his authority as the central figure for potential alliances among the Kurdish tribes. It is this role among the Kurds of the region, which he was hoping to leverage for his independence aspirations, and the castle served this purpose well.

During Cochran's one-week visit in 1880, he was warmly received by Sheikh Obeidullah. Respecting Cochran's preferences and Western norms, the Sheikh insisted on providing him a chair and asked Cochran to sit by him. The two men engaged in theological conversations. Cochran noted that Obeidullah had read the Bible and described him as open-minded. Elaborating on his general appearance, Cochran provided the following description:

> The Sheikh is fifty-three years old, rather prepossessing in his appearance and manners. He dresses in flowing robes of broadcloth, and wears a white turban. He is a man well read in Persian and Arabic literature. He has also read most of the Bible, a copy of which we sent him last year. He is a man who is ambitious to have the civilized world know that even here in wild Kurdistan there is a little kingdom whose laws are superior to those of her neighbours, Persia and Turkey, and that she has the power to carry them out. He is a very pious man, constantly speaking of God, and trying, he says, to do His will, according to his religion.[267]

The close relationship between the two men meant that Cochran was trusted a great deal by the Sheikh. The sense of trust became more critical as he sought to secure channels of communications with Western powers. Obeidullah was seeking international support for the establishment of an independent Kurdish state. Elaborating further on his 1880 visit, Cochran wrote:

> Two weeks ago I returned from a trip to Nochea, a district in Kurdistan, two and half days distant. I went to pay a visit to Sheikh Obeidullah, who considers himself the third man in ecclesiastical rank in Islam. He is also the civil monarch of the Kurds. He has seemed disposed of some years past to get into closer relations with us and the civilized world. He regards the

---

[267] Speer (1911), *The Hakim Sahib*, p. 79.

Turks and Persians as deceptive people, not living up to their religion, and altogether too depraved to hope that they will ever again hold the position they once commanded among the other nations. Regarding them in the light that he does, and situated as he is between them, he wishes to have the moral, if not material, support of a better people and government. To this end, he has several times sent to us, asking that we put him in a way of getting such help from the British government. Last year before entering on a campaign against the Turks, to whom he had up to that time paid tribute, he sent confidential agents to us repeating this request. Not desiring to be complicated in such affairs at such a time, we referred them to the English consul at Tabriz.[268]

The persistence of Sheik Obeidullah in seeking Western support and in stirring up unrest in Kurdish regions of Persia and Turkey continued. In August of 1880, a large entourage of his associates, including his second son Sheikh Abd al Qadir, visited the Urumia region. They dined at the Cochran residence in the village of Seir. Their conversations with the Europeans had not been fruitful in receiving any form of reassurance of support in establishing an independent Kurdish state.

Although Obeidullah was unable to gain the support of the West for his cause, he had many sympathizers among the Kurds in the border regions of Persia and Turkey. This created the pretext for significant unrest and instability in the months to come. Specifically, as noted by McDowall, given that Sheikh Obeidullah's son, Abd al Qadir, was his representative, and given that many of the Kurds in this region of Persia were followers of the Nihri Sayyids, Abd al Qadir was considered by the Persian governor of Urumia as their intermediary in cases of local conflicts or tensions involving Sheikh Obeidullah's followers in Persia.[269]

As it turns out, several Kurdish chieftains in the Persian territories were punitively treated by Persian government officials for alleged wrongdoings. Abd al Qadir was not consulted on this matter by the Persian government, although by way of tradition, as the representative of Obeidullah, he should have been. This created the pretext for

---

[268] Ibid., p. 75.
[269] McDowall (2007), *A Modern History of the Kurds*, p. 53.

Obeidullah's invasion since by not responding, Obeidullah's spiritual standing as the head of the Nihri Sayyids in the entire region would have been put into question. In Obeidullah's mind, this justified an attack. In reality, he was most likely using the incident involving the unauthorized punishment of the Persian Kurds by Persian government officials as an excuse for occupying lands that he had hoped would someday become part of his independent Kurdish state.

By the fall of 1880, the Sheikh's army had begun its plans to invade Persia and Urumia. However, due to Cochran's close friendship, the Sheikh had promised to spare the American missionaries and the Christians in the region. Cochran firmly believed in this reassurance, as evident by the following correspondence by his wife, dated October 6, 1880 in which Sheikh Obeidullah is referred to as a "friend":

> It seems that war is to follow famine. Our friend, the Sheikh, is at war with Persia. When Joe was with him, he told him that he wished to gather in all the Kurdish districts lying around Urumia, and form a consolidated Kurdish nation. On this mission, his son came last summer, when we entertained him a Seir. What the result of this interview with the government was, we do not know, but probably unfavourable to the Sheikh's project, for a large Kurdish army has long been mustering, and within the last few days, with the Sheikh's son at the head, has come down and taken some of these Kurdish districts. He has carried all before him so far, and is now around the southern end of the Lake.... It is reported that he means to take Tabriz. We think he would do it only to frighten the Persians into making terms with him. Don't be alarmed; they won't touch us even if they do come to Urumia. The Sheikh is our friend.[270]

One of these correspondences was forwarded by Cochran to the British Consul in Tabriz, in response to Obeidullah's request. Sheik Obeidullah's message to William Abbott (the British Consul-General in Tabriz) explained his motivations for independence:

> The Kurdish nation ... is a people apart. The religion is different [from that of others], and their laws and customs are distinct ... the Chiefs and Rulers of Kurdistan, whether Turkish or Persian subjects, and the inhabitants of Kurdistan, one and all are united and agreed that matters cannot be carried on in this

---

[270] Speer (1911), *The Hakim Sahib*, p. 82.

way with the two Governments [Ottoman and Qajar], and that
necessarily something must be done, so that European
Governments having understood the matter, shall inquire into
our state. We also are a nation apart. We want our affairs to be
in our own hands.[271]

As detailed by McDowall, Abd al Qadir proceeded to occupy
Mahabad. Persian Kurdish forces to the south of Mahabad joined him.
He then moved 10,000 of his troops to the southern side of Lake
Urumia and invaded the town of Mianduab. Then, in mid-October,
Sheikh Obeidullah's first son moved his forces from the Hakkari region
of Turkey into Persian territory toward the western side of Lake
Urumia. A separate contingent led by Sheikh Obeidullah himself
mobilized the Hakkari Kurds and moved southward.

The fact that there were regular communications between Cochran
and Obeidullah did not go unnoticed by the locals. Couriers and
intermediaries were involved and aware of such communications.
These communications created misunderstanding among the local
Persians, as some incorrectly assumed that Cochran was in support of
Obeidullah's attacks. The correspondences of Katharine Cochran in
October of 1880 reveal the complications, as well as the atrocities
being carried out by forces allied with the Sheikh in Persia:

> "We are placed in a rather difficult position. Of course we
> ought to maintain a neutral position, being friends of both
> parties, but the Sheikh keeps sending Joe letters, which makes
> the Persians think that we are in league with him, and of course
> if we betray anything to the Governor, the Sheikh would be
> displeased.... The report is now that 150 villages were sacked
> by the Sheikh's son at the time the city of Mianduab was taken,
> and the inhabitants massacred, and over 4,000 people must have
> perished in all. And to think, that the man who ordered all this
> cruelty sat at our table at Seir a few months ago.[272]

Despite the massacres and military battles taking place in the area,
Cochran continued his communications with Obeidullah. He was able
to negotiate a deal with Obeidullah so that his forces would not rob or
hurt Persian Christians. Jwaideh, a renowned scholar of Kurdish
nationalist movements, asserts that Sheikh Obeidullah's initial overtures

---

[271] McDowall (2007), *A Modern History of the Kurds,* p. 53.
[272] Speer (1911), *The Hakim Sahib,* p. 84.

to the Christians and his assurances to them that they would not be attacked was intended to inspire sympathy and support from the European powers and to manipulate the dialogue about his intentions in Western circles.[273] According to Jwaideh, he honored this promise and did not attack the Christian population of the Urumia plain. However, most of the Christian population was indirectly affected by regional instability and was displaced, resulting in a refugee crisis. In describing the exodus, Cochran's mother wrote on October 21, 1880:

> All the people from the neighboring Nestorian village of Hussar came rushing over with beds on their backs, driving cows, buffaloes, and sheep into our premises.... There are no soldiers here in Urumia, no one to fight but the city rabble, and there sits the immense wild Kurdish army not six miles distant from them. Joe and the British consul then went into the city to try to induce the Persians to surrender, but they desired Joe to go again to the Sheikh and ask for one more day to consider the matter.[274]

When asked by the Persians in Urumia what they should do, given that Obeidullah's forces were positioned outside the town and were ready to attack, Cochran responded: "Surrender, if you cannot keep the city. If you can, then fight; that is your duty."[275] The closeness between Cochran and Obeidullah eventually came to benefit the Persians. At the request of the governor of Urumia, he was able to convince Obeidullah to delay his attack.[276]

The delay of one day, which Cochran managed to convince Sheikh Obeidullah to provide before attacking Urumia, was instrumental to Urumia's, and possibly all of Persia's, defense. It is one of those moments in history, without which an entire city, and in this case, possibly the national integrity of all of Persia could have been forever compromised. It is this interval of time, forgotten by many today, consisting of precisely 24 hours that Cochran had asked for and was able to receive because of his trusting relationship with Obeidullah, from which Urumia and all of Persia benefited.

---

[273] Jwaideh (2006), *The Kurdish National Movement*, pp. 82-85.

[274] Speer (1911), *The Hakim Sahib*, p. 85.

[275] Ibid., p. 87.

[276] Present at the meeting where this request was made was John Haskell Shedd, the head of the Urumia Mission, as noted in Shedd (1912), *The Life of John Haskell Shedd*, Chapter 16.

The time he bought helped prevent an all-out massacre of Urumia's population. Thousands of people of all backgrounds may have been butchered by Obeidullah's forces and their allies. The massacres in Mianduab and Mahabad carried out by his allies indicate what could have happened in Urumia, had the attack not been delayed. Most of the victims of the massacres in Mianduab and Mahabad were civilian Moslems.[277] The one-day delay enabled the Persian army to reposition and establish its reinforcements in Urumia. The Persians were able to boost their defensive arsenal of cannons and guns, and regroup the necessary battalions for a defensive posture.

To most observers, it is fascinating that Obeidullah agreed to Cochran's request to delay his attack on Urumia. Obeidullah was hoping that during the one-day delay, the residents of Urumia would make a decision to surrender. However, because of the delay, he significantly reduced his own chances of military success. There is little doubt that the trust and respect that he had developed for Cochran was the primary reason for his agreement to delay. Speer elaborated on the strength of the trust between the two men and Cochran's role in saving Urumia: "His romantic relation to the great Sheikh Obeidullah, who led the Kurdish invasion of Persia in 1880, and his part in saving the city of Urumia from capture by the invaders could have but the one effect of exalting still further his position in the minds of the people and of enlarging his influence for good."[278]

The Persian and Ottoman governments, realizing their mutual interests in removing Obeidullah due to his threats to both countries' territories, reached an agreement to jointly eliminate him. They both had a common interest in making sure the mountains within their national boundaries do not become a haven for an independent Kurdish nation. The Turkish forces took primary responsibility, and by late October of 1880, troops had arrived at the Persian border. They instructed Sheikh Obeidullah to stop his attacks and summoned him to

---

[277] Sheikh Obeidullah had promised not to attack Christians. This was most likely so that he would not lose his chances for attracting Western sympathy for his cause. He sought to avoid repeating Bedir Khan, who (as discussed in the chapters related to Asahel Grant) in the 1840s had massacred thousands of Christian villagers in Turkey's Kurdish mountains, resulting in European intervention to have Bedir Khan removed.
[278] Speer (1911), *The Hakim Sahib*, p. 73.

Constantinople. He ignored this request and executed an all-out attack on Persia.

By early November of 1880, Obeidullah's forces were pushed out of the Urumia region. The roughly 20,000 Kurdish fighters that he had been able to muster earlier from Hakkari and Persian territories had shrunk to only about 6,000. Many of the fighters had collected their war spoils and simply returned to their villages, thereby abandoning the battlefield altogether.[279] To counter the 6,000 remaining troops of Obeidullah, there were 7,000 Persian soldiers who had moved from the southern side of Lake Urumia and 5,000 more who had moved south from the western side of the lake. To his west, he was being attacked by Turkish forces. Once he realized that he was surrounded in the mountains by Persian and Ottoman troops, he gave in to the Ottoman government's demands, ceased the military campaign, and removed himself to Constantinople. He eventually escaped from Constantinople but was detained by the Turks later and removed to Hejaz (in modern-day Saudi Arabia), where he died in 1883.

By agreeing to Cochran's request to delay the attack on Urumia, Obeidullah placed himself in a position of military weakness against the freshly reinforced Persian army, resulting in his eventual defeat. Nevertheless, he continued to view Cochran as a friend, even while in detention. As Cochran's wife wrote in her correspondences in 1882: "He [Sheikh Obeidullah] seems to consider Joe his firm friend."[280] However, the horrors of the attack on the local population of Urumia and elsewhere became embedded in peoples' collective memories. In describing the horrors of Sheikh Obeidullah's invasion of the region, Mary Lewis Shedd wrote:

> The year 1880 had been a memorable one in the history of Urumia Station. Terrible famine had been followed by the Kurdish raid of Sheik Obeidullah. Until the World War all events in Urumia dated from the *Coming of Sheik*.[281]

Sheikh Obeidullah's plans for creating an independent Kurdish state, intended to be a noble cause, turned into a murderous act of desperation. Prior to his attack on Persia, he had asked Cochran to

---

[279] McDowall (2007), *A Modern History of the Kurds*, p. 55.
[280] Speer (1911), *The Hakim Sahib*, p. 101.
[281] Shedd (1922), *The Measure of a Man*, p. 45.

mediate the conversations related to Kurdish independence with the British. Cochran had no interest in mediating such conversations and redirected Obeidullah to the British. However Obeidullah sabotaged the possibility of Western support through his butchery. The massacre of thousands of civilians in Mianduab and Mahabad made it impossible for any European power to justify supporting him. It seems that in his desire to push for an independent Kurdish state militarily, he may have won the military battles but had lost the war by losing European support for his cause. The end result was very similar to that of Bedir Khan's massacre of the mountain Nestorians of Turkey in the 1840s, which destroyed Bedir Khan's image in the eyes of the West, eventually resulting in his downfall. As articulated by Samuel Wilson, the attack by the Sheikh: "destroyed whatever sympathy may have been felt for the Kurds."[282]

The most impactful outcome of Obeidullah's attack on Urumia, from an American perspective, was that it served as a catalyst for the establishment of formal diplomatic relations between Persia and America. The American government became aware of the risks that its citizens in Urumia and Tabriz were under and recognized the need to have direct lines of communications with Persian government officials by establishing its own embassy in Tehran. Up until that point, all diplomatic matters of America in Persia were handled primarily using British diplomatic resources.

Cochran described the influence of John Haskell Shedd, head of the Urumia mission at that time, and his wife in affecting political sentiments in Washington, to initiate the diplomatic relations: "It seems that Dr. and Mrs. Shedd's letters, giving an account of the precarious condition in which our Mission stood at the beginning of hostilities, had reached Mrs. Shedd's brother, General Rufus Dawes, who then was member of Congress."[283] The efforts of Congressman Dawes resulted in the establishment of an American embassy in Tehran, in 1883.[284]

---

[282] Wilson (1895), *Persian Life and Customs*, p. 110.

[283] Speer (1911), *The Hakim Sahib*, p. 100.

[284] The first American ambassador assigned to Persia in 1883, Samuel Benjamin, was the child of American Protestant missionaries. Being a missionary child, he had grown up in the Ottoman Empire and elsewhere in the Middle East and was well-versed in the region's cultures and languages.

Cochran served in Urumia until 1888. In April of that year, he and his family left for America on a one-and-a-half-year furlough. They stopped over in London for the wedding of his younger sister, Emma, and then took a steamer to New York City and arrived there in July. During this furlough in America, Cochran made numerous trips to identify candidates to serve as missionary physicians in Persia. He was especially interested in recruiting a physician to serve the mountain Assyrians, a population group that had also been of great interest to Grant nearly half a century earlier. Cochran also raised funds to set up a women's ward at Urumia's Westminster Hospital. As a result of this effort, he received $2,000 from Mrs. Ellen Howard of Buffalo, which eventually resulted in the construction of the Howard Annex at the hospital.

In October of 1889, the family sailed back to Persia and arrived in Urumia in November.[285] The furlough had re-energized Cochran's ambitions for the Urumia mission station. However, the entire decade of the 1890s was to be a period of rapid political change in Persia and growing unrest in the Urumia region. In 1892, cholera spread to major cities in Persia and eventually found its way to Urumia, despite attempts to quarantine travelers wishing to enter the city. The Cochrans' little daughter died in August of that year, and in March of 1893, his mother also passed away.[286]

References and Related Readings

Bird, Isabella L. (1891). *Journeys in Persia and Kurdistan.* London: John Murray.

Curzon, George N. (1892). *Persia and the Persian Question.* London: Longmans, Green & Co.

Hurewitz Jacob C. (1956). *Diplomacy in the Near and Middle East: A Documentary Record 1914–1956.* Princeton, NJ: Van Nostrand

Jwaideh, Wadie (2006). *The Kurdish National Movement: Its Origins and Development.* Syracuse: Syracuse University Press.

---

[285] This was not to be their last trip to Buffalo, as a decade later, in 1898, the family visited America again.

[286] Neither of the two deaths was related to the outbreak of cholera.

McDowall, David (2007). *A Modern History of the Kurds.* New York: I.B. Tauris & Co.

Shedd, Mary Lewis (1922). *The Measure of a Man: The Life of William Ambrose Shedd, Missionary to Persia.* New York: Gordon H. Doran Company.

Shedd, William A. (1912). *The Life of John Haskell Shedd.* Unpublished manuscript.

Speer, Robert (1911). *The Hakim Sahib.* New York, Fleming H. Revell Company.

Wilson, Samuel G. (1895), *Persian Life and Customs.* New York: Fleming H. Revell Company.

Chapter 23

UNREST IN THE MOUNTAINS AND THE CITY

During the 1890s significant changes were taking place in eastern Turkey which subsequently affected Urumia. In 1891, Sultan Abdul Hamid II established the Hamidiya Cavalry, conveniently named after him. It was an irregular mounted force, consisting of regiments of Kurdish tribes that had proven to be loyal to him over time. The Hamidiya was needed in order to counter Russian military presence in the region. As McDowall suggests, the Kurds benefitted from being part of this force in several ways, one of which was that they would be exempt from conscription into the Ottoman army and therefore enjoyed greater freedoms.[287] The Hamidiya forces were primarily deployed between Erzurum and Van where a large concentration of Armenian settlements existed, and as such most of their early conflicts involved the Armenians.

The Hamidiya were generally not effective on the battlefield since they were an irregular army and lacked extensive military training and disciplined leadership. Given their local priorities, they were unlikely to engage in battles far away from their own settlements. The tendency to disengage was further reinforced because their regiments, typically consisting of about 600 fighters, were headed by leaders who would place their own tribal interests above Turkey's national strategic

---

[287] McDowall (2007), *A Modern History of the Kurds,* p. 59.

interests. Since the Kurdish tribes contributing to the Hamidiya forces were numerous and geographically dispersed, they were generally not a united force. As a result, the various Hamidiya regiments associated with different Kurdish tribes could often engage in internal skirmishes among themselves, making it very difficult for Ottoman commanders to lead them as a united force on the battlefield.

Due to the poor state of its finances, the Ottoman government often had difficulty making payments to the Hamidiya troops. Over time, instead of making cash payments to the troops, the Ottoman government granted them tax collection rights. This began to give the Hamidiya troops a degree of civil authority far beyond what an army's traditional roles in society were. The task of tax collection in the Kurdish regions of the Ottoman Empire where the Hamidiya operated was delegated to unsophisticated, illiterate, heavily armed fighters with little or no understanding of civilized administrative processes.

As such, the simple task of tax collection from individual citizens could easily become a bloody and violent scene. For example, in 1894, Hamidiya troops killed over 1,000 Armenians while conducting tax collection operations in Armenian villages. Such incidents prompted protests by the European powers. Moreover, they gave rise to the militarization of Armenian resistance, including an 1895 protest in Constantinople with many casualties. In response to Armenian protests and armed resistance, the Hamidiya became even more brutal in its ways. The end result was the mobilization of their forces against Armenian villages, leading to years of violence, some of which indirectly affected Urumia.

The spirit of lawlessness that the Hamidiya Cavalry had created spilled over to the Persian side of the Turco-Persian border and seemed to have become a norm in the entire region in the 1890s. On the Persian side of the border, violence toward Christian villagers grew. By 1893 aggression towards the Christians (both Armenian and Assyrian) in Urumia was captured in missionary logs, as evident by Cochran's writing in a letter from August of 1893:

> Last week there was a dreadful murder by a mob in the market, of an Armenian Christian. Until to-day all Armenians have

closed their shops from fear, and the city is in rather a disturbed state. Soldiers are guarding the Christian quarters. Friendly Mussulmans have sent word to our prominent Nestorians not to be out in public much... The roughs who committed the murder fear punishment, and if they do not get it may make trouble. Joe is sending a letter to the Crown Prince to-day, hoping he will believe his word as to the occurrences here and not all the stories that he has been told. The consuls, too, have all been informed.[288]

In another letter, Cochran's wife described how quickly some in Urumia had even turned against her husband because of his faith. Meanwhile, an outpouring of Assyrian and Armenian refugees from the Kurdish mountains of Turkey had begun. Some of those fleeing took refuge in the villages surrounding Urumia. In many cases they were not welcomed by the local villagers due to limited resources, religious differences, and prejudice. Between 1894 and 1896, the atrocities in eastern parts of the Ottoman Empire grew due to political turmoil in the region, oppressive Ottoman policies with its minorities, and lawlessness attributed to the Hamidiya Cavalry.

A Refugee Crisis in Urumia

By 1896 due to the instability in the Ottoman territories, thousands of Assyrians from the Kurdish mountains had flocked to the Assyrian villages surrounding Urumia. This made the demands for the services of the Mission considerably greater than before, as resources were limited since the amount of donations coming from America had also dropped. This further constrained the ability of the Mission to provide assistance to the refugees. Fortunately, there were special relief funds secured by the British.

By the fall of 1897 in the mountain ranges of Turkey and Persia, the Armenians had become militant against the Kurds. Some of the tensions were linked to hostilities provoked by the Hamidiya Cavalry in Turkey in earlier years. At the same time, religiously inspired tensions in the Urumia plain and surrounding mountains were on the rise. Some

---

[288] Speer (1911), *The Hakim Sahib*, p. 176.

of the incidents which signifying the extent of the violence are noteworthy. In 1897, during the holy month of Muharram, Christians were forbidden to appear on the streets. The Russian mission, which had been constructed earlier that year and where Russian Christian missionaries resided, was also attacked during that month.[289] On another occasion, in retaliation for the death of a man visiting a village to collect a debt, the governor beheaded a Christian man without any proof of guilt or a trial. Villages in the Christian area of Geog Tapa were looted in late 1897. As a result of the growing hostilities, the inflow of refugees into Urumia fleeing the violence continued. In the fall of 1897, Cochran estimated that about 6,000 refugees were in Urumia. The influx of refugees in such large numbers created significant operational and financial challenges for the Mission.

Improvements in the Legal Rights of Christians

The ever-present violence had resulted in a fearful state among Christians of all denominations in the Urumia region. It also gave additional reasons for the Russian Orthodox Church to expand its operations in the Urumia plain. In 1897, the Russian Mission began to establish its foothold in Urumia. It aggressively attempted to convert members of the Old Nestorian Church, the Syrian Evangelical Church, Armenians, and Catholics into Russian Orthodox Christians. There was widespread misinformation that by joining the Russian Orthodox Church, one would enjoy greater levels of protection from Russia. Some of the prospective converts were under the incorrect impression that such a conversion would imply the granting of Russian citizenship. There were even speculations that Russia may take over this part of Persia. William Shedd, a missionary which will be discussed in the coming chapters, reflecting on this issue, wrote:

> The methods of the Russian priests were interesting. The first thing on reaching a village was to reconsecrate the Nestorian church which they took possession of without discussing the question of legal rights. Those who had given their names were

---

[289] Shedd (1922), *The Measure of a Man*, p. 64.

then received individually and made their confession to a priest. Later the 'converts' gathered in the churchyard where the formal reception rite was performed. The people through a representative and by kneeling in assent, renounced the errors of Nestorianism and accepted the Russian Orthodox Church. Then all attended communion service in the church.[290]

It is important to point out that at that time, the idea of Russian takeover of the region would have been quite easily imaginable to many. This is because Russian Cossack forces were active in Persia, the Persian Cossack Brigade was under Russian influence, the Persian government had grown in its dependence on Russia, and Russia had recently demonstrated its military strength through its defeat of the Ottoman forces in the Russo-Turkish War of 1877-78.[291] Shedd believed that the Russian Orthodox Church's activities in Urumia were primarily motivated by politics rather than religion. He felt that this further agitated the local Moslem population of Urumia against all Christians since there was generally a negative popular sentiment regarding Russia which was viewed as a Christian force.

Refugees in the Russian Consulate in Urumia

---

[290] Ibid., p. 64.
[291] The Persian Cossack Brigade was stablished using Russian advisors in 1879.

Shedd's point regarding Russian attempts to influence the political dynamics in Urumia is validated by a statement made by the Russian ambassador in Constantinople who wrote: "Nestorians appear essential instruments to enable the spreading of our influence in Kurdistan."[292] In later years, the Russians claimed that by the start of the First World War, nearly 20,000 Assyrians in the region had become members of the Russian Orthodox Church. The history of Qajar Persia's relations with Russia during the nineteenth century would also confirm Shedd's assessment regarding the predatory attitudes of Russia. Persia's losses of its northern territories and water rights of the Caspian Sea to Russia as a result of the 1813 Treaty of Gulistan and the 1827 Treaty of Turkmenchay were never forgotten by the Persian public.

Russia's grip on Persia's finances and its constant military presence in northern Persia caused great mistrust and fear about anything or anyone related to or supported by the Russians. As a result, any Persian group favored by the Russians would have been looked upon negatively by the rest of the Persians. This translated into a ripple effect, whereby Persians' dislike of Russians in northwestern Persia turned into a dislike for Persian Christians in that region. The growing gap between Christians and Moslems in Persian Azerbaijan, and the politicization of Christianity by the Russians, placed the Christian population of the Urumia plain at great risk of mistreatment in Persia's official courts and legal matters.

A notable example of mistreatment by Qajar courts is the case of Shushan Wright. She was a Persian Assyrian who had married Reverend John N. Wright, an American missionary based in a mission school in the Salmas district. Mrs. Wright was stabbed to death in her home in 1890 by a handyman.[293] The handyman, who was a Christian escaped but was later arrested and put to trial. Despite the clear evidence and eye-witness accounts at the trial pointing to the murderer, he was not given a death sentence as would have been the typical

---

[292] Gaunt (2006), *Massacres, Resistance, Protectors*, p. 17.
[293] Rankin (1895), *Memorials of Foreign Missionaries of the Presbyterian Church*, pp. 394-395.

punishment for murder.[294] Instead, he received a lighter sentence of life imprisonment, and having only served several years, he escaped from prison, never to be seen again.

In 1898, the legal rights of the Assyrians in the Urumia region improved due to changes in judicial procedures, advocated by Cochran. He was able to improve the processes by which legal disputes among Assyrians were settled, especially as it related to civil (rather than criminal) cases.[295] Up to that point, in order to settle civil cases among members of the Syrian Evangelical Church, the church had established a Legal Board consisting of its qualified members and one missionary to examine each case. This was done to allow legal disputes to be settled internally among Christian subjects who were members of the church, rather than to move these disputes for arbitration in provincial Persian courts, where they could be stalled or entangled.

However, the legal bearing of decisions made by the Legal Board could be contested. Cochran was able to improve the authority of the Board, as articulated by Mary Lewis Shedd:

> In 1898, the provincial authorities, including the representative of the Foreign Office and the Crown Prince, who represented the Shah in Azerbaijan, at the request of Dr. Cochran, issued an order which gave full recognition of the rights of the Legal Board to adjudicate matters in the Protestant Church. Thus the Legal Board was formally recognized by the Persian Government. To this court were brought all sorts of cases between Christians, except those purely criminal, which were settled in the civil courts, and the Board's decision was accepted as final by the Persian authorities.[296]

This was a significant accomplishment on legal processes and the administration of justice among the Assyrian evangelical community members. The reason for the Persian government accommodating this

---

[294] See for example, the US State Department correspondences related to this case from 1890, available in the State Department digital archives discussing the legal proceedings: https://history.state.gov/historicaldocuments/frus1890/d419 (accessed on 2/22/2021).

[295] Therefore, this change in legal processes would not have been applicable to cases such as Shushan Wright's murder, but would have affected cases such as those related to property disputes, inheritance, and business transactions.

[296] Shedd (1922), *The Measure of a Man*, p. 74.

change was that many legal matters, such as divorce, finances, and inheritance, were subject to religious norms, and as such, the Syrian Evangelical Church would be more qualified to evaluate these cases. The Legal Board of the Church generally followed the Canon law of the Old Nestorian Church in administering its decisions. Following the establishment of the Legal Board of the Syrian Evangelical Church, similar boards for settling civil matters among Christians were established by the French and Russian missions.

The Passing of Katharine Cochran

In addition to turmoil in the Kurdish mountains and Urumia making life difficult, the 1890s were an especially difficult time for the Cochran family due to the passing of his wife. She passed away from complications related to a severe case of "grippe" (flu) on March 21, 1895. The losses kept mounting, as three weeks later, Dr. John Haskell Shedd who was the head of the Urumia Mission at that time, also passed away. His loss made Cochran the most senior active missionary, creating additional responsibilities for him at a time when he was challenged at home taking care of his young motherless children and grieving the loss of his wife. Following his wife's passing, Frederick Coan and his family moved into the Cochran residence to help look after the children and provide Cochran with the support he needed in this difficult time. Reflecting on the supportive nature of the Coan family in these trying times, Emma Cochran-Ponafidine wrote:

> The sorrow and desolation of my brother were lessened somewhat by the sympathetic helpfulness of Mr. and Mrs. Coan, who moved into his home with their children and did much to brighten the lives of the motherless young ones. This action of the Coans seemed a quite natural one, for there was a peculiarly close bond between many of the younger missionaries, since many of them were of the second generation. This was true, for instance, of the Coans, the Shedds, the Labarees and the Rheas.[297]

In some ways, the emotional pain felt by Cochran resembled what Grant felt after the passing of Judith Grant. The sorrow of the loss of a spouse, the demands of missionary work, combined with the

---

[297] Ponafidine (1932), *My Life in the Moslem East*, p. 191.

responsibility of looking after young motherless children in a foreign land can be overwhelming, even for those of the soundest mind and strongest faith. Similar to Grant, who briefly visited Tabriz after his wife's passing, Cochran visited Tabriz for a short while. Also, as had been the case for Grant, Cochran proceeded to visit the mountain Assyrians following his wife's death. He visited them in the summer of 1895. It is unclear whether Cochran was even aware of the similarities of his actions with those of another missionary physician who had passed away half a century earlier, wrestling with the same life struggles that he was facing. Nevertheless, the similarities are, at the very least, noteworthy.

Similar to Grant, it was at this stage in his life that Cochran struggled with the important question of what he should be doing for his children, who no longer had a mother. The two older children needed to be in America for their education. Stephen Merrell Clement, Cochran's childhood friend from Buffalo, suggested that the children should move to America. He agreed to cover all their schooling expenses. Therefore, Cochran took Clement and Lillie with him, first to Russia to see his sister Emma for three weeks, and then to London. In London, the children boarded a steamship to America by themselves. Cochran could not accompany the children to America as he was not on furlough and had to return to Persia.

References and Related Readings

Gaunt, David (2006). *Massacres, Resistance, Protectors: Muslim-Christian Relations in Eastern Anatolia During World War I.* Piscataway, NJ: Gorgias Press.

McDowall, David (2007). *A Modern History of the Kurds.* New York: I.B. Tauris & Co.

Rankin, William (1895). *Memorials of Foreign Missionaries of the Presbyterian Church, U.S.A.* Philadelphia: Presbyterian Board of Publication and Sabbath Work.

Shedd, Mary Lewis (1922). *The Measure of a Man: The Life of William Ambrose Shedd, Missionary to Persia.* New York: Gordon H. Doran Company.

Speer, Robert (1911). *The Hakim Sahib.* New York, Fleming H. Revell Company.

Chapter 24

ANTI-IMPERIALISM SENTIMENTS AND THE MOOSHIE DANIEL MURDER

At the turn of the twentieth century, the attitudes of the general population in many developing countries had turned against imperial powers. America was also experimenting with imperialism at that time, through its colonization of the Philippines.[298] In many developing countries, the negative sentiments stemmed from changes that were being brought about under Western pressure and affecting weaker nations' economies, cultures, and ways of life. One place where this was evident was thousands of miles to the east of Urumia, in China, where the Boxer Rebellion was taking shape.[299] This was a rebellion by a group of local militants who opposed the economic, political and social pressures placed upon the people of China by several European nations.

In Cochran's writing, there appears to be a clear recognition of the potential impact that such a mindset might have had on how the Persian population viewed Westerners. He was also concerned about similar forces negatively affecting religious minorities, such as the Assyrians

---

[298] McKenna (2017), *American Imperial Pastoral: The Architecture of US Colonialism in the Philippines.*

[299] Preston (2001), *The Boxer Rebellion.*

and Armenians, who received protection and support from Western missionaries:

> What then is a missionary to do? Is he not to show his
> sympathy with the oppressed and the down-trodden? Is he not
> commanded to 'relive the oppressed, judge the fatherless, and
> plead for the widow'? In the light of the events transpiring in
> China at present, this question becomes more than usually
> important. Some go so far as to believe that the rising against
> the foreigners by the Chinese is the direct outcome of the
> relation which the Roman Catholic missionaries have sustained
> toward the government and their converts. In China, as in
> Persia, they have made a general offer to those whom they wish
> to win as converts, that the missionaries will stand between
> them and litigations on the part of native authorities. They have
> in many places in China given out the impression that a sort of
> protectorate has been established by them over all their
> converts. No such criticism can be justly made of the methods
> pursued in this regard by our Mission. At the same time, we
> have many times made the authorities feel and sometimes say
> that it was a question whether we had the right to interfere in
> affairs between themselves and their subjects. The relation
> existing at present between the authorities of all classes and
> ourselves is extremely pleasant; perhaps they were never more
> so. At the same time, what can we do to retain their good will
> and at the same time to show our sympathy for our people when
> they are oppressed by their rulers or by public marauders?[300]

The rebellious attitudes prevailing in places like China were also becoming visible in Persia in the early 1900s. To further complicate matters in Persian Azerbaijan, by September of 1901, Ottoman forces had begun attacking the border region and occupied several villages on the Persian side of the border. The Russians were also taking greater control of Persia. By December of that year, it was clear to Cochran that Russia's grip on Persia was tightening. To him, this was evident in the completion of the Erivan railroad which had significant logistical implications on the dominance of Russia in the region. In his writings from the time, he had expressed concerns about the large loans that Russia was offering to Persia, Russia's forceful advancement of commerce with Persia, and the growth in Russian banking and finance

---

[300] Speer (1911), *The Hakim Sahib*, p. 308.

operations in Persia. At the same time, the opposition of the masses in Persia to foreign influence was growing.

There was also a strong public desire for changes in the governance structure of Persia. The public's desire was for a balanced legislative process, which at that time was driven by orders of the Shah's court rather than a democratic parliamentary process. Aspirations to develop a constitution and to have the Persian people represented in a democratic form of government were strong.[301] These democratic aspirations amplified patriotic themes in the public discourse. Though well-intended from a general societal perspective, these aspirations had the side-effect of enflaming the anti-foreign sentiments of the Persian public, which resulted in further deepening of the religious and ethnic lines of divisions that existed in Persian society. These divisions were more evident in parts of the country where greater diversity was evident, such as Persian Azerbaijan and the Urumia region.

The very fact that it would be possible for those in favor of democracy and establishing a constitution to be inclined to oppress minorities seems counter-intuitive and surprising. The Persian Constitutional Revolution, which took shape during the first decade of the twentieth century, was in reaction to the influence of European powers, and the economic and territorial failures of Qajar rulers. The inability of the Qajars to prevent these failures was a result of their own incompetence and their genuine lack of concern for the nation's wellbeing. Given the Qajar kings' poor management of the country's finances, their overindulgences, and their administrative inefficiencies, there was much for the Persian public to be unhappy about. The attribution of some of these failures to Western Christian powers is where the Persian public's discontent with Westerners was at times misdirected to Persia's own Christian minorities.

Tensions came to a head during the first decade of the twentieth century. Constitutional revolutionists took over Tehran and forced Mozaffar ad-Din Shah to accept a consultative assembly called the "majlis." A constitution was drafted, which the Shah signed into law in 1906. However, Mozaffar ad-Din Shah died in 1907, leaving the Persian throne to his son, Mohammad Ali Shah. The following year, Mohammad Ali Shah reversed all democratic efforts, abolished the

---

[301] Keddie (2012), *Qajar Iran and the Rise of Reza Khan.*

constitution, arrested the constitutional leaders, and used Russian forces to bomb the Parliament building. This led to a period of violent clashes between the Persian government and the revolutionists, resulting in the July 1909 overthrow of Mohammad Ali. He fled to Russia and was replaced by his thirteen-year-old son, Ahmad Shah, and the 1906 constitution was reinstated.[302]

During the revolutionary years, to facilitate democratic processes at the local and municipal levels, "anjumans," consisting of groups of interested individuals from the general public, were formed. In major cities and population centers, members of the local anjuman would discuss governance matters and at times could be active in manifesting their opinions through enforcement actions, in some cases using force and violence.

The anjumans had no legal standing, yet they received considerable public encouragement and support as they were perceived to be advocating a democratic process whereby the people and not the rulers determined what was right and what was wrong. The possibilities for anarchy, corruption, and lawlessness were abundant. As evident in the missionary writings from that time, the power of the anjumans and the scope of their influence in the Urumia area were excessive and at times they seemed out of control. No formal guidelines or procedures existed for the control of the anjumans' actions and this resulted in concerns regarding human rights, legal protections entitled to citizens, and the equitable administration of justice.

The Mooshie Daniel Murder

The overall effect of the forces at play in the years leading to and during the Persian Constitutional Revolution was chaos in Persian Azerbaijan. Often, under the honorable banners of revolution and democracy, long-held prejudices combined with anti-European sentiments translated into violence applied to Christian minorities of the area, which was especially evident in the Urumia region. As early as January of 1903, forces who claimed to be associated with what eventually became the Persian Constitutional Revolution were targeting minorities in the Urumia region. This is evident, for example, by a

---

[302] Browne (1910), *The Persian Revolution of 1905-1909.*

January 20, 1903 letter, in which Cochran described the shooting of two Armenian brothers by revolutionists. Cochran had to medically attend to the two men and wrote: "These revolutionists have been the means of the greatest losses to this plain. In the past seven years it is estimated that they have killed openly and secretly, and hidden or buried, not less than two hundred Armenians."[303]

The fact that some of the supporters of a movement inspired by democratic values were causing harm to Persia's minorities in areas such as Urumia, is in contrast to conventional understanding about the honorable motives behind the Persian Constitutional Revolution. However, it is important to recognize that with northwestern Persia being somewhat of a wild-west due to its geography and topography, lawlessness under any banner would have been easy to implement. In the years leading to, and during the Constitutional Revolution, conflicts between the Kurds and the Christians in the mountain villages surrounding Urumia were rising. This was especially true in a region referred to as Tergawar, to the west of Urumia, consisting of villages in mountainous areas in the vicinity of the border between Persia and Turkey. In a correspondence from June of 1903, Cochran described some of these incidents, providing a graphic account of the scale of violence that was at play:

> The week has been full of work and anxiety for the Christians of Tergawar. Shebani, Balulan, Hekki, and Dostullan have been burned after the people fled from them. In Dostullan, Selbi, Kasha Onar's mother (she graduated from Fiske Seminary in the first class) was burned to death with three other women. In Shebani twelve men were cut off from the rest and were killed. At present all the Syrians of the villages of northern Tergawar are flocked together in Mawana surrounded by not less than 1,000 Kurds.[304]

Similar incidents were taking place elsewhere in the Urumia region. In 1903, in the Dasht region to the northwest, skirmishes between Assyrian and Kurdish villages broke out. In a letter from September of 1903, Cochran described the gradual escalation of the conflict as such:

---

[303] Speer (1911), *The Hakim Sahib*, p. 243.
[304] Ibid., p. 246.

A comparatively small affair had been exaggerated, and had become the starting-point for a most serious attack upon the Christians of Tergawar, a little district of six Christian and three or four Kurdish villages lying over the foothills, some twenty miles from the city. The southern end of this valley or plateau is called Dasht, where there are more than twice as many Kurdish villages, with several hundred Christian families living in them with the Kurds. The Kurds of Dasht united to crush or drive out the Christians of Tergawar. These Christians are brave and warlike, and not unlike their Kurdish neighbours in dress, manners, and morals. But as the government did not come to their aid as it usually has done in the past when they have been attacked, they were badly beaten. They took refuge together in the largest village, and there they have been huddled together since June… The Kurds along the border emboldened, threatened to overrun the country in a general raid, and now both Christian and Moslem, thoroughly frightened, began to desert their villages and move their goods within the city walls.[305]

The tensions took a deadly and personal form when an Assyrian man closely associated with the Mission was murdered by someone of the Dasht tribe. Cochran provides a detailed account of this murder in a correspondence from September of 1903:

Selbi and Her Son Kasha Onar (c. 1892)

---

[305] Ibid., pp. 254-255.

The past week has witnessed the murder, in cold blood, of one of the best educated and most respected of the Syrians of the country, Mr. M. G. Daniel of this place. After graduating from the Mission schools this man had been our High School teacher, and later college teacher. He then spent eleven years in the United States and Canada, chiefly in the study of theology. On the day of this tragedy, he was overseeing workmen in his vineyard when a notorious outlaw, Sayid Ghafar, who has been terrorizing the community without let or hindrance, shot him down because he would not give up his watch.[306]

While the violence in Tergawar was a source of general concern, the murder of Mooshie G. Daniel made the nature of this more directly relevant to the Mission. He was highly educated, a naturalized citizen of Britain, a member of the Syrian Evangelical Church, a former professor of ancient Syriac at Urumia College, a graduate of McCormick Seminary in Chicago, and an author. Being a British subject elevated the significance of his murder. Also, given that Daniel was a member of the Syrian Evangelical Church, his murder required special attention by Joseph Cochran, who was on the Legal Board of the Church. Daniel's murder, as typical as it may appear in the larger context of violence and death affecting the area, would result in a chain-reaction of events which would engage Cochran, the Urumia Mission, Persia, Turkey, and the United States for years to come.

Mooshie G. Daniel (c. 1901)

---

[306] Ibid., p. 257. Note that the proper spelling of the name is *Ghaffar*; however, due to the common use of *Ghafar* in missionary correspondences, for consistency, the latter spelling will be used here.

References and Related Readings

Bird, Isabella L. (1891). *Journeys in Persia and Kurdistan.* London: John Murray.

Browne, Edward G. (1910). *The Persian Revolution of 1905-1909.* Cambridge: Cambridge University Press.

Daniel, Mooshie G. (1901). *Modern Persia.* Toronto: The Carswell Co. Ltd.

Keddie, Nikki (2012). *Qajar Iran and the Rise of Reza Khan.* Costa Mesa, CA: Mazda Publishers.

Lawrence, T.J. (1935). *Seven Pillars of Wisdom.* Garden City: Doubleday, Doran & Company.

McKenna, Rebecca T. (2017). *American Imperial Pastoral: The Architecture of US Colonialism in the Philippines.* Chicago: University of Chicago Press.

Preston, Diana (2001). *The Boxer Rebellion: The Dramatic Story of China's War on Foreigners that Shook the World in the Summer of 1900.* New York: Berkley Books.

Said, Edward W. (1994). *Culture and Imperialism.* New York: Vintage Books.

Said, Edward W. (1979). *Orientalism.* New York: Vintage Books.

Speer, Robert (1911). *The Hakim Sahib.* New York, Fleming H. Revell Company.

Chapter 25

THE BENJAMIN WOODS LABAREE MURDER

Cochran joined the Anglican Mission of Urumia to bring the violent murder of Daniel to the attention of the governmental authorities in Tabriz and Tehran. He requested Richmond Pearson, the American minister in Tehran, to apply all his powers and influence to have Ghafar arrested and prosecuted. However, since Ghafar was a sayid (a lineal descendent of the Prophet), he enjoyed "exemption from the more common punishments, or for any offence against."[307] Prosecuting him would have been a challenge, even with the greatest application of Persian power and authority. Ghafar was still on the loose, and it took some time to detain him. Recognizing that Joseph Cochran was actively advocating for his arrest and was appealing to the authorities for swift action, Ghafar enlisted the help of his fellow nomadic tribesmen to assassinate Cochran.

On March 4, 1904, a group of Westerners headed out from Urumia to Khoi, approximately 100 miles to the north. The group was to be led by Cochran and included a teacher of the American missionary children and missionaries from Germany and Sweden. However, it was decided last-minute that Benjamin Woods Labaree, a fellow American missionary, would lead the group and Cochran would stay behind.

---

[307] Speer (1911), *The Hakim Sahib*, p. 257.

Benjamin Woods Labaree (seated at the table to the left) visiting an Assyrian Village (c. 1900-1904)

Labaree was born in Urumia and was the son of a missionary (also named Benjamin Labaree). Later in life, he attended Marietta College in Ohio and then went on to Hartford Theological Seminary where he received a Doctor of Divinity degree.[308] Ghafar's men were under the impression that Cochran would be leading the group on this trip and therefore mistook Labaree for Cochran. They were unaware that instead of Cochran, it would be Labaree who would be in charge and that Cochran would not be traveling. They had planned to follow the group and then assassinate Cochran once outside of the Urumia district. Cochran, in his report regarding this matter, provided further details, following an investigation:

> The party of Kurds divided up into three companies, which held
> the three different roads, and on the 9th, the Sayid and three

---

[308] Hence his designation as "Dr." in much of the missionary writings from that time period. He moved to America but returned to Persia on the insistence of Cochran.

Kurds attacked Mr. Labaree and his servant as they were
approaching Salmas, before they were out of the mountain pass.
Israel was shot down, some of his clothing stripped off, and his
horse, with Mr. Labaree's journey outfit taken, and Mr. Labaree
was carried off toward the other passes, and finally murdered in
a most cruel manner, with daggers and sword blows (thirteen in
all), about five miles distant from where his servant's body lay.
Travelers who had seen them on the other side of the pass, and
came after them, now recognized Israel's body as they came
upon it, and reported the murder to our preacher in Salmas.
This preacher, with a physician who is a graduate of our
schools, obtained government horsemen, and recovered the
body of the servant, and finding the fresh tracks of the horsemen
in the snow and muddy grounds across the hills, came upon the
body of Mr. Labaree in a wild and sheltered valley.[309]

Labaree died on March 9, 1904, five days into what should have
been a peaceful trip to Khoi. He left behind a grieving widow and two
young children. Records of the American State Department's
correspondences indicate that when Mozaffar ad-Din Shah was
consulted on this matter by Pearson in November of 1904, the Shah
expressed that it would be impractical to execute Ghafar. He argued
that by doing so, in retaliation, the life and safety of Christians in the
Urumia area would be at risk.[310] As an alternative, the Shah
recommended a life imprisonment sentence for Ghafar, the execution
for his accomplices, and financial compensation for Labaree's widow.

Despite the Shah's recommendation, the Persian authorities did not
move decisively to arrest any of the wrongdoers in time. They escaped
alongside their entire tribe to the Turkish side of the border. The
American dissatisfaction with Persian inaction peaked as President
Theodore Roosevelt and the American State Department contemplated
moving warships into the Persian Gulf. For a while, it seemed that
within a little over two decades from the commencement of formal
diplomatic relations between America and Persia, the relationship could
end abruptly and violently.

Labaree's widow recalled when Cochran eventually, by pure
coincidence, came face-to-face with Ghafar, the man who had

---

[309] Speer (1911), *The Hakim Sahib*, p. 260.

[310] Yeselson (1956), *United States-Persian Diplomatic Relations: 1883-1921*, p. 70.

murdered M.G. Daniel, plotted Cochran's assassination, and mistakenly caused the death of her husband. She wrote:

> One day, some six or eight months after Mr. Labaree's death, doctor went to see a prominent patient, who had come from Tabriz for an operation for cancer, and, on entering the room, saw, to his dismay -------, the man who had plotted his death. It was a situation to try the greatest diplomat or the most Christlike character. Dr. Cochran was both, but he suffered intensely during that interview when ------- spent his time in Oriental flattery, and assured his host that if ever he (the host) had need for any medical aid he would surely find Dr. Cochran the finest and most skillful of physicians. The doctor told his wife that never to his dying day should he get over that thought that his life had been so plotted against, and that another had died in his stead.[311]

The Return of Benjamin Woods Labaree's Body through One of the Gates of Urumia (c. 1904)

---

[311] Speer (1911), *The Hakim Sahib,* p. 275; Note the "----" in the passage is from the original correspondence. The name of the individual (Ghafar) was intentionally left blank by Mrs. Labaree.

With the possibility of American warships moving to the Persian Gulf, the prospects of war between America and Persia was becoming likely. This constituted the very first time in the history of the two countries that war was an openly discussed topic. However, before the deployment of American warships could be further contemplated, Ghafar was arrested. It took the Qajar authorities five months to arrest him, despite having had many opportunities to do so earlier. He confessed to the murder of Daniel and the plotting of the assassination attempt, which resulted in the death of Labaree. He was sentenced to life in prison, as Mozaffar ad-Din Shah had initially recommended.

However, the thirteen assailants who ambushed and killed Labaree, under Ghafar's instructions, were on the loose. In describing the attackers and their revengeful tendencies, which resulted in further tensions, Cochran wrote: "These Kurdish chiefs of Tergawar are not a large force, but they have repeatedly been in open rebellion against the government." The fact that the Kurds were openly defying the government suggests that they were not fully under the rule of the Persian authorities, and in fact in some cases, the Persian authorities were fearful of the revengeful acts they might take in retaliation for Persian attempts to enforce the law.

Some of the murderers had been spotted in the Urumia region, but no genuine efforts were made by the Persian officials to arrest them. Therefore, Cochran had to appeal to the representatives of foreign governments to persuade Persian officials to take action. Complaint letters were sent to the American minister in Tehran and the British consul-general in Tabriz. The common theme in all of these correspondences was that there was indisputable evidence as to who the murderers of Labaree were, that the complaints to the Persian officials have been left unaddressed, and that Persian officials were intentionally ignoring these calls for justice.

The uncooperative attitude of Persia's Qajar government in enforcing justice must have brought back dark memories of the case of Shushan Wright, the wife of an American missionary who was murdered in her home in the Salmas district. Her murderer was detained and sentenced to life in prison, instead of the typical punishment for such a crime, which was the death sentence. The failure of the Qajar justice system in Shushan's case may have served as a reminder to partially explain the weaknesses of the Persian authorities in handling the Labaree and Daniel murder cases.[312]

Cochran and the Mission were not satisfied with the state of affairs and insisted that the death sentence must be pursued for Ghafar. Because of his insistence along with other American missionaries, the American State Department pressed on, asking for the death penalty for Ghafar. In addition, on Cochran's recommendation, some of the members of Ghafar's tribe were kept as hostages in Tehran, to make sure his fellow tribesmen do not retaliate or inflict harm to the missionaries and those related to them in the Urumia area. This may have been a short-term attempt to control the reaction of the tribe and their allies and to prevent them from taking revengeful actions, but in the long term it was not sustainable.

Joseph Plumb Cochran on a visit to Persian government officials. To his right, near the window, is Benjamin Labaree Sr. (father of Benjamin Woods Labaree), and to his left is Frederick Coan, a fellow missionary. (c. 1904-1905)

---

[312] As described by Yeselson (1956, p. 80), the extent of the discontent of the American missionaries with the Qajar government's lack of response and Richmond Pearson's inability to persuade a response was so great that they went so far as to petition the American State Department to have Pearson removed from his job as the American minister to Persia altogether. Their petition did not succeed but was a clear sign of the missionaries' deep discontent with how matters were mishandled.

Realizing the vulnerability that a retaliation could present to the lives of the American missionaries, their families, and the Assyrians they were associated with in Urumia, there was a sudden and drastic change of heart. The fear of retaliation caused a reversal of the position being advocated by Cochran and his missionary colleagues. According to Cochran, complaining to the authorities had only further provoked the offenders: "Representations had to be made to the authorities here and in Tabriz in behalf of the poor Christians, and this with the constant active opposition of the enemies, has created much bitter feeling against me in particular, and against foreigners and Christians generally." [313]

The extent of the bitter feelings grew and became more personal for Cochran, as he became a highly prized target. He was in constant need for a security detail and armed protection against potential assassins. Since America did not have diplomatic representation in Urumia, British protection was sought. In 1904, amidst the tensions in Tergawar, a refugee crisis in Urumia, and the lack of progress in prosecuting the murderers of Labaree, Cochran married Bertha McConaughy. She was also a missionary stationed in Urumia, who had served as a teacher for the children of the American missionaries.

In December of 1904, to provide for stronger official representation of America on the Labaree case, the American Consul at Harpoot, Turkey arrived in Urumia. This was temporary relief for Cochran as it would reduce the need for him to be the sole advocate for this case. However, for personal reasons, the consul had to leave before a settlement of the case could be reached, leaving much of the responsibility for settling the case back to Cochran.

The stress of these times on him was significant. The words of those around him and his family photographs from the time indicate that his hair grew white, wrinkles appeared on his face, and he lost a noticeable amount of weight. The internal struggle was complicated for him since the Kurdish tribe responsible for the murders was one he had taken good care of for many years and believed he was on very good terms with them. The biggest source of agony for him was not the dangers aimed at himself but the fact that Labaree had died in his place. He felt a great deal of personal responsibility, since if he had kept his

---

[313] Speer (1911), *The Hakim Sahib*, p. 261.

original plans to lead the party leaving Urumia for Khoi, and had he not asked Labaree to be his replacement, Labaree would have still been alive.

References and Related Readings

Coan, Frederick G. (1939). *Yesterdays in Persia and Kurdistan.* Claremont, CA: Saunders Studio Press.

Daniel, Elton L (2012). *The History of Iran.* Santa Barbara: Greenwood.

Ryder, C.H.D. (1925). "The Demarcation of the Turco-Persian Boundary in 1913-14," *The Geographical Journal*, Vol. 66, No. 3, pp. 227-237.

Speer, Robert (1911). *The Hakim Sahib.* New York, Fleming H. Revell Company.

Sykes, Percy (1969). *A History of Persia.* New York: Barnes & Noble.

Yeselson, Abraham (1956*). United States-Persian Diplomatic Relations: 1883-1921.* New Brunswick: Rutgers University Press.

Chapter 26

JOSEPH PLUMB COCHRAN'S LEGACY

In January of 1905, there was an assassination attempt on Cochran's life. Intruders quietly entered the College compound at night. They looked for Cochran. Failing to find him, due to the extreme cold temperatures, they decided to withdraw from the compound and left. By March, Cochran had to have British bodyguards protect him in his daily movements. Complaints to the governor of Urumia did not result in any action to protect him, and reliance on British protection had become essential.

In April, Cochran escorted Labaree's widow and her two children on their way to Tabriz. She and her children were headed to Russia, on their way back to America. During this short trip to Tabriz, Cochran came to grips with the practical difficulty of achieving justice in the case of the murders of Labaree and Daniel. He had also recognized the support that the locals gave Ghafar, the plotter of the murders, by petitioning to have him released from prison. Most importantly, he had realized that the odds were not in favor of the missionaries if matters were to escalate any further:

> On arriving here I find Mr. Wratislaw has come to the same
> conclusion that we had arrived at, independently of him,
> namely, that since there is every reason to believe that the Kurds
> are not going to be thoroughly punished, we had better come to
> some terms with them, for the present condition of affairs in
> Urumia is intolerable and fraught with danger to all of us and to
> our people…. We in Urumia feel that we had much better
> appear to be the ones to get him [Ghafar] pardoned and returned

from here than to have him secure his return in any other way. I have been asked, therefore, to stay in here [Tabriz] another week until we shall get instructions from the British Legation, and if it seems best still to do so, to give him the opportunity to come to the British consulate, and in the presence of other Persians, make his apologies and promises, and I will intercede in his behalf in a formal way, and we will let him return to Urumia. At first glance this all may appear like receiving much less than the original demands. It is less, but it is better than to get nothing more, and to leave matters in a very unsatisfactory condition. At the same time, much has been done. The Sayid is in prison, two noted chiefs who have had much to do with the murder or the affairs connected with it ever since that event are also under arrest in Teheran; this very influential man has been removed from Urumia, notwithstanding the fat that every effort has been put forth to save him by his people and by the Crown Prince, and a large indemnity has been paid over, and the late Governor has been dismissed, and is now in exile.[314]

The above statements reveal a sense of realism in how Cochran came to see matters. The widow of Labaree had received a $30,000 payment for the loss of her husband. This amount was considerably larger than the $16,000 she had initially asked for. Ghafar was already in prison for having instigated the crimes.[315] The practical difficulty of arresting and prosecuting the remaining assailants who had fled to Ottoman territories alongside their tribe remained a lingering issue. It was to affect the relationship between Turkey and Persia for years to come. The inability to prosecute the 13 assailants due to the lack of cooperation of the Ottomans was an unfortunate reality that Cochran seemed to have come to terms with.

Despite efforts to assassinate Cochran, it was not a bullet that would take his life, but a common illness to which many American missionaries and their family members in Urumia had fallen over the years. In late July of 1905, he began to develop a fever and felt aches in his body. The symptoms continued for several days. He had contracted typhoid fever from a patient he was attending to. He passed away on August 18, 1905.

---

[314] Speer (1911), *The Hakim Sahib*, p. 278. Note that A.C. Wratislaw mentioned in this passage later became a member of the Turco-Persian Boundary Commission.
[315] He remained in prison until his death due to natural causes in 1907.

Joseph Cochran with a Patient at the Dispensary (c. 1905)

Joseph Cochran with Kurdish Visitors in Front of Westminster Hospital of Urumia (c. 1905)

Reflecting on his personality and traits, as evident in the writings of others who knew him well, tolerance was a commonly attributed characteristic of Cochran. On many occasions, despite how he or his family members may have been mistreated, he exhibited forgiveness and compassion when such individuals were under his care as patients. He truly embodied the code of ethics by which all physicians abide to. His actions also exhibited the generosity commonly associated with missionary work, as he removed himself from personal grievances with others as much as humanly possible.

He also had a unique sense of calmness in his demeanor. In his biography of Cochran, Robert Speer mentions a particular incident in which the doctor was shot at in the Salmas district. He was approaching Salmas to attend to a patient. Due to poor visibility, a group of locals on the road assumed that he was a robber, and with no advanced notice, a dozen bullets were shot in his direction. Upon gaining better visibility, the men doing the shooting realized it was Cochran. Knowing him personally, they greeted him and began conversing. Cochran "talked with them as if nothing had happened." What may have rattled any other person seemed not to have shaken him one bit.

Cochran was also uniquely capable of putting old grievances aside. He was on very good terms with the Anglican missionaries stationed in Urumia. The intense conflicts which existed between Anglican missionaries and American missionaries in the days of Grant, which are a defining part of the history of missions in that part of the world, did not influence Cochran's interactions with them. The relationship that he had developed with them was cooperative and collegial. He would regularly invite the Anglican missionaries to his home for meals and was, on several occasions, their travel companion.

In terms of his personal interests and activities, recollections from his children and close friends indicate a highly active lifestyle. His son, Clement, recalled his father's love for mountain climbing: "His love of a wide outlook was that of a mountaineer, as indeed he was by birth and boyhood, and I think he was seldom happier than when able to look from some commanding position as far as his vision could carry."[316] His hobbies and interests also affirm a very active lifestyle and

---

[316] Speer (1911), *The Hakim Sahib*, p. 174.

included cycling, horseback riding, listening to music, and excursions in scenic areas.

Cochran was known to be a practical joker, especially with his close friends. In one instance, when his best friend, Stephen Clement, from Buffalo had come to visit him in Urumia, Cochran asked several of his local native friends to stage a mock armed robbery without Clement knowing it is a hoax. He scared Clement dearly, following which Cochran appeared at the scene of the affair as a practical joke to entertain Clement, all of this happening when both men were fully grown adults. On another occasion, he played a practical joke with a fellow missionary on April fool's day. Robert Labaree (the brother of Benjamin W. Labaree), was anxious about the weather conditions for his intended journey from Urumia to Mosul. The potential for bad weather would have forced him to cancel his travel plans, causing great inconvenience. As an April fool's hoax, Cochran arranged for someone to send him a telegram stating: "New snows, blocked road, impossible for a month." Interestingly, Robert Speer noted in his biography of Cochran that as much as he liked to play practical jokes on others, he was not a happy recipient and that Cochran "loved nothing better than a good practical joke, although he very much disliked being teased."

Cochran Contemplating Whether or Not to Ride a Bicycle (c. 1895-1905)

One of the notable aspects of Cochran's life was his unique ability to interact with the full spectrum of social groups and social classes. Because his work had brought about advanced medical practices to the region, he was frequently visited or called upon by Persian royalty. During his lifetime, he had interacted with all of the Qajar kings of his time. In 1887, Naser al-Din Shah gave Cochran and another American missionary physician who was based in Tehran, awards to recognize their contributions to Persia. In the fall of 1890, Cochran had a formal visit with Naser al-Din Shah. His son, Mozaffar ad-Din (when he was the crown prince) and grandson Mohammad Ali, had sought Cochran's medical advice while visiting Urumia on several occasions. Ahmad Shah, the very last Qajar king, had also sought the medical advice of Cochran, while visiting Urumia.

Despite the attention he received from royalty, he never lost sight of those in need. In the final months of his life, he adopted a little beggar boy who was an orphan and severely ill. Cochran had noticed the child, while walking the streets of Urumia. He brought the boy to his own home and took care of him, and kept him with his family.[317]

It is also important to recognize that despite being a missionary physician with access to royalty, Cochran viewed himself as a physician and teacher for the people. Nearly half of his patients were local Moslems, and the same ratio holds for his medical students. In the fall of 1901, the Crown Prince (Mohammad Ali) joined Cochran in endorsing the graduates of Urumia Medical College during their graduation ceremony.

As expressed by Frederick Coan, his childhood friend and fellow missionary: "One of the reasons why the Persians respected and loved Dr. Cochran so much, was his strict observance of their etiquette."[318] His understanding of the unique protocols in Persian culture and the traditional norms and requirements of communication demonstrated his respect for Persia. It made him a welcome person in any circle, among the poor and royalty alike.

---

[317] Ibid., p. 326. After Cochran's passing, the child was taken care of in an orphanage.

[318] Coan (1939), *Yesterdays in Persia and Kurdistan*, p. 6.

Joseph Cochran with the Orphan Beggar Boy Rescued from the Streets of Urumia (c. 1904-1905)

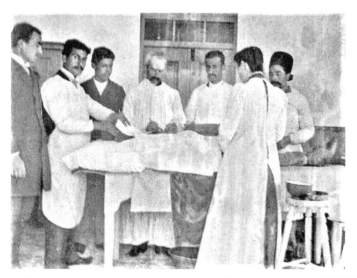

Joseph Cochran Teaching Autopsy to His Medical Students in Westminster Hospital (c. 1900-1905)

Cochran believed the education of Persia's doctors to be a means of creating social equity and prosperity: "As I have pointed out at other times, the mission of teaching the medical science to the young men of this nation here, and right here in their homes."[319] His emphasis on the education of Persian medical students taking place in Persia rather than abroad was based on his belief that seeking medical training in foreign lands may make the Persian students disconnect from their culture and less able to effectively labor in Persia once they finish their studies abroad. This is one of the many reasons he had established Persia's first medical college in Urumia. He was a physician of immense skills, whose healing hands removed pain and suffering from thousands in Persia. His visionary mind helped create Persia's very first medical college and elevated the norms and expectations for public health in all of Persia.

In addition to his many qualities as a physician and educator, Cochran was highly trustworthy. Being able to speak multiple languages, and having grown up in both Persia and America, he was uniquely capable of helping and relating to people of diverse backgrounds. His most memorable demonstration of this ability came in 1880 when Sheikh Obeidullah was about to invade northwestern Persia. Having earned the Sheikh's trust, he was able to request from the Sheikh a 24-hour delay in the Sheikh's planned attack.

This allowed the Persian army to reposition into a defensive formation and resupply its forces to prevent the invasion of northwestern Persia. Through his ability to communicate with both sides, Cochran bought Persia one of its most precious 24 hours because, without it, the possibility of Persia becoming a much smaller country would have been very real.

Joseph Plumb Cochran is buried in the American Cemetery in the village of Seir. His home still stands, as part of the Urumia University campus, for remembrance, and as a symbol of Iran's enduring respect for him.

---

[319] Speer (1911), *The Hakim Sahib,* p. 271.

References and Related Readings

Coan, Frederick G. (1939). *Yesterdays in Persia and Kurdistan*. Claremont, CA: Saunders Studio Press.

Ryder, C.H.D. (1925). "The Demarcation of the Turco-Persian Boundary in 1913-14," *The Geographical Journal*, Vol. 66, No. 3, pp. 227-237.

Speer, Robert (1911). *The Hakim Sahib*. New York, Fleming H. Revell Company.

Sykes, Percy (1969). *A History of Persia*. New York: Barnes & Noble.

Wigram, W. A. (1920). *Our Smallest Ally*. London: Society for Promoting Christian Knowledge.

Chapter 27

WILLIAM AMBROSE SHEDD

William Ambrose Shedd was born to American missionary parents who served in Urumia. He spent his early childhood years in Persia, and in his later years was in constant transition between there and America. As such, similar to Cochran, he was able to experience both nations' cultures, traditions, and social norms. He became a leading figure in the Urumia mission station in the years leading to the First World War and had extensive contact with authority figures among Persian government officials, Kurdish leaders, and the communities that the Mission served.

One of the unique aspects of Shedd was that in contrast to all other American missionaries in Persia, he took on an official role as a diplomat. He served as the American Vice-Consul in Urumia during the closing months of the First World War in 1918. He had conflicting demands placed on him, which required him to attempt to balance diplomatic norms of neutrality against the pressing concerns of humanitarian and missionary work in the Urumia region. He was well-versed in theological matters related to Islam and its relations with Oriental churches, and he wrote and lectured on it while he was a visiting scholar at Princeton University in 1902.

During the First World War, Shedd was entrusted with administering the Near East Relief Fund in the Urumia plain. The relief efforts supported by this fund had begun in 1915 in recognition of the needs of displaced Armenian refugees from Turkey. Later on, the efforts expanded to address the greater needs of all displaced refugees in the area, affected by the war.[320] As the administrator of the funds, Shedd was also able to serve as an eye-witness to the outcomes of a devastating war, manifested in the form of large-scale religious and tribal violence. Having taken on the role of the American Vice-Consul in Urumia, he fled, alongside nearly fifty thousand refugees, to escape the treachery of the invading Ottoman forces and their Kurdish allies that overtook the city in the summer of 1918. He died during this exodus, only weeks before the official end of the First World War.

---

[320] The Near East Relief efforts resulted from collective fundraising campaigns under the banners of the Persian War Relief and the Syria-Palestine Relief Fund. The leadership and much of the financial backing behind this effort in America were provided through leading Presbyterian industrialist families, such as the Rockefellers and the Rockefeller Foundation.

Family Legacy

William Ambrose Shedd was born on January 24, 1865, in the village of Seir, near Urumia. Although thousands of miles away from his ancestral lands, he grew up among American missionary families living in Seir. His ancestral heritage and family lineage are among the most illustrious of all American missionaries who served in Persia, dating back to individuals who participated in the American Revolution and the Boston Tea Party. During the years of the American Civil War, fifty-two members of the Shedd family, including three of his uncles, participated on the Union side.[321]

Shedd's grandfather, Reverend Henry Shedd, was a vocal supporter for the abolition of slavery and temperance and was a strong-minded man known for baring a slave owner from communion. His strength of conviction passed down the generations and was an attribute that William Shedd also clearly demonstrated in his life. Shedd's father, John Haskell Shedd, graduated from Marietta College in Ohio and attended Andover Theological Seminary in Massachusetts, graduating in 1859. In that year, he became a missionary for the ABCFM and married Sarah Jane Dawes.

There was considerable family history on his mother's side as well. She was the granddaughter of Congressman Manasseh Cutler, who in 1787 crafted legislation to prohibit slavery in territories northwest of the Ohio River. Her brother, General Rufus Dawes, was a United States Congressman who was instrumental in pressing the case for establishing official diplomatic relations between the United States and Persia in 1882. Shedd's cousin was Charles Gates Dawes, a prominent banker, politician, and musician, who eventually served as the vice president of the United States between 1925 and 1929, under President Calvin Coolidge. For Shedd, considering his ancestral heritage from both parents' sides, there were high standards to live up to. His parents were assigned by the ABCFM to serve in Persia, where in 1859 they began their missionary labors.

---

[321] Shedd (1912), *The Life of John Haskell Shedd*, chapter 1.

Youth, Persia, Charlotte, and Marietta

Born in the village of Seir, southwest of Urumia, Shedd spent the first few years of his life there, alongside his older brother Charles. His father was then reassigned to America, and the entire family moved there when Shedd was five years old. The stay in America turned out to be longer than initially planned as his mother became ill, making a return to Urumia impossible for several years. When William was seven years old, the family moved to Charlotte, NC as his father had been reassigned to Charlotte to work with freed slaves, working under the umbrella of the Biddle Institute.[322]

The significance of carrying out missionary work in the South following the American Civil War cannot be overstated. Even after the abolition of slavery, there was still discrimination, persecution, racism, and violence against freed slaves. Similar conditions applied to the missionaries assisting them in their integration into post-abolition American society through educational, religious, and social programs. Families of these missionaries were socially ostracized, and their children were banned from attending white schools. Shedd, recalling his childhood in Charlotte, wrote:

> My own memories as a boy tell of no friends among the white children of the place. We children were sent to the white Presbyterian church of the town.... The doctor had the privilege that doctors have of ignoring social conventions, and he was a friend.... I have no memories more delightful than those of going with my father behind the steady mare, Julia, to the country churches under his care. Communion services were sometimes held in the woods, the communicants sitting on either side of rough plank tables under the trees; and there was a solemnity and simplicity about it that laid hold on the imagination. At noon picnic dinners were spread and the lapse of years has not dimmed the memories of fried chicken, sweet potato pies, cakes and other dainties made by cooks who had learned the art in the great houses of the slave plantations.

---

[322] Which later became Biddle University and is now part of John C. Smith University.

These things played a larger part in the boy's life than in his father's.[323]

Exposure to the aftermath of slavery in America, being considered an outcast by other white communities in Charlotte, and being warmly received by the community of freed African-Americans, gave Shedd a rare inside perspective on the pains that discriminated populations experience. He felt well-integrated with the children of those families that his father helped. This not only broadened his views of life but most likely influenced his appreciation for diversity and inclusion as an adult.

While living in the South, Shedd was often ill and weak. He was an avid reader with a special interest in international affairs. In 1878, his mother returned to Persia with the younger children who were born in America, while he and his older brother remained in America and moved in with their grandmother and aunt in Marietta, Ohio. William made many friends in Marietta. They called themselves the "Hill Crowd." At that young age, there was only one girl among the Hill Crowd. She recalled William's bravery, how he believed in defending her rights within the male-dominated group, and how social equity guided his convictions from an early age:

> I counted on Will to defend me when I needed defense. His
> ready wits were used for my benefit against any of the boys
> when we argued or quarreled, and I counted definitely on his
> size and his brains as a help in trouble. I remember once when
> he contended that the fact that I was a girl didn't disqualify me
> from participating in their society on a basis of equality. This
> was when one of the boys had objected, on the score of sex, to
> my tagging along. It is all forgotten except my gratitude to Will
> because he respected me in spite of the fact, the bitter
> humiliating fact, that I was a girl. Will looked more like my
> father than any of his sons, and his keen brown eyes that saw
> everything but were so soft and smiling to his friends, were like
> my father's, as were his thin, small, brown hands.[324]

Shedd entered Marietta College in Ohio at the young age of 15, the same institution where his father had received his doctorate. While there, he was also a tutor and was recognized by fellow students for

---

[323] Shedd (1912), *The Life of John Haskell Shedd*, chapter 13.
[324] Shedd (1922), *The Measure of a Man*, p. 41.

being very patient with the younger students who were having learning difficulties. As his third wife, Mary Lewis Shedd points out in her biography of William Shedd, his kindness and care towards those left out and considered "black sheep" were widely recognized at Marietta. This was demonstrative of his patience and tolerance, which were some of the valuable characteristics that were to define him for his entire life. She believed that his compassion and tolerance for those who were so different from him explained why he was uniquely gifted to deal with the social and political complexities of Urumia.

Before Shedd was able to complete his studies at Marietta, at the age of 17, his parents asked him to return to Persia. The unrest caused by Sheikh Obeidullah's 1880 attack on northwestern Persia, and the refugee crisis had placed great demands on the Urumia mission station, where his father was the head missionary. The Shedd family had suffered a great deal during the year of the Obeidullah invasion, and their youngest son died in this period.[325]

Despite the immediate need for his return to Persia in 1882, the stay of many years with his aunt and grandmother had a great influence on William Shedd. They were a source of spiritual strength and provided him with the moral grounding that guided much of his adult life. Exposure to other members of his maternal family during his stay in America, especially his uncle, was uniquely influential. His uncle, General Rufus Dawes, was a Congressman in Washington, DC. While visiting Washington, he wrote back to his aunt describing the visit to the city's many sites and his interactions with his uncle:

> I sent off a letter this morning to you, which brought things up
> till Friday evening. That evening Aunt Mary and Uncle Rufus
> took all of us over to the Observatory. We did not see the
> largest telescope (which is the largest in the world), but we each
> had a look through a smaller, but-quite-large one. We looked at
> the moon and at one of the fixed stars. He also showed us the
> clock that keeps the stars and time for the United States and
> explained the system to us (or rather to Uncle Rufus). The
> telescope was in a dome with a revolving room and other
> fixtures.[326]

---

[325] Although not due to the invasion.

[326] Letter dated April 4, 1882; Archives of the Presbyterian Historical Society, Philadelphia; Shedd Family Archives, RG 19-0504.

For the young William Shedd, visiting his uncle, a highly respected congressman and a former general in the Union Army, must have created quite an impression. It possibly also affected his aspirations and expectations in life. It is important to point out that his uncle was the primary political force in Washington who later that year successfully championed the formation of formal diplomatic relations between the United States and Persia. His political efforts resulted in the establishment of the American Legation in Tehran the following year.

Urumia Apprenticeship

Shedd returned to Urumia in 1882. These were years of growing demands for the Mission's services. The Westminster Hospital construction, led by Dr. Cochran, had just been completed, and the Mission facilities had expanded. Only two years earlier, Sheikh Obeidullah's attacks on northwestern Persia had resulted in a massive influx of refugees from the mountain villages.

Upon his return to Urumia, at the age of 17, William was heavily involved in a range of Mission activities. He served in the libraries of the Mission and was also a teacher. The academic exposure he gained during this period as a librarian and a teacher may have inspired his own interests in comparative religious studies, which many years later led to his writing of a related book on the relationship between early Islam and Eastern Christianity. To sharpen his local language skills, he also improved his Syriac and Persian during this time period. The Mission was also entering a landmark period in 1885, having been established for nearly half of a century.

After a little over two years of service in Urumia, at the age of 20, Shedd returned to Marietta College to finish his studies, graduating in 1887. He returned to Urumia in the fall of that year, where he remained for two years. These two years created a transition point in developing his skills from teacher to administration. He taught and also began to take on administrative roles. He was assigned the critical role of accounting and record-keeping for the Mission.

The Jubilee Celebration of the Urumia Mission Station in 1885

The administrative knowledge he gained and the language and people skills he developed during his previous two-year apprenticeship in Urumia, were instrumental to the sharpening of his leadership abilities. In addition, although still very young, Shedd had to develop a great deal of independent thinking and decision making skills. His parents had left for America on furlough, leaving him with many important Mission tasks to manage on his own. He seemed to be concerned about his lack of preparedness, stating: "I need guidance and especially moderation. I wish I knew how to be firm and yet gentle. More and more I feel my weakness in comparison with the work given me to do. Maybe this feeling will help me."[327] His openness in acknowledging his weaknesses demonstrated his continued desire to develop and learn.

After his second apprenticeship in Urumia, Shedd returned to America in the summer of 1889 to attend Princeton Theological Seminary. At Princeton, his classmates affectionately called him "Sheddy." He did not participate in sports a great deal and was considered somewhat quiet and reserved. One of his joys was teaching fellow classmates the Syriac grammar, a language which he considered

---

[327] Shedd (1922), *The Measure of a Man,* p. 49.

to be a mother tongue to him. In 1892, at the age of 27, he returned to Urumia.[328]

References and Related Readings

Guilak, Hooshang (2011) *Fire Beneath the Ashes: The United States and Iran: A Historical Perspective 1829-1947.* Xlibris Publishing.

Rockwell, William W. (1916). *The Pitiful Plight of the Assyrian Christians in Persia and Kurdistan.* New York: American Committee for Armenian and Syrian Relief.

Shedd, Mary Lewis (1922). *The Measure of a Man: The Life of William Ambrose Shedd, Missionary to Persia.* New York: Gordon H. Doran Company.

Shedd, William A. (1912). *The Life of John Haskell Shedd.* Unpublished manuscript.

Wilson, Samuel. G. (1896). *Persia: Western Mission.* Philadelphia: Presbyterian Board of Publication and Sabbath-School Work.

---

[328] In 1907 he was granted the degree of Doctor of Divinity by Marietta College, and from thereon, he was addressed as Dr. William Shedd in most of the official correspondences. Marietta was also John Shedd's alma mater, where he too had obtained his Doctor of Divinity degree decades earlier.

Chapter 28

SHEDD'S GROWING ROLE IN THE URUMIA MISSION STATION

By 1892, the health of Shedd's father was deteriorating. John Haskell Shedd had to gradually remove himself from many of the duties associated with being the head of the Urumia mission station. Similar to how Cochran's decision to return to Urumia was motivated by the need to fill the gap by the passing of his father, Shedd was also compelled to be present in Urumia due to his father's failing health.

The year 1892 was a difficult one in Urumia and the entire region due to the resurgence of cholera. In addition to the health risks posed by the national outbreak of cholera, Persia was beginning to feel political unrest due to public protests against the Tobacco Concession, which had been granted to Great Britain by Naser al-Din Shah two years earlier. This fifty-year concession gave the British monopolistic powers over the production, sale, and export of tobacco products. It would force local producers to sell their products to agents of this concession, under unfavorable terms. Price controls over tobacco products were also to be handed over to the concession agents. The unfavorable terms for Persians created economic distress and social unrest. They prompted Persia's Islamic authorities to announce a religious ruling ("fatwa"), whereby the consumption of tobacco was banned. The public resistance to the concession represented a landmark event in Persian politics, whereby the orders given by Persia's Islamic clergy effectively superseded concessions made by a king. The end result was the cancellation of the concession in 1892.

The success of the Islamic clergy to force a reversal of the Shah's agreement with the British opened a new chapter in Persian politics. It demonstrated the immense power of Islam in controlling politics and society in Persia. The following extract from an 1892 dispatch from the American Legation in Tehran to the American State Department summarizes the American views on the monopoly and how it helped increase anti-foreigner sentiments throughout Persia:

> When the foreign tobacco monopoly commenced its work in Persia, the mollahs, Persian priests, announced to the people that tobacco was unclean. They forbid them to smoke while tobacco was handled by foreigners. The leading priest represented to the King that the concession he had given to a company of foreigners to control the cultivation and sale of tobacco in Persia was inconsistent with the doctrines of the Koran and of Islam. They demanded an abolition of the concession.... the attempt to control its sale by an English company had influenced the fanatical hatred here of all foreigners.[329]

As evident from the above communication, one of the end effects of the tobacco concession was a dislike for foreigners by sectors of the Persian public. As noted in earlier chapters, Cochran had also mentioned this effect in his correspondences from this time period. In the years to come, the scale of concessions given to European powers by the Shah would increase, resulting in more protests by the Persian public. In 1901, the Qajar government granted extraction rights to William D'Arcy, a British subject. The concession allowed D'Arcy to explore, extract, transport, and market petroleum from Persia's oil fields for a period of sixty years. The terms of the concession were highly unfavorable to the Persians, who would only receive 16% of the generated profits.[330]

---

[329] Source: US Department of State Digital Archives: https://history.state.gov/historicaldocuments/frus1892/d295 accessed 1/8/2021.
[330] Since the Persian revenue intake was based on a fixed percentage of D'Arcy's generated profits (rather than revenues), it was affected by questionable accounting practices in computing the costs of the drilling and oil extraction operations, which

It took decades before the Persians could cancel the oil concession. The D'Arcy and tobacco concessions, along with other Western-inspired influences in Persia caused public resentment against Western powers. Similar sentiments were felt elsewhere in the world, where imperial powers exercising their economic leverage had caused anti-Western sentiments. A notable example of this was the Boxer Rebellion in China, which was in motion at approximately the same time period.[331] It was a result of discontent with Western influences around the end of the nineteenth century and was initially in reaction to the favorable terms that Western missionaries were able to arrange for their converts in China.[332]

Upon his return in 1892, Shedd was placed in charge of several critical roles at the Urumia mission station. He served as treasurer, head of the Mission press, and the superintendent of the churches, village schools, and outfields. As he entered his late 20s, the expectations of him taking on leadership responsibilities like his father were becoming more apparent. However, the mentoring he would have received from his father was not to last long, as John Shedd passed away in April of 1895. This was only several weeks after Cochran had also lost his wife. The two men shared a great deal of grief and pain in these trying times. In 1896, Shedd's mother returned to America after serving in the Mission for a quarter of a century.

Recognizing the challenges of the tensions, instability, and growing violence in the Urumia area, Shedd was often called upon to villages and towns where such violence was directed at the communities that the Mission served. He wrote about his relief work in the Salmas-Khoi region, reflecting on the difficulty of being an observer to the human suffering resulting from the violence, much of which related to cross-border tensions in the region:

---

were not subject to Persian audit, and at the mercy of D'Arcy's choice of cost accounting methods.

[331] Preston (2001), *The Boxer Rebellion*.

[332] It is important to note that the Boxer Rebellion (1899-1901) was initially mobilized in reaction to the presence of Western missionaries from various Christian denominations. The rebels believed that the missionaries had facilitated favorable social terms for their converts, unavailable to the average Chinese citizen, and that they were promoting the replacement of Chinese values with those of the West.

I never saw such pitiful creatures, poor little children, fatherless and motherless. I was glad to have something to help them.... It is all 'unstable equilibrium' till some righteous revenge is taken for the blood spilled in Turkey. Things can't be settled till they're settled right, and Persia cannot entirely escape the consequences of affairs in Turkey.[333]

Returning from this trip, Shedd was so disturbed about the darkness he had witnessed that he at one point seemed to have questioned God altogether. The fact that in his writing, Shedd was reflecting on his struggles in finding God is a unique display of genuine expression, especially for a man of strong faith. He wrote:

It seemed as if the Lord was wrestling with me and I must not let Him go. It was to me a conviction of sin, of righteousness and of judgment — a revelation of my worthlessness, weakness and sinfulness. One sin after another was shown to me in its true hideousness. At the same time I felt God very near; perhaps in the way meant in saying 'He that is near Me is near the fire.' It was a revelation of my utter inability to do anything and God's readiness to do everything. The Lord has humbled me as I have never been humbled before.[334]

In Shedd's view, the Persian Constitutional Revolution, despite its good intentions, had managed to force distress in the Urumia area. In some cases, the local government in Urumia, in order to retaliate against the revolutionists, would punish the innocent in their place:

As is always the case with this poor misgoverned land, the innocent suffer with the guilty, or oftener instead of the guilty. I saw one poor man in the street in front of the Governor's door who was dying and did die a few hours later. He was an innocent man who had been arrested to fill the vacancy of an escaped Revolutionist. He died from the effects of the beating and branding he had received in the Persian prison.[335]

The form of punishment that Shedd was describing is a form of an-eye-for-an-eye punishment, central to the modes of justice in tribal settings. As unjust and primitive as this appears, what Shedd had witnessed was consistent with the tribal mindset of the region at that

---

[333] Shedd (1922), *The Measure of a Man*, p. 62.

[334] Ibid., p. 63.

[335] Ibid., p. 62.

time and was a practice commonly used in the mountains where institutionalized judicial systems were absent and armed tribal engagement were commonplace.

Interestingly, Shedd's observation was consistent with what Grant had witnessed in his journeys through the Kurdish mountains of Turkey decades earlier. In one case, Grant had described staying overnight in a Kurdish village in 1839. The villagers were in a quarrel with a neighboring village to equalize their human losses, which they had incurred in an earlier dispute. Grant's description has great similarity to Shedd's:

> At night we lodged in a Koordish hamlet, where the people had a blood-feud with another village through which we passed, and which lay in sight. Three men had been killed from one of them, and only two from the other, and now the former were trying to make up the balance by deliberately murdering their neighbours, and thus the quarrel would finally be settled.[336]

Other incidents of similar nature were noted by Grant among Nestorians. Grant described an account of a quarrel between the sons of two Nestorian brothers in the family of his host in the Hakkari region:

> One of these boys went out to cut down a valuable tree, in the absence of the parents of both, who were brothers. His cousin forbade him, saying the tree belonged to his own father. But the first boy persevered, while the other went and brought out his gun, and deliberately shot his cousin dead upon the spot. An indelible stain would now rest upon the family of the murdered boy, unless vengeance was satisfied according to immemorial usage; and the bereaved father, who was the legal avenger of blood, could accept of nothing but the blood of his brother's child, and they were both buried in one grave before the setting of another sun! [337]

In the case that Shedd was describing, the innocent man was treated as a proxy for the guilty individual who could not be found and arrested. This required him to receive the punishment for them, creating a sense of balance between the two conflicting sides (in this case, the Revolutionists and the Urumia government). This is despite the fact that the individual being punished was actually innocent, and his only

---

[336] Grant (1841), *The Nestorians, or, the Lost Tribes,* pp. 44-45.
[337] Ibid., p. 72.

fault was that he was suspected of being a Revolutionist. The insanity of this situation demonstrates that while embedded as a means for administering justice, this approach to establishing justice cannot achieve peace, and as will be seen later in this book, resulted in an incomprehensible escalation of tribal and religiously-inspired violence in the years leading to the First World War.

Furlough to America

The turn of the century had introduced added challenges to Shedd's life. In 1901, his first wife, Adela L. Myers, passed away after having been ill for several years. The couple had married in Urumia in 1894 and had two young daughters, Susan and Margaret (Daisy). Related to her death, Shedd wrote: "In some ways the difficulties all come over me as time passes, especially as regards my children. They are beautiful little girls, three and six years old, and I realize how hard it is to mother them and how much they need what I can give them so imperfectly."[338]

In 1902, having served for the past ten years in Urumia, Shedd left Urumia, on furlough to visit America. He was in America for a little over a year. During his visit, he taught a course on the *Historical Relations of Islam and the Oriental Churches* at Princeton University. The lectures eventually became the basis for his book titled *Islam and the Oriental Churches*.

In 1903, he traveled to California and married fellow missionary Louise Wilbur, who was also on furlough in America at that time. They married in April of that year. The two had been missionary colleagues in Urumia, where Louise was a teacher of the missionary children for several years, and then became the principal of the Fiske Seminary. In the years that followed, the couple had two daughters, Bertha and Louise, both born in Urumia.

---

[338] Shedd (1922), *The Measure of a Man,* p. 69.

The Shedd Family (April 1908):
William Shedd and Louise Wilbur Shedd with their Four Children (left-to-right):
Daisy (Margaret), Bertha, Louise, Susan

References and Related Readings

Grant, Asahel (1841). *The Nestorians, or, The Lost Tribes.* London: John Murray.

Lottridge, Celia B. (2010). *Home is Beyond the Mountains.* Toronto: Groundwood Books.

Preston, Diana (2001). *The Boxer Rebellion: The Dramatic Story of China's War on Foreigners That Shook the World in the Summer of 1900.* New York: Walker & Company.

Said, Edward W. (1994). *Culture and Imperialism.* New York: Vintage Books.

Said, Edward W. (1979). *Orientalism.* New York: Vintage Books.

Shedd, Margaret (1967). *Hosannah Tree*. Garden City, NY: Doubleday & Company.

Shedd, Mary Lewis (1922). *The Measure of a Man: The Life of William Ambrose Shedd, Missionary to Persia*. New York: Gordon H. Doran Company.

Chapter 29

SHEDD AND THE LEGAL BOARD OF THE EVANGELICAL CHURCH

After his return to Urumia and Cochran's passing in 1905, Shedd had to take on a growing role in representing the Mission on various matters related to the Persian government. He also had to take on responsibilities that Cochran used to have with the Legal Board of the Syrian Evangelical Church. At the time of Cochran's passing, the frequency and intensity of tribal clashes in the area were on the rise. There were also violent political factions who associated themselves with the Constitutional Revolutionists, which caused chaos and lawlessness in Persian Azerbaijan. In this new environment, Shedd would spend a great deal of his time on cases associated with the Legal Board.

Shedd's increased responsibilities at the Mission required him to be the Mission's spokesperson with the Persian government. Regular contact with Persian government officials and Urumia's local leaders allowed him to apply his unique relationship-building skills. The experience helped him develop further into a resourceful authority figure that many people approached for advice and guidance, especially in times of turmoil.

Shedd's labors with the Legal Board were essential since at that time the legal protections that applied to non-Moslems were different from what applied to the Moslem population of Persia. The Legal Board's task was to settle issues among church members so that they could be settled without the need to resort to Persian courts. Membership on the Board was decided by a church committee, elected by its members, and one missionary was also designated to be on the Board.

Lawlessness Resulting from Border Skirmishes

One of the reasons for Shedd's increased engagement in the Legal Board was that the degree of lawlessness in the Urumia region was on the rise during the early 1900s. Being so close to the Turkish border, the region was constantly agitated by forces allied with the Ottomans. Some of the turmoil was a result of the deployment of 1,500 Persian soldiers as an expeditionary force to retrieve the 13 accomplices that had participated in the murder of Benjamin Woods Labaree in 1904. These men had worked under the instructions of Ghafar, who himself had murdered an Assyrian man (M.G. Daniel) the same year, as detailed in earlier chapters.

On the insistence of the American government, the Persian expeditionary force had been deployed to retrieve and bring to justice the 13 men. However, these men had escaped across the border to Turkey, alongside their nomadic tribe. The presence of the Persian expeditionary force resulted in numerous skirmishes in the border region and agitated some of the Kurdish tribes, causing them to side with the Turks in repelling the Persian troops. On the Persian side of the border, sympathizers with Ghafar's tribe were revengeful toward some of the Christian villages of the highlands to the west of Urumia.

These sympathizers in the border region were being encouraged by the Ottomans to attack the Urumia region, and when they complied, they took over much of the countryside to the west of Lake Urumia. The mobilization of these Kurdish forces was made under increased Pan-Islamist rhetoric that the Ottoman Sultan, Abdul Hamid II, had advocated over the years. His religiously fueled messages gave those sympathizing with Ghafar encouragement and a marching order to attack the villages in the Urumia area where many Christians lived.

Despite the fact that Persian territory was being compromised, the local government forces felt conflicted in their desire to counter these attacks, and did not put up a convincing defense to deter such attacks. One reason was the Persian concern that by reacting swiftly, they would be escalating the conflict further and provoke Persia's Kurds. This, the Persians feared, could mobilize Persian Kurds so that the entire region would become a hotbed for an independent Kurdish state.

The other reason for Persia's lack of a forceful defense was aspirational rather than strategic. Among the local Persian and Kurdish masses in Persian Azerbaijan, the Russians were viewed as Christian occupiers. During the early 1800s, Russia had taken over parts of northwestern Persia, such as Dagestan, Baku, Shirvan, and Ganja. The Turks shared the same experience with Russia in having lost territories to Russia in the nineteenth century. For decades, the Russian policy towards both Persia and Turkey was one of intimidation and domination. This was further reinforced in Persia, when Persian efforts for seeking a democratic constitutional government were crushed, at times directly using Russian military forces.[339] As such, Persia's masses and the Turks historically shared an intense animosity toward the Russians, and by proxy, their Christian allies in the region, among whom were the Christian minorities of Persian Azerbaijan.

The closeness felt between the Persians of northwestern Persia and the Turks was further strengthened by the fact that the common language of communication in this region is Azari (a dialect of Turkish). In fact, Persians from this region were (and still are) referred to as "Turks." The cultural, linguistic, and historical connections between Ottoman Turks and the Persian Turks of northwestern Persia made it less likely for the Persians to repel attacks by Turks or their Kurdish allies. By repelling the Turks, the Persians would have strengthened the Russians, which in their minds were uninvited occupiers of Persia. Therefore, the Turkish-inspired push by their Kurdish allies into the Urumia region was not effectively repelled by the Persians.[340]

---

[339] For example, in 1908, only two years after the 1906 signing of the Persian Constitution, Russian troops bombed the Iranian Parliament building in Tehran.

[340] This theme was to continue for many years, including the years of the First World War.

The Persian Constitution of 1906

Shedd's assignment to the Legal Board coincided with drastic changes in the national politics of Persia. During the first decade of the twentieth century, the hunger for establishing a constitution led to protests and civil unrest throughout the country. A constitution was established and signed into law by Mozaffar ad-Din Shah in 1906. The preparedness of the Persian public, who from time immemorial had been ruled by oppressive monarchs was in question. Democratic institutions had the potential to propel the nation into an elevated state of political maturity, and could have facilitated social equity and prosperity. However, such a drastic change had never been successfully implemented before in Persia, or the region.

The most recent example in this part of the world would have been the 1876 establishment of a constitution in Turkey by the New Ottomans, which was abandoned within two years. The big question in 1906 in Persia was whether a constitutional form of government would bring order or anarchy. Mary Lewis Shedd reflected on this question:

> The Persian Revolution, which began in Teheran, soon reached Urumia, and what was at first a general unrest became an active protest against the prevailing order of political corruption, feudal oppression, and despotic injustice. The people, following the lead of Teheran and Tabriz, demanded a representative government. An *anjuman* or council of the people, was formed in which were represented the various classes of society. The movement, though unexpected, was popular and patriotic, intellectual as well as political. It was inevitable that such a revolution among a people to whom the idea of representative government was so foreign and for which they were wholly unprepared, should lead through anarchy and chaos to collapse. The granting of the Constitution by the Shah was celebrated in Urumia by the illumination of the bazaars, where large crowds gathered full of enthusiasm for the new day that had dawned for *Iran*. Mullahs and sayids were enthusiastically talking of liberty and equality, with little conception of their meaning, but the road between Oriental despotism and democracy is not traveled in a day nor in a generation.[341]

---

[341] Shedd (1922), *The Measure of a Man,* p. 80.

In 1906, after much public pressure and years of social unrest, the Persian Constitution was signed into law by Mozaffar ad-Din Shah. He died in 1907. His son, Mohammad Ali Shah, in 1908, abolished the constitution and banned the Parliament, with direct Russian assistance.[342] The time period between the events leading to the initial signing of the constitution and its reinstatement at the end of the decade was one of great turmoil, and is referred to as the Persian Constitutional Revolution. Those advocating for the constitution and its return were referred to as Constitutional Revolutionists. Despite their common interests, the political sentiments and organizational structure of the Constitutional Revolutionists varied significantly from one part of the country to the other.

Citizen Army or 'Fidais' in Tabriz (photo taken by William Shedd in 1907)

---

[342] The abolition of the Persian Constitution and the disbanding of the Persian Parliament by Mohammad Ali Shah within two years of the establishment of the 1906 constitution have close resemblance to the timing of the same sequence of events with respect to the Ottoman Constitution of 1876, which was abolished by Sultan Abdul Hamid II in 1878.

Democratic efforts in Persia, such as the establishment of a constitution, were viewed negatively by the Russians, as they would weaken Mohammad Ali Shah. The establishment of democratic institutions could also weaken Russia's grip on Persia and reduce Russia's ability to benefit from economic and military concessions granted to it by Mohammad Ali Shah. Therefore, it was no surprise that Russia supported Mohammad Ali Shah's efforts in abolishing the 1906 constitution and disbanding the Parliament.

In 1909, Mohammad Ali Shah was forced out of power by the Persian Constitutional Revolutionists, and the constitution was reinstated. Russia's forceful and manipulative treatment of Persia and its support of the deposed Shah created strong anti-Russian sentiments within the Persian population at that time. Due to Russia's oppressive actions prior to and during the Constitutional Revolution, the general Persian public viewed Russia as an occupier and oppressor.

Position Reversal on the Murderers

In 1907, one of the lingering issues affecting the American missionaries in Urumia was the punishment of the 13 men who had participated in the murder of Labaree. While the Constitutional Revolution was in progress throughout Persia, Kurdish sympathizers to these men in the highlands to the west of Urumia, had revenge on their minds. They were especially disturbed by the presence of the Persian expeditionary force deployed to the area at the insistence of the American missionaries and the American government. Skirmishes with the expeditionary force were not uncommon, and to the Kurds, the presence of this force appeared as a form of occupation.

Because of the potential for revengeful actions by these sympathizers, there was a great deal of insecurity felt by the American missionaries and their families in Urumia. The Mission went as far as asking the newly appointed American Consul in Tabriz, William Doty to negotiate a peaceful settlement with the Kurds to bring down the temperature. The proposal was for Doty to accompany Persian government forces entering Turkey (with Turkey's consent) to meet with the accused men and let them know that the American government no longer sought punishment against them.[343] Doty was willing to carry out this dangerous task, but was not given approval by the American State Department.

At the same time, the Mission asked the American ambassador in Turkey to ask Turkey to persuade its Kurdish allies in the Urumia region, who were among the sympathizers of Ghafar to cease their attacks on Christian villagers. The Mission clearly wanted to lower the tensions and not aggravate the situation any further. However, Persia's intent in deploying the expeditionary force may have been to achieve more than just the arrest of the accomplices who had participated in Labaree's murder. The Persian army used this situation as an opportunity to strengthen its military deployment in areas where border tensions with Turkey were rising. The presence of the Persian expeditionary force in pursuit of those protecting the accused men became the pretext for Turkey to react by invading northwestern Persia.

Ottoman Forces in Persia with Captured Persian Cannon (photo taken by William Shedd in 1907)

---

[343] Yeselson (1956), *United States-Persian Diplomatic Relations: 1883-1921*, p.74.

In August of 1907, Ottoman troops alongside their Kurdish allies crossed the Persian border and entered Persian Azerbaijan. While they did not attack or occupy Urumia, they took over most of the territory to the west of Urumia.[344] At that time there were 14 American missionaries and their families living in Urumia. This caused great concern in Washington, especially in light of the missionaries' earlier plea for a peaceful ending to the Labaree case.

Ottoman intrusion into Persian territory began a long period of border disputes between the two countries. The Ottoman action prompted the constant presence of Russian troops in northwestern Persia. The Turkish occupation of the area also upset relations between Persia and America. Persian diplomats and government officials blamed America for being the cause of the Turkish invasion. They argued that America's insistence on capturing the assailants that had taken refuge in Turkey was the reason for the deployment of the Persian expeditionary force. The presence of this force in response to American insistence is what provoked Turkey to retaliate by invading parts of northwestern Persia. Persian citizens died as a result, and massive property losses had also occurred.[345]

Having America blamed for the Turkish occupation of Persia was not helpful in improving the Persian public's perceptions of the American missionaries in Urumia. In 1907, Persian distrust of foreigners continued to grow because of a secret agreement between the British and Russians regarding Persia. The two had agreed to divide the country into northern and southern spheres of influence. This was done without the Persian government's approval or the knowledge of the Persian public. In effect, the scope and boundaries for economic concessions and military deployments of Russia and Britain were pre-defined by this secret agreement. In some parts of Persia, news of the secret deal caused Persian nationalism to be confused with anti-Christian bigotry. For some sectors of the Persian population, the British and Russians were primarily viewed as Christian powers. To them, the 1907 agreement reflected negatively on all Christians, including their own. These sentiments were further amplified in northwestern Persia, where due to Ottoman intrusion beyond the Turco-Persian border, Russian forces were constantly present on Persian

---

[344] They remained there until 1912.
[345] Yeselson (1956), *United States-Persian Diplomatic Relations: 1883-1921*, p. 77.

lands. Therefore, while the changing attitude toward Christians may not have been a national matter, it was uniquely evident in northwestern Persia, where most of the country's Christians lived and Russian presence was constantly felt.

The public discontent produced by the 1907 secret agreement between Britain and Russia was further compounded by a general state of disorder in the country, resulting from a shift from a pure monarchy to a constitutional form of government. The potential for chaos in this rapidly evolving and seemingly ungoverned political climate was significant. Mary Lewis Shedd elaborated on the loss of control experienced by local Persian government officials in light of the growing powers gained by forces claiming pro-democratic positions in Urumia. The result was a rise in lawlessness and increased potential for anarchy in the city:

> *Fidais*, or devotees, organized with parades of armed men, drill and political meetings. There were popular organizations composed of representative of the bazaar, shopkeepers, artisans, porters and the like. Each organization demanded a share in the government which was divided among the Governor, *anjuman* leaders of the *fidais*, and representatives of the trade. Sometimes the Governor by exercising great tact in keeping on speaking terms with the various elements was able to retain some of his authority. Sometimes there was no government at all, with disorder and crime uncontrolled and constant danger from mobs.[346]

The Martyrdom of Howard Baskerville

By 1908, the official American position was that if the escaped nomadic tribesmen responsible for Labaree's murder were to return to Persia and were not punished, the American government would not object. America no longer had an interest in pursuing redemption because Labaree's widow had been paid a large compensation for his death and Ghafar had died of natural causes in prison. As such, the decision as to whether or not there would be any form of punishment for the 13 accomplices who had now escaped to Turkey was left with

---

[346] Shedd (1922), *The Measure of a Man*, p. 82.

the Persian government. It was a matter in which the American government no longer desired to intervene.

In 1909, the death of Howard Conklin Baskerville, an American citizen working in northwestern Persia would engage America again.[347] Mohammad Ali Shah had, in the previous year, abolished the constitution. His actions had sparked a revolutionary fire within Persia. Armed resistance against his government had engulfed the nation, creating a period referred to as the Persian Constitutional Revolution. Tabriz had become a role model for all of Persia for resistance against Mohammad Ali Shah. A sizeable armed contingent of Constitutional Revolutionists, led by a legendary commander named Sattar Khan, had gained control of the city. Tabriz was then surrounded by Persian Cossack army forces, which were trained and led by Russian officers. The forces encircling Tabriz were further reinforced with Russian troops. Due to the military encirclement of Tabriz, the city was deprived of essentials and food, and a state of famine ensued.

Howard C. Baskerville

---

[347] Shafaq (1976), *Howard Baskerville.*

Baskerville was a young, energetic, passionate 24-year-old from Nebraska. He had graduated from Princeton University in 1907, where he had been a student of Woodrow Wilson.[348] After graduation from Princeton, he came to Persia to work as a teacher in the American Memorial School, run by the American Presbyterian Mission in Tabriz. Having seen the devastation caused by the famine, attributed to the military encirclement of Tabriz, and having spent time with a fellow Persian teacher at the American Memorial School, Baskerville developed strong pro-revolution sentiments.

The murder of his fellow teacher emboldened his commitment to militant resistance and the cause of the Persian Constitutional Revolution. When Samuel Wilson, the head of the Presbyterian Mission in Tabriz found out about Baskerville's intentions to take up arms alongside the Constitutional Revolutionists, he discouraged him from interfering in the internal matters of Persia. Wilson pleaded with Baskerville to focus on his regular duties as a teacher. A similar and even more direct request was expressed by William Doty, the American Consul in Tabriz, who attempted to confiscate Baskerville's American passport.

Baskerville ignored both men and in 1908 resigned from his post as a teacher. He continued with his military training in preparation for armed engagement with the Russian-backed forces surrounding Tabriz. His former students from the American Memorial School who also had pro-revolution sentiments joined his training regiments. He was also joined by an Irish journalist named W.A. Moore, who was working as a reporter in Tabriz on behalf of a British newspaper.

In the early hours of the morning of April 19, 1909, Baskerville was joined by a small number of revolutionists to attempt to break the siege in order to smuggle food into Tabriz. In the darkness of the morning hours, Baskerville advanced close to the outer boundaries of the city. A shot was fired in his direction. He fired back. Lacking military experience, he had not realized that he would be giving away his exact position to the enemy by firing his weapon at such a dark hour, and was shot in the chest by a sniper. He died that morning in the

---

[348] Woodrow Wilson was the president of Princeton University and a professor while Baskerville studied there. He later became the United States president.

arms of one of his former students who had come to aid him. Moore lived to report and write about the incident.

The next day, mass ceremonies were held in Baskerville's honor in Tabriz. He instantly became a national hero for Persians and was recognized as a martyr for the Persian Constitutional Revolution. Shortly after his funeral, under the premise of intending to break open the city to provide food supplies to its citizens, Russian-backed government forces entered Tabriz and occupied the city. Baskerville's siding with the Persian Constitutional Revolutionists and his sacrifice have made him a legend for Iranians. He is still today considered a martyr by modern Iranians and there is a memorial sculpture dedicated to him in Tabriz to honor his memory.

While the Persian Constitutional Revolutionists were in awe of Baskerville's sacrifice, his actions countered the policy of non-interference of the American mission stations in Persia. This is especially important to recognize since he was a teacher at the American mission station in Tabriz. Prior to his death, Baskerville had been given several warnings not to engage in armed action by Doty and Wilson, which he ignored.

Even though the Tabriz mission station mourned his loss, the fact that Baskerville had taken up arms put his legacy at great odds with the policies of the Presbyterian Board of Foreign Missions and American diplomatic norms in Persia. Similar to the Urumia mission station, the Tabriz mission station had benefited from protection by the Russians and the Persian government, especially at times when Mission facilities and staff were in danger. Having one of its teachers take armed action against Russian-backed Persian government forces was out-of-line with the norms of the Presbyterian Board's mandate in Persia.

While Baskerville was recognized by the Persian public as a martyr for supporting Persia's democratic cause, his death did not get nearly as much attention by Americans in Persia or America. The American missionaries believed that Baskerville should have kept himself out of Persia's internal matters altogether. Therefore, while Baskerville became a national hero for Persians, his mention is rarely found in American missionary writings. He was mostly forgotten, even though he was a teacher at an American mission school, a Presbyterian, and an

American. In a letter addressed to renowned Orientalist Edward G. Browne, a year after Baskerville's passing, William Shedd wrote:

> I think that there is no doubt whatever of Mr. Baskerville's worthiness to be ranked as a martyr, perhaps the more so as he found a good deal to disappoint him and still held on. The Mission, of course, is precluded by its position from espousing a political cause, and Mr. Baskerville's act was a private one.[349]

Continued Anarchy in the Urumia Region

In the Urumia region, the dynamics of the interactions between the invading forces of Turkey, the Kurds, the Persians, the local Constitutional Revolutionists, and the Islamic clergy of Urumia created a confusing political climate and contributed to chaos and human suffering. As a result, invasion efforts by Kurdish forces backed by Turkey and by Turkey's own troops were not effectively repelled by genuine efforts by the Persian defenders. Instead, the attacks on predominately Christian villages resulted in masses of refugees fleeing to Urumia. Thousands of refugees flocked the Mission compound to seek protection and shelter. To create some balance, the Persian government decided to arm some of the Christians so that they would be able to defend themselves. This was a helpful measure in keeping a balance in the short-term, but further militarized the region in the long-term.

To demonstrate the degree of lawlessness, Mary Lewis Shedd cited a case in 1909 of the arrest of the governor of Urumia by a constitutional revolutionist leader, who came there overnight.[350] He forced the sitting governor into exile and announced himself as the new one. He was in charge of the city for several weeks, and in that time, exhorted large sums of money from Urumia's affluent families. However, after a few weeks, with no advance notice, he left town overnight, taking with him all the exhorted money. In the morning, no one knew who was in charge. The previous governor returned a few weeks later, with the armed support of the very same group that had put the bandit make-shift governor in place. The lines of loyalty and

---

[349] Browne (1910), *The Persian Revolution of 1905-1909*, p. 441.
[350] Shedd (1922), *The Measure of a Man*, p. 82.

political alliances were blurred, contributing to confusion, chaos, and lawlessness.

References and Related Readings

Afary, Janet (1996). *The Iranian Constitutional Revolution, 1906-1911.* New York: Columbia University Press.

Browne, Edward G. (1910). *The Persian Revolution of 1905-1909.* Cambridge: Cambridge University Press.

Keddie, Nikki (1980). *Iran: Religion, Politics, and Society.* London: Frank Cass and Company Ltd.

Ryder, C.H.D. (1925). "The Demarcation of the Turco-Persian Boundary in 1913-14," *The Geographical Journal*, Vol. 66, No. 3, pp. 227-237.

Shafaq, S.R. (1976). "Howard Baskerville," in Ali Pasha Saleh (ed.), *Cultural Ties Between Iran and the United States.* Tehran: Bistopanj-e-Sharivar.

Shedd, Mary Lewis (1922). *The Measure of a Man: The Life of William Ambrose Shedd, Missionary to Persia.* New York: Gordon H. Doran Company.

Yeselson, Abraham (1956). *United States-Persian Diplomatic Relations: 1883-1921.* New Brunswick: Rutgers University Press.

Chapter 30

"THE STRANGLING OF PERSIA"

By the end of 1909, Shedd had developed incipient tuberculosis. He was generally weak for most of the following year. The family traveled to Switzerland for several months in 1910 so that he could rest and rejuvenate. They then headed to America and stayed there until the fall of 1911. At the time of their return, Persia was still experiencing significant challenges due to the country's rapidly declining economic state. The finances of the country were in disarray, due to the government's inability to collect taxes and the overwhelming weight of loan obligations to the Russians and the British.

The Persians could not trust either the British or the Russians to advise them on treasury and taxation matters. On numerous occasions, Britain and Russia had both taken advantage of Persia's economic vulnerabilities, as noted in earlier chapters. Finding an appropriately experienced and trustworthy treasurer to resolve the nation's finances became a necessity. The Persians hesitated to assign a Persian citizen to this task due to potential conflicts of interest that could arise and a shortage of candidates with the necessary technical skills to lead the nation's treasury operations.

Unable to rely on the Russians, the British, or their own, the Persians approached the American State Department for help in identifying a competent American administrator to take on the role of

Treasurer General of Persia. Several candidates were considered, and an American named Morgan Shuster was identified and introduced through the Persian legation in Washington.[351] Though only 34 years old, Shuster had an outstanding resume and had demonstrated an ability to bring order to chaotic systems of administration. He had established an effective taxation system in the Philippines and later served as the director of customs in Cuba. He had a reputation for being a person of high integrity, and the Persian Parliament enthusiastically approved his three-year appointment. Shuster was to serve as a private American citizen and was not a representative or agent of the American government. The Persians were hopeful that he would help them clean up the corruption and mismanagement that had drained the nation's treasury.

Morgan Shuster

---

[351] Shuster was commonly addressed using his middle name, as Morgan Shuster, omitting his first name, William. In his writings he would identify himself as W. Morgan Shuster.

Shuster arrived in Tehran in May of 1911. Despite a warm early reception, his work quickly became increasingly difficult due to resistance from wealthy Persians and government officials who were troubled by his ability to quickly identify and isolate cases of mismanagement and internal government corruption. His appointment was also problematic for the Russians and the British, who viewed him as a catalyst for change, through which they could see their own loss of control over Persia's finances.

The most pressing concern for Persia's treasury related to tax collection. It was a process administered through a hierarchy of local and regional tax collectors, who often pocketed most of the collections. To address this issue, Shuster began plans for the establishment of a gendarmerie of over ten thousand men, purely dedicated to the task of tax collection. He saw this as the only way to establish an effective and transparent tax collection system in Persia.

While attempting to improve the country's finances and modernize budgeting and taxation processes, Shuster seemed to have offended many powerful groups. He had also aggravated Russian and British agents and diplomats, who were offended by his directness and persistence. The Russians were especially disturbed by Shuster's decision to assign a non-Russian as the head of the gendarmerie in charge of tax collection. Shuster's efforts to root out corruption were resisted by those who flourished in the old system, including Persia's wealthy and bureaucrats.

By November of 1911, the Russians seemed to have had enough of Shuster. With implicit approval of the British, they insisted that he must resign and leave the country. Russia threatened that if Shuster did not leave, it would invade northern Persia. The Persian Parliament voted to determine a response to Russia's ultimatum and rejected it. Russia's proposal represented a clear violation of Persia's independence. Russian forces were deployed and reached north of Tehran. They also surrounded Tabriz and continued their demand for Shuster's departure. British troops had also begun deployment in southern Persia, starting earlier in 1911, to counter potential Russian movements further south toward the Persian Gulf.[352]

For the Persian nation, it seemed that just because of Shuster, despite his good intentions, the entire country was being invaded. Russian troops occupied Tehran, and the 14-year-old Ahmad Shah was forced by the Russians to dissolve the Parliament and expel Shuster. Shuster's departure was under the escort of the Shah's personal motorcade.

He later described in detail the financial and administrative mischiefs that he had witnessed, in his book titled the *The Strangling of Persia*. His recollections of the events that he observed and the individuals he interacted with document in detail the depth of corruption that plagued Persia's finances. Shuster's mission to Persia was demonstrative of the chaotic nature of Qajar rule and the absence of central administrative authority in Persia at that time.

The Persia that Shedd was returning to was the one that Shuster was escaping from. It was a growingly unstable country, especially in the Urumia region. It was in this area where the issue of the exact line of separation of Turkish and Persian lands had caused an international dispute in 1904.[353] This dispute had been elevated by the events that followed the murder of Labaree and the Persian army's pursuit of the men responsible for his murder.

The Persian expeditionary force deployed to the region engaged in skirmishes with Ottoman border posts and their Kurdish allies, which reignited long-held territorial disputes. The presence of Russian forces in northern Persia further ignited military confrontations in the area. The pursuit of the men responsible for Labaree's murder also resulted in the death of Persian and Turkish soldiers and civilians and the

---

[352] The British sought to prevent a possible Russian invasion of northern Persia from continuing southward, thereby threatening British interests in the Persian Gulf and India. This was consistent with Britain's strategic approaches to counter anticipated Russian approaches to India, under the umbrella of what is referred to as the "Great Game" as described by Hopkirk (1992), *The Great Game: The Struggle for Empire in Central Asia*.

[353] Although the Turco-Persian border had been agreed upon in the 16th century, much of the one-thousand-mile border which extended from Mount Ararat down to the Persian Gulf had been unmarked, and as a result, the exact dividing line between the two countries was undetermined in many sections of the frontier.

revival of concerns over the poorly defined Turco-Persian boundary. Determining the exact position of the boundary was essential, as northwestern Persia had great logistical value.

The road system in this region connected the Russian Railway through its station in Julfa to critical travel hubs such as the Persian town of Khoi and the Turkish city of Van. Therefore, from a logistical perspective, especially as it relates to troop and supply movements, it was a prized territory. Settling the exact line of division between Persia and Turkey was of immense strategic importance for both countries. The more land each country could claim, the greater its influence would be in this strategic region.

To resolve the border dispute, a multi-nation commission which consisted of British, Russian, Turkish, and Persian representatives had to settle the matter. Despite numerous meetings and considerable diplomatic efforts, the commission could not agree on the exact position of the border. Neither the Russians nor the Turks were in a rush to establish the border. They both benefited from the confusion that existed regarding the dividing line between Persia and Turkey. It took until 1913 before some form of agreement could be reached.

Turco-Persian Border Commission at Work

As a result of the long delay in marking the border, the Urumia region and the Persian frontiers to its west were lands of great confusion with regards to territorial rights. Clashes between villagers and nomadic tribes were not uncommon, and the Ottomans benefited from the instability. During this time, Russian presence in the region was essential to the Persians in order to ensure that Turkey does not permanently occupy the Urumia region. Furthermore, whenever the Russians were in occupation of the Urumia region, there was a greater level of safety and security for the Christians and the missionaries. The fact that Russia was a Christian nation and that the Russian Orthodox Church had aspirations of expansion by converting Assyrian Christians meant that Russia was naturally supportive and protective of the Assyrian population of the region.

It was only after the Constantinople Protocol of 1913, and the marking of the border using pillars the following year, that a formal agreement on the exact location of the boundary was reached. The thousand-mile border was eventually marked. The Ottomans were to lose the territory they had conquered in the Urumia region during their earlier occupations of the region, and their dissatisfaction led to additional border clashes. Shortly after the marking of the border, the entire region was engulfed in all-out war, during the opening scenes of the First World War, in 1914.

References and Related Readings

Daniel, Robert L. (1970). *American Philanthropy in the Near East: 1820-1960*. Athens, OH: Ohio University Press.

Hopkirk, Peter (1992). *The Great Game: The Struggle for Empire in Central Asia*. Tokyo: Kodansha International.

Keddie, Nikki (1980). *Iran: Religion, Politics, and Society*. London: Frank Cass and Company Ltd.

Ryder, C.H.D. (1925). "The Demarcation of the Turco-Persian Boundary in 1913-14," *The Geographical Journal*, Vol. 66, No. 3, pp. 227-237.

Shedd, Mary Lewis (1922). *The Measure of a Man: The Life of William Ambrose Shedd, Missionary to Persia*. New York: Gordon H. Doran Company.

Shuster, William Morgan (1912). *The Strangling of Persia*. New York: Century Company.

Chapter 31

OTTOMAN OCCUPATION OF URUMIA IN 1915

The First World War broke out in the summer of 1914. The Persian government declared neutrality but saw its lands used as battlefields and occupied at various times by the Ottomans in the northwest, the British to the south, and the Russians to the north.[354] Battles between Ottoman and Russian forces over the Caucasus eventually expanded into northwestern Persia. It had immediate effects on the Urumia region. Kurdish forces in Turkey's eastern regions were encouraged by the Ottomans to attack beyond the Persian border, which was still in dispute despite the Turco-Persian border agreement.

While coordinating the attacks with the Ottoman forces, the Kurdish forces under the leadership of Bedir Khan Bey's grandson also had aspirations of carving out an independent Kurdish state for themselves.[355] Just like Sheikh Obeidullah, who had invaded northwestern Persia in 1880 with the hopes of creating an independent state between Persia and Turkey, similar aspirations seemed to have motivated the Kurdish chieftains to take part in this attack.

---

[354] Keddie (1981), *Roots of Revolution*, p. 79.

[355] As discussed in earlier chapters, Bedir Khan was a Kurdish chieftain with whom Asahel Grant interacted in the early 1840s, and who was responsible for the massacre of Christians in eastern Turkey in 1842, 1843 and 1846. He was later exiled by the Ottomans, under European pressure.

Since the border between Turkey and Persia was still unstable, and the Ottomans desired the Persian territory to the west of Lake Urumia, Kurdish forces allied with the Ottomans were used as a proxy force, under Ottoman command, to advance into these lands. At that time, the Russian army was in control of the city of Urumia. However, early on in the war, much of the Russian troops in Urumia had to be redeployed to the northern parts of Persia for broader regional strategic reasons. Russian military presence in Urumia thinned down, and to defend Urumia, fortifications were built around the city. Meanwhile, Kurdish and Ottoman forces surrounded Urumia. By September of 1914, the majority of the population of the Christian villages in the areas surrounding Urumia had fled into the city for protection. Mary Lewis Shedd described the opening scenes of the conflict as such:

> Before Turkey's public entrance into the War, early in October, an attack under Turkish officers was made upon the city of Urumia. The Russians brought their mountain guns into action from a position near our Mission. As we watched the battle from our roof, we could follow the flight of the cannon balls through the trees and with our telescope could see them strike among the rocks where the enemy was stationed on the opposite hills.[356]

Some of the Russian troops returned to protect Urumia and prevent its invasion. However, as Mary Lewis Shedd observed: "There was a widespread sympathy on the part of Persians for the enemies of Russia, partly because they hated the Russians and partly due to Turkish agents getting ready for war with Russia."[357] William Shedd explained the source of this hatred as such:

> The Nationalist movement in Persia, which had begun a decade previously, and which succeeded in establishing the form of Parliamentary government, was a genuine popular movement, but it failed. It neither established a stable, representative

---

[356] Shedd (1922), *The Measure of a Man*, p. 138.

[357] Ibid., p. 139. It is important to point out, that as argued by Zirinsky (2002), earlier occupations by Russian forces in the regions west of Urumia and their attacks on Moslem villages in Persia may have damaged the relationship between Urumia's Persians and the Russians, and negatively influenced Moslem-Christian relations in the entire region. Keddie (1981, p. 79) also argues that the anti-Russian sentiments may have been further fueled by German and Turkish influence in hopes of mobilizing the Persians to fight against the Russian occupation of northern Persia.

government nor produced an enlightened despot. It left behind it in Persia a smoldering Nationalist aspiration, disconnected because of its failure, for which it largely blamed Russia. Russian influence antagonized the popular feeling, though it tended to secure order in the country. It left behind it also a set of professional revolutionists, men of some enterprise but no principle. Many of these were forced to flee and found an asylum in Turkey and in the war were active Turkish partisans.[358]

By the end of 1914, the Russians had to completely withdraw from Urumia since their regional strategic needs required their forces to be redeployed elsewhere. They gave no advance notice to the residents of Urumia and left overnight on January 1, 1915. The next day, when Shedd rushed to the Russian Consulate to find out what had happened, he found it to be abandoned. Although there was an American Consulate in Tabriz, communication lines were cut off, and reaching it on foot would be dangerous given the encirclement of Urumia. There was no assurance that Tabriz would be in a better shape than Urumia.[359]

With the departure of the Russians, Shedd immediately recognized the possibility that anarchy could take over unless some organization and leadership was quickly put in place. Among the very first things he did was to reach out to the Moslem clergy of Urumia.[360] He urged them to create a temporary government to maintain order. But the clergy could not agree amongst themselves, and no government was formed. By January 2nd, Christian villagers in the Salmas district (approximately 100 miles north of Urumia) had found out that the Russian troops had left Urumia. Instead of heading south to Urumia, many of these villagers headed north to Julfa, a border town near the Russian border.[361] By the next morning, most of the villages in the Salmas district had been abandoned.

---

[358] Ibid.

[359] Tabriz was also under attack at that time and was overtaken by Ottoman forces one week later.

[360] For further details of the timeline of events during the 1915 occupation of Urumia, interested readers are encouraged to examine Mary Lewis Shedd's book, *The Measure of a Man*, which is used as a source in this and the following chapters.

[361] There, they were supported by Assyrians and Armenians in southern Russia and received stipends from the Russian government to sustain themselves.

The departure of the Russian forces and foreign nationals put the Mission in a unique position, whereby it took on the truly unusual role of safekeeping others' belongings. Personal possessions, cash, jewelry, and other valuables would be brought to the Mission compound and entrusted to the missionaries in hopes that the American flag would prevent any invaders from entering the compound. For example, the Belgian head of customs brought his rugs and a piano for safekeeping on Mission grounds and the Russian missionaries also sent along some of their belongings. Within a few days of the Russian army's departure, Hugo Muller, the Mission's treasurer, was entrusted with nearly $20,000 for safekeeping. The understanding was that the received sums of money would be repaid without interest after normal conditions returned, but in the meantime, the Mission was allowed to use this money for emergency expenses.

By Sunday, January 3rd, no Russian soldier was in sight in Urumia. People from the villages in the Urumia plain were entering the Mission compound and taking spots on the grounds. The weather was frigid. It was snowing, and the temperature was well below freezing. To prepare for the developing humanitarian crisis, the Mission staff emptied the school rooms and other rooms that could be spared. To provide heat, a large study hall in the Fiske Seminary was emptied, and fire pits were made to provide warmth for the incoming crowds. Mary Lewis Shedd described the rapidly deteriorating conditions in great detail:

> By the morning of January 3, the people began pressing into our yards in crowds. The larger part of them had been stripped of everything but the few clothes on their backs. It was winter with snow and slush, the temperature often ten to twenty degrees (Fahr.) below freezing, and many suffered greatly on the road. We emptied all the school-rooms and store-rooms, to get ready for the rush. The big study-hall of Fiske Seminary was full of desks and not thought suitable for living quarters. Here fires were built and the shivering women and children brought in to get warm. They remained here for months and many of them were carried to their graves from that room. On the desks and under them, on the platform and in the aisles, they lived and sickened and died. The church filled up with mountaineers. The Press, administration building, boys' school at Sardari, college and hospital buildings all filled up. Still they came, first from the nearer villages, then from the more distance

ones, till every hallway, washhouse, cellar, and closet was packed full, not lying-down but sitting-up full.[362]

She estimated that nearly fifteen thousand people, the majority fleeing the Assyrian and Armenian Genocides which were well underway, took refuge in the Mission compound within the first few weeks of the occupation.[363] Frederick Coan described the Mission compound during the first few days of the occupation as such:

> As the college had been dismissed for the holidays, we packed away in its empty rooms ten times their ordinary capacity. The chapel, school rooms, cellars, wood rooms, store-rooms, closets, stables, both on the college as well as the hospital side, were filled. We then took all we could into our own homes. One missionary had fifty-four guests and we had thirty. In the city we annexed all the Christian yards between our compound and the city gate. The gateways into the street were barricaded and we knocked holes in the intervening walls so as to give access from yard to yard. Over them all we raised the American flag.[364]

By the third day, the Turkish forces had occupied Urumia, and control of matters was passed on to the Turkish Consul. The Persian governor was still in town, but he now had to serve on behalf of the Turkish Consul. The situation in Tabriz was also about to turn for the worst. Tabriz was surrounded by Ottoman forces and on January 14th they took over the city.[365]

The American flag was a clear signal for the occupiers of Urumia to avoid the Mission compound and all those who had sought refuge in it. During the five-month siege, the missionaries took turns in making sure at least one of them was awake at night so that matters do not get worse. During this time, Shedd was in constant contact and negotiations with the Turkish officials, Kurdish chiefs, and the Persian governor of Urumia. One of the issues of contention was a demand made by the Turks to have the American flag removed from the compound. This demand was never met.

---

[362] Shedd (1922), *The Measure of a Man*, p. 144.

[363] An additional 10,000 people took refuge in the French mission compound.

[364] Coan (1930), *Yesterdays in Persia and Kurdistan*, p. 245.

[365] They remained in control of Tabriz until they were removed by Russian troops in February of 1915.

During the five-month occupation of Urumia, the Mission was cut off from communications with the rest of the world. It also was running out of funds and would have run out completely had it not been for its safekeeping role and the money it was allowed to borrow against some of the kept funds. The funds were needed for the purchase of food for the thousands of refugees who were under its protection. The obligations were massive. The purchase of bread for the daily feeding of the thousands of refugees was the largest expenditure of the Mission during the occupation.

The condition of the refugees within the Mission compound was unbearable. There was no bathing or washing facilities and no sewage or underground drainage. In addition, most of the refugees were mountaineers who lived primitive lives with poor hygiene habits. The conditions on the Mission grounds were the perfect environment for the spread of disease. A range of health epidemics affected the Mission occupants, resulting in significant human suffering and death. Twice every day, the dead were gathered and placed in a room set up as a morgue. This makeshift morgue was located near the gate of the compound and allowed for quick removal of the bodies on a regular basis. The dead were then put on carts and buried in trenches. In total, 3,000 people died within the Mission premises during the 1915 occupation of Urumia.

As a count, on the day of the attack (January 1, 1915), the number of Americans associated with the Urumia mission were as follows: 18 adults, nine children, and three additional Americans at the Christ's Home for Children. By the time the five-month siege of the town was over, 14 adults and two of the children had become ill at some point during the siege, and three had died of illness. The primary sources of illness among the Americans were typhoid and typhus. A Swiss teacher named Madelaine Perrochet, who was in charge of teaching the American missionaries' children, died on February 25th. Also, Mary McDowell, the wife of Edmund McDowell, died on April 16th. In addition to the American lives affected by the occupation, there were massive human losses among the refugees. The Ottoman army disarmed Urumia's Christians, and the Mission collected and handed over the Christians' weapons to the Turkish forces. Despite this gesture of peace-seeking, Shedd noticed many forms of poor behavior from the Ottoman soldiers, including confiscation of property belonging to the

Christians, selling promissory notes of protection, and arresting men and keeping them for blackmail until sums of money were paid.

During the occupation, Shedd and the Mission were regularly involved in negotiating the release of those arrested for ransom. They were also constantly appealing to those who have the means, the funds, or food stocks to be donated to the refugees. The Mission was also seeking justice on behalf of those who were being unjustly punished by the occupiers. In February, several uniquely disturbing incidents took place. In one case, 50 men were taken from the French Mission and shot outside Urumia, by orders from Ottoman commanders. During the same month, missionaries saved the life of a bishop of the Russian Orthodox Church by hiding him in the roof of the church on the Mission compound. He was later found and arrested by Ottoman officers, and was eventually released after a large ransom was paid. On another occasion, 50 men from the village of Gulpashan (six miles from Urumia, near Lake Urumia) were taken from their homes and killed.[366]

In the final weeks of the occupation, Shedd contracted typhoid fever, and was taken care of in the residence of a fellow missionary physician. He recovered, but while he was ill, his wife (Louise Wilbur Shedd) also fell ill. She died on May 17, 1915, only a week before the return of the Russians and the liberation of Urumia from Ottoman occupation. In his personal calendar, Shedd noted the following log for May 17, 1915: "Louise passed from us 10 a.m."[367] One week later, the Russians regained control of Urumia.

Russia's Return to Urumia

On May 24, 1915, the Russian army, consisting of a thousand Cossacks, entered Urumia, freeing it from Ottoman occupation. Shedd, accompanied by representatives from the other Christian missions in Urumia, greeted the arriving Russian troops. Reliance on Russian support for protection was quite clear to him, and the return of the Russians was a source of relief for the missionaries. It is estimated that

---

[366] Platt (1915), *The War Journal of a Missionary in Persia,* pp. 28-29.

[367] Source: Archives of the Presbyterian Historical Society, Philadelphia, PA; Shedd Family Archives, RG 19-0504.

there were 30,000 Christians in the area when the conflict began. Of these, 5,000 left for Russia. Of the remaining 25,000, approximately 4,000 died. In other words, within the five months of the occupation of Urumia (January to May of 1915), about twenty percent of the 25,000 Christians that did not flee to Russia had died.[368]

In June of 1915, a new Russian Consul, Basil Nikitine described as "a man of ability, sincere sympathy, and fine character" arrived in Urumia.[369] Nikitine, was a man of brilliance and deep intellectual curiosity.[370] He had a genuine desire to understand the ethnic and religious variations of the area, and in later years of his life, proved to be a prolific author on the topic. Nikitine's arrival in Urumia, and the years that he shared the city with Shedd, created many opportunities for the two men to closely collaborate on humanitarian matters. Nikitine and Shedd worked together to visit the ravaged villages, assess their conditions, and administer aid to the refugees.

Nikitine directly or indirectly affected many of the important decisions that Shedd was to make in the following years. Nikitine's intellectual depth, along with his genuine interest in helping relieve human suffering in Urumia, was evident in his actions. He was an Orientalist, coming from a family of Orientalists. He had a practical interest in the people of the area.[371] Furthermore, the fact that as a Russian diplomat he was able to utilize the support of his country to procure and facilitate aid must have resonated well with Shedd. As will be seen shortly, Shedd eventually took on the same path, by becoming a diplomat in order to demand similar types of support from America to relieve the human suffering in Urumia.

---

[368] Shedd (1922), *The Measure of a Man*, p. 152.

[369] Ibid., p. 199.

[370] Also spelled Niktin in some scholarly outlets where he has been cited for his scholarly works on Kurdish culture and history.

[371] Nikitine remained in Urumia until the spring of 1918. After his departure, he continued his scholarly studies on the Kurds, and became a world-renowned authority on Kurdish culture and nationalism. He wrote extensively on the topic (mostly in French scholarly journals).

Last American Furlough

In September of 1915, Shedd left for America with his two young daughters (Bertha and Louise) from his marriage with Louise Wilbur Shedd, who had passed away earlier that year. His other two daughters from his first marriage (Susan and Margaret) were already in America. They traveled through Moscow on their way to America. The main reason for the visit was to bring Bertha and Louise to America, where they would be able to continue their schooling in a safe environment. The other reason was for him to increase Americas' awareness of the grave situation in Urumia and Persia and gather American support for the thousands of refugees displaced by the war.

The balance of 1915 and most of 1916 (until August) was spent traveling within the country, fundraising, and meetings with influential Americans to gather support for the refugees. Shedd worked closely with the American Committee for Armenian and Syrian Relief as part of the Near East Relief fundraising efforts.[372] By October of 1916, the total amount of collected funds was over $1,000,000. This was a significant achievement, since the year before, the Urumia mission station was only able to distribute $105,000 in relief aid to the refugees.[373] Also noteworthy is the fact that the Rockefeller Foundation provided nearly one-third of the funds raised. Considering that the Rockefeller Foundation was only established three years earlier, their support demonstrated the extent that the Rockefeller family, who were influential Presbyterian industrialists, cared about the cause that Shedd was advocating for.

The day before his return to Urumia, Shedd attended a one-day conference at Columbia University in New York City. The conference, held on August 16, 1916, was organized by his friend, Dr. Abraham Yohannan, who was a faculty member at Columbia. The conference was attended by some of the leading American figures in the refugee

---

[372] The Near East Relief Committee, shortly after its formation in 1915, consolidated the Persia and Syrian War Relief Committees which were formed in America earlier that year. It eventually encompassed other relief organizations focused on addressing the massive level of human suffering in the Near East resulting from the First World War. It also developed a working relationship with the American Red Cross. For additional details, consult Barton (1930), *Story of Near East Relief.*

[373] Rockwell (1916), *The Pitiful Plight of the Assyrian Christians in Persia and Kurdistan,* p. 58.

relief effort.[374] The next day, Shedd boarded a steamship to head back to Urumia. It was to be the last day he would see America.

References and Related Readings

Barton, James L. (1930). *Story of Near East Relief.* New York: MacMillan Co.

Bryce, Viscount (1916). *The Treatment of Armenians in the Ottoman Empire.* London: Hodder and Stoughton.

Gaunt, David (2006). *Massacres, Resistance, Protectors: Muslim-Christian Relations in Eastern Anatolia During World War I.* Piscataway: Gorgias Press.

Keddie, Nikki (1981). *Roots of Revolution: An Interpretive History of Modern Iran.* New Haven: Yale University Press.

Platt, Mary Schauffler (1915). *The War Journal of a Missionary in Persia.* New York: The Board of Foreign Missions of the Presbyterian Church in the U.S.A.

Rockwell, William W. (1916). *The Pitiful Plight of the Assyrian Christians in Persia and Kurdistan.* New York: American Committee for Armenian and Syrian Relief.

Shedd, Mary Lewis (1922). *The Measure of a Man: The Life of William Ambrose Shedd, Missionary to Persia.* New York: Gordon H. Doran Company.

---

[374] Yohannan was from Urumia, had attended the Mission schools in Urumia, and received his higher education, including his doctorate degree, in America. He was instrumental in organizing this conference, the proceedings of which are summarized in Rockwell (1916).

Chapter 32

WILLIAM SHEDD, THE DIPLOMAT

On August 17, 1916, having left his children in good hands in America, Shedd began his return voyage to Persia. Reflecting on his long visit to America and the rapidly changing social and political landscape of the country, he wrote: "America is to me a place that I don't altogether understand, though I know well enough that it is the finest place in the world."[375] He was expressing a concern about America's hesitation to become a participant in the war. The country had not yet officially entered the First World War at that time. Shedd felt that with the absence of American military might on the battlefields of the First World War, a sense of "complacency of conscience" may have contributed to the war atrocities:

> I think that I hate war as much as any one, but I don't seem to
> set peace as the greatest good in the way that many people do.
> With the American people, I'm a great deal more afraid that they
> won't have the zeal they should have than that they will learn to
> love war. There is a kind of peace that is a negative kind of
> thing, like a good deal of the prevailing complacency of
> conscience.[376]

Upon his return to Urumia in the fall of 1916, Shedd resumed work as the head of the American School, teacher, and Legal Board member.

---

[375] Shedd (1922), *The Measure of a Man*, p. 203.
[376] Ibid., p. 202.

He had a large responsibility in dealing with the challenges facing those who relied on the Mission for aid and protection. At stake were the lives of thousands of refugees. At that time, the total number of displaced people who had entered the Urumia region through the northern parts of the Urumia plain was estimated at 35,000. Most of this population came directly to Urumia. Another group of several thousand people, instead of coming to Urumia, had headed north and taken refuge in the areas surrounding Khoi, in proximity to Russian lines of protection.

Shedd's responsibility and authority were enhanced by the fact that the fundraising efforts in America under the banner of Near East Relief had resulted in the financial resources needed for the humanitarian work of Urumia. Being in charge of the distribution of the relief funds in the Urumia region increased his authority on local matters. He was often approached by a range of individuals from various backgrounds seeking aid. This helped him bring a sense of common interest among conflicting groups. The Russians also provided financial support to those who were displaced. Despite the inflow of relief funds, there were many demands for aid, not just from the mountain tribes, but also from those in all walks of life in Urumia and elsewhere. Reflecting on his gatekeeping role, Mary Lewis Shedd wrote:

> The mountaineers were not the only protégés of American generosity. Our yards and often our houses were filled from day to day with the most grotesque and varied specimens of humanity. Kurds driven from their villages by famine and war came to Urumia to appeal to the Americans. There were Kurds from the south in full bloomers, wrapped with a girdle from thigh to armpit and armed with *hanjar* or dagger, and the warrior who proudly boasted rifle and cartridges. The Persian *khan* was there to beg a loan in time of distress. There were hundreds of poor, miserable women with their starving babies and naked children clinging to them. There were Mohammedan ladies, each with a special petition, sometimes presented through one of the missionary ladies, but oftener by direct appointment with Dr. Shedd.[377]

The fact that Urumia was occupied by Russian soldiers increased tensions between the Moslems and Christians of the city. To the city's

---

[377] Ibid., p. 208.

Moslems, the Russians were viewed as a Christian occupying force, in war with the Moslem army of Turkey. The heavy-handed approach that Russia used in fighting back the Persian Constitutional Revolution and its occupation of northern sections of Persia over the years had made it an unwelcome occupier.

Furthermore, some of the Russian soldiers in Urumia had been unprofessional in their treatment of the locals. They had displayed cruelty and harshness, which seemed to have been more focused on the Moslem population of the city. Incidents, including the looting by Russian soldiers of bazaars in Urumia in 1917, and cases involving their rough handling of the local population contributed to strong anti-Russian sentiments.

Since the Russians were viewed as a Christian force, the negative feelings generated by the poor behavior of these Russian soldiers resulted in anti-Christian sentiments toward the Armenians and Assyrians of the city. Some of the Russian soldiers were simply not the best representatives for Christianity in Urumia, and their actions aggravated the already raw nerves of the city's Moslem residents.[378] The anti-Russian sentiments were further fueled by the fact that in 1915 and 1916 Russian forces had occupied parts of eastern Turkey and had carried out outrages against Kurdish villages, in some cases massacring large portions of the population.[379]

The Impact of the Russian Bolshevik Revolution on Urumia

In February of 1917, protests in St. Petersburg, which at that time was the capital of Russia, began. The protests were due to the discontent of the Russian public and Russian soldiers with Russia's losses in the war. By then, the First World War had been underway for nearly three years. The poor performance of the Russian forces on the battlefield was attributed to organizational inefficiencies, shortage of military supplies and weapons, and lack of financial resources, resulting in massive

---

[378] For a more detailed account of the Persian perspective on the Russian forces' mistreatment of the Persian population in Urumia, consult chapter 12 of Kasravi (1998). Also see Browne and Javadi (2008), *Letters from Tabriz: The Russian Suppression of the Iranian Constitutional Revolution*.

[379] Joseph (1961), *The Nestorians and their Moslem Neighbors*, p. 136.

Russian casualties. The Russian army, disappointed with the leadership of the country, was about to enter a state of mutiny.

There were also other concerns contributing to the uprising, such as the economy, growing poverty, government corruption, and food shortages. With poor leadership exhibited by Tsar Nicholas II, the Russian Parliament took control of the country to avoid further chaos. A provisional government was formed, but only lasted until October of 1917, when it was overthrown by masses of workers and soldiers, and the Bolshevik Party then seized power.[380]

The effects of the Bolshevik Revolution were felt as far away as Urumia. Between February and October of 1917, the issue of who the Russian soldiers would take orders from was a primary source of confusion. The command structure of the Russian army was in disarray. This weakened the protections that Russian troops provided Christian minorities in northwestern Persia. Debates in Russia began surrounding the question of whether or not Russia should even continue to be part of the war effort. As a result, a weakening of Russian presence and reinforcements in Urumia was being felt.

The political turmoil in Russia compromised the effectiveness of the Russian forces in Urumia. Some of the Russian soldiers became less controlled, harsher, and more violent against Urumia's local population, which fueled greater degrees of animosity towards Russia. The actions by these soldiers also increased the tensions between the Moslems and Christians of Urumia. Unable to directly respond to the violence inflicted on them by rogue Russian soldiers, some of the local Moslems became revengeful against the local Christians of Urumia, contributing to the ramping up of religiously inspired violence in the Urumia region.

As the Russian revolution proceeded, Russian soldiers retreated from Urumia. However, Russian military supplies in Urumia remained in place. The stockpile of the Russian weapons left behind was sold by some of the remaining soldiers who did not sympathize with the Bolshevik Revolution and had chosen to remain in Urumia. In their enterprising mindset, they sought to profit from the sale of these weapons personally. The weapons were sold to the highest bidder, regardless of background. The privatized black market sale of Russian

---

[380] Smith (2002), *The Russian Revolution.*

weapons to the diverse population of Urumia helped militarize the city, making it more susceptible to large-scale violence and civil war.

Recognizing that the Christian population of Urumia was gaining access to Russian weapons, the Urumia Democrats were alarmed. The Democrats were a political party, prominent in northwestern Persia at that time, with strong anti-Russian sentiments, resentment toward cultural, linguistic and political pressures placed on Azari (Turkish-speaking) Persians by the central Persian government, and their own reform aspirations.[381] To them, the idea of an armed Christian population in Urumia who may sympathize with the Russians was a difficult proposition to peacefully accept. They therefore called for greater levels of arming of the city's Moslem population, with an explicit intent to keep the armed Christian groups in check.

Taking on a Diplomatic Role

America's diplomatic relations with Persia had formally begun in 1883 with the establishment of the American legation in Tehran. In 1907, the American Consul in Tabriz began its operations. However, no such representation existed in Urumia. The need for American representation in Urumia was felt strongly by Shedd. He was of the belief that America's lack of attention to the human suffering in this corner of the world had created a humanitarian disaster.

In April of 1917, America entered the First World War and thereby formally became an adversary of Turkey. In the fall of that year, Shedd wrote:

> I pray that America may strike with all her force to end this war
> and that her heart may be made pure to meet the momentous
> issue of it and to see her way clearly. I am glad we are in the
> war and yet I tremble, not for the loss but for the responsibilities
> that it seems to bring on us. You know that I am not a pacifist,
> and I am inclined to believe that our country will exert the
> greatest influence for peace and bring it more quickly and make
> it more stable by putting her strength and conscience into
> righteous war than in any other way.[382]

---

[381] Keddie (1981), *Roots of Revolution*, pp. 83.
[382] Shedd (1922), *The Measure of a Man*, p. 213.

His sentiments were shared by Gordon Paddock, the American Consul in Tabriz, and John Caldwell, the American Ambassador in Tehran. On Paddock's insistence, Shedd was appointed "Honorary Vice-Consul" for America in Urumia, in January of 1918. This was an important role since, in addition to the American missionaries and their families, there were approximately 50 families of naturalized American citizens living in Urumia at that time. They were in need of consular services, ranging from diplomatic representation before Persian government officials to the issuance of passports and the notarizing of official documents. Furthermore, various properties such as the Mission's buildings and land were American-owned. This required official American representation in the city, especially in the chaotic state that Urumia was in at that time.

In addition to the issue of American representation in Urumia, other equally important factors contributed to Shedd's decision to become America's diplomat in Urumia. As indicated earlier, he firmly believed that America should take an active role in matters in the region. His early life experiences had convinced him of the power of political influence in advancing social, national, and global conversations. One of these observations dated back to his youth, when in 1882 at the age of 17 he had visited his uncle, General Rufus Dawes, in Washington. General Dawes, who at that time was a congressman representing the state of Ohio, successfully advocated for the establishment of diplomatic relations between the United States and Persia. By the following year, an American legation began operating in Tehran. Knowing that his uncle successfully championed this historic event, and being able to see him in action in Washington, must have planted the seeds in Shedd's mind that political forces can be put to good use.

In more recent years, the interactions between Shedd and Nikitine, the Russian Consul in Urumia, may have also contributed to Shedd's decision to take on the role of American Vice-Consul. Shedd's close collaboration with Nikitine on refugee relief efforts, Nikitine's superb intellectual abilities, his deep knowledge of the Kurds, and his genuine desire to reduce the suffering of the refugees in Urumia, clearly impressed Shedd. The two men shared numerous intellectual interests, with Shedd being a scholar in comparative religion and Nikitine being a scholar in Oriental studies. Both were intellectually inspired to explore leading-edge social questions that were dramatically affecting the region.

Nikitine and Shedd also had very similar passions for humanitarian work. Nikitine constantly made efforts to reduce the suffering of refugees using Russian government support. Being a Russian government representative, Nikitine had demonstrated to Shedd how he was able to channel and manage Russia's resources to this effect. Shedd's collaboration with Nikitine on humanitarian efforts may have convinced him of the enabling power that American government representation in Urumia could have on mobilizing humanitarian aid.

The position of American Vice-Consul was not only a new role for Shedd, but it was also an extension of the role of a missionary far beyond the normal boundaries of Mission responsibilities. With this added role, Shedd now had three senior-level responsibilities to three different organizations. He was the senior missionary in Urumia, the chairman of the Relief Committee, and the senior diplomatic representative of the United States in Urumia. With America having just entered the First World War, the latter role put him in direct opposition to the Ottoman government, with its army only miles away from Urumia. With their massive deployment of forces stationed nearby, the risks to Shedd and the Mission significantly grew due to his new role as an American diplomat.

It is therefore no surprise that with the United States having entered the First World War, and with Shedd having taken on the role of America's official representative in Urumia, that he would be closely watched and harshly criticized by those locals who sympathized with the Ottomans. Issues related to humanitarian aid, which Shedd would have freely been able to resolve as a missionary, were now considered untouchable by a diplomat who should seek non-intervention. As an American diplomat, he was experiencing constraints rather than freedom in helping reduce the human suffering in Urumia. This was the exact opposite of what he had hoped for when he had accepted the role of Vice-Consul.

References and Related Readings

Browne, Edward G. and Hassan Javadi (2008). *Letters from Tabriz: The Russian Suppression of the Iranian Constitutional Movement.* Odenton, MD: Mage Publishers.

Bryce, Viscount (1916). *The Treatment of Armenians in the Ottoman Empire.* London: Hodder and Stoughton.

Daniel, Robert L. (1970). *American Philanthropy in the Near East: 1820-1960.* Athens, OH: Ohio University Press.

Joseph, John (1961). *Nestorians and their Muslim Neighbors.* Princeton: Princeton University Press.

Kasravi, Ahmad (1998). *Eighteen Year History of Azerbaijan.* Tehran: Saad Moaser Publishing. Farsi manuscript reprint.

Keddie, Nikki R. (1981). *Roots of Revolution: An Interpretive History of Modern Iran.* New Haven: Yale University Press.

Shedd, Mary Lewis (1922). *The Measure of a Man: The Life of William Ambrose Shedd, Missionary to Persia.* New York: Gordon H. Doran Company.

Smith, Stephen A. (2002), *The Russian Revolution: A Very Short Introduction.* Oxford University Press.

Chapter 33

OTTOMAN REOCCUPATION
OF URUMIA IN 1918

In July of 1917, amidst all of the turmoil, Shedd married his third wife, Mary E. Lewis. She had been a missionary colleague of Shedd for well over a decade. The couple began their married life in one of the most unwelcoming settings imaginable. By the fall of that year, most of the Russian army soldiers had left Urumia, creating the context for chaos. There was a weakening of the Russian command structure in the region due to the Bolshevik Revolution. However, a sufficient number of soldiers, mostly those who did not sympathize with the Bolshevists, had remained in Urumia. While these remaining forces were not well organized, they were essential to the defense of the city and the protection of Russian interests in Urumia.

The Russians did not have full control of the internal affairs of Urumia and were primarily deployed to provide the city's exterior defenses. In the interior, the Democrats, which had anti-Russian sentiments, were discontent with the remaining Russian presence and viewed the Assyrians and Armenians as Russian allies. Among the Assyrian and Armenian refugees from Turkey, some had been armed and trained by the Russians in earlier military campaigns elsewhere. They had combat experience and were effective fighters. However, some of these men were difficult to control, which further aggravated the Democrats. The conflict between these two groups contributed to the explosive nature of the violence that was about to erupt within the city.

The departure of the bulk of the Russian army had resulted in the pillage and black market sale of stores of their weapons, which contributed to the arming of the population of Urumia. The Christian forces were a militia consisting of armed Assyrian and Armenian men. According to Shedd, some of the elements of this militia lacked the discipline to revert from violence. In a letter to Robert Speer (Secretary of the Presbyterian Board of Foreign Missions), Shedd acknowledged the difficulties in controlling this militia: "The Christians have been guilty of atrocities, not by any means on the same scale as was the case three years ago but enough to make one feel very much humiliated. I have not heard of crimes against women but there have been many murders and much looting."[383]

As a result, violence between Moslems and Christians grew dramatically in Urumia during the first few weeks of 1918. On February 22nd, all out civil war broke out. By the following day, the city was under the control of the Assyrian and Armenian militia. Peace was temporarily achieved, and the upper hand was with the Christian forces. The Christian forces were concerned about giving up control of the city to Moslems, and the Moslem forces were discontent with Christian control. Shedd moderated negotiations to bring peace to the city, and an agreement was reached. A mixed council of Christians and Moslems, representing the various groups within Urumia, was formed to ensure

---

[383] Source: Archives of the Presbyterian Historical Society, Philadelphia. Letter from William A. Shedd addressed to Robert Speer, dated February 27, 1918. Shedd Family Archives, RG 19-0504. Note that in this letter, Shedd refers to prior cases in which violence applied by the Christians on Moslems had taken place. These unpublished correspondences indicate the escalation of violence between the two groups, in the middle of which the American missionaries seemed to have been caught. The inability of the missionaries to control the violent elements among the Christian militia, as suggested by this and other correspondences, had harmful effects on Mission relations within Urumia. Kasravi (1998; chapters 14 and 15) also points to the complications and escalation of tensions resulting from the violence exercised by the rogue elements of the militia. In the long-term, as argued by Ghazvinian (2021) and Zirinsky (2002), this contributed to apathy among the local Moslem population in Urumia. For example, following the end of WWI, there was a long delay of several years before the return of the American Mission to Urumia became possible, partially due to the locals' opposition to the re-establishment of the Mission.

order and peace. The council was able to achieve some degree of control of the city for a short period of time. Shedd wrote:

> The *Democrats* are doing all they can to get up an army to exterminate the mountaineers. The crimes that in ages past have been done in the name of autocracy are now being committed in the name of democracy, that being the name to conjure by.[384]

As can be implied from Shedd's descriptions of the growing violence inside the city, the truce was short-lived. The Urumia plain was surrounded by multiple armies from various directions. From the east, forces allied with the Democrats blocked boats on Lake Urumia. To the south, it was the "Karapapakhs," or "black hats," forces belonging to southern Turkoman tribes, who blocked the southern borders of Urumia. Simku, the chieftain of the Shikkak confederation of Kurds, contributed to the encirclement by repositioning his forces to other surrounding areas of Urumia. For Shedd and the mission station, all lines of communication with the outside world were cut off.

Meanwhile, the influx of refugees to Urumia continued. The refugees were not all just Assyrians or Armenians. Among those fleeing to Urumia due to famine and war were thousands of Moslem villagers. In the Mission yards, there were approximately one thousand Kurds and Persians, in addition to the thousands of Christian refugees. Some of the Kurds and the Persians were escaping violence targeted at them by Christian militia in the mountains. Revengeful acts of violence by Christians on Moslems were adding to the killing and the refugee crisis. The Mission's task, therefore, included protection and feeding of both Christians and Moslems, all of whom were victims of tribal and religiously inspired violence.

Among those who had been displaced to Urumia was Mar Shimon Benjamin, the Assyrian patriarch. He had to flee his residence in the Kurdish mountains of Turkey, alongside thousands of his Assyrian subjects. With the Assyrian patriarch in Urumia and with the Christians having a commanding position in Urumia, the patriarch's blessing would be essential to achieving peace in the region. Simku had a different view. He sought to take advantage of the instability and find means for subduing the Assyrian and Armenian militia.

---

[384] Shedd (1922), *The Measure of a Man,* p. 237.

Assyrian and Armenian Militia of Urumia (c. 1918)

William Shedd with the Refugees (c. 1918)

Simku baited the patriarch by asking him to visit him in a mutually agreed upon location in the Salmas district to make peace, and the patriarch obliged. He greeted the patriarch with warmth and affection, and they had a friendly meeting. The two men conversed over tea. Simku gave him his word that they will be in peace and kissed the patriarch upon departure. As the patriarch was about to leave with his party, Simku signaled his men who were hiding out of sight to shoot down the patriarch, his bodyguards, and the entire entourage.[385] The patriarch and his party were instantly massacred. However, several of the men managed to escape and brought back the news of the assassination of the patriarch.

Mar Shimon Benjamin (Assyrian Patriarch between 1903 and 1918)

---

[385] The Persians' accounts of this meeting, as described by Kasravi (1998), are slightly different from Western writings. Kasravi (chapter 16) suggests that based on subsequent statements made by Simku, the meeting was called for by the patriarch and not Simku, and the context of the meeting was the possibility of coordinating a joint effort by the Kurds and the militia in Urumia to carve out an independent territory for their collective use. Also, according to Kasravi, Simku claimed that he himself shot the patriarch. Others have suggested that senior Persian officials may have requested Simku to kill the patriarch (Shedd 1922, p. 238). While the Qajar government may have had concerns over the growing military strength of the Assyrian and Armenian militia in Urumia, no clear evidence has survived to assess these accounts, as Simku's residence was burned down in retaliation, and he was eventually assassinated by the Persian government under orders by Reza Shah in 1930.

Casualties in the Streets of Urumia (c. 1918)

The news of the patriarch's killing caused an immediate escalation of violence between the Christians and Moslems. For a region of the world where tribal warfare, an-eye-for-an-eye punishment, and violent retribution were the most common ways of seeking justice, tit-for-tat revenge was the only way known to move forward. The observation that Grant had made in 1839 on how two neighboring villages balanced their scores by making sure equal numbers of men were killed from each village was now about to be demonstrated on a far larger scale. Violence between Christians and Moslems in the region grew, with the former revengefully carrying out atrocities against the latter, many of the victims being innocent civilians. According to Shedd, out-of-control elements among the militia who had taken refuge in Urumia, in their primitive, tribal, and violent ways, contributed to much of the senseless violence in Urumia.[386] The entire area, including places such as Khoi, Dilman, and Salmas, was soaked in seemingly endless cycles of revengeful violence, triggered by Simku's treacherous act. He had successfully achieved his goal of creating instability in the area, hoping that someday he would take control of the region himself.[387]

---

[386] Based on Persian accounts, Zirinsky (2002) estimates the number of casualties associated with this specific incident at approximately ten thousand. See also Shedd (1922), *The Measure of a Man*, p. 253.

[387] He continued to contribute to violence and instability in the region until his death in 1930.

The Second Ottoman Invasion of Urumia

By April of 1918, Shedd was the only representative of the Allied forces in Urumia. The British, French, and Russians, who were at war with the Ottomans, had withdrawn all their senior diplomats for fear of an Ottoman invasion of the city. The chaos within Urumia did not go unnoticed by the Ottomans who had stationed themselves in the outskirts of the city. With the thinning out of the Russian forces, by June of 1918, Ottoman troops had reached within a few miles of the city. What prevented an Ottoman occupation was the Assyrian and Armenian militia. At risk were the lives of approximately 80,000 refugees who could be massacred if the city's defenses failed. About two-thirds of these refugees were from the Turkish mountains, and the rest were from the Urumia plain.

Ottoman forces and their Kurdish allies had surrounded Urumia on three sides. The Assyrian-Armenian militia was fed using funds supplied by the Near East Relief Committee. This represented a conflict of interest since the relief funds were under the control of Shedd, who was now also the American Vice-Consul in Urumia. By feeding the militia, he was using the relief funds, which were intended for the refugees, to support an armed group. He was also overstepping his role as an American diplomat by influencing what was fundamentally an internal conflict on Persian soil.[388] Shedd justified his decision to support the militia as such:

> I have given up all pretense to neutrality and keeping out of military affairs. The people here are not fighting the people of Persia, and will not fight them, unless they are attacked. They are repelling an attack by an invading foe, and our lives and safety depend on the result of the effort to drive them off.[389]

As early as December of 1917 the British had already defeated the Ottoman forces north of Baghdad, resulting in a general withdrawal of the Ottoman army from that area. By July of 1918, the British began to advance their troops through Mesopotamia (modern day northern Iraq).

---

[388] It is important to recall that by then, all lines of communication between Tabriz and Urumia were cut off, and there were no means for Shedd to receive guidance or instructions from Gordon Paddock (the American Consul in Tabriz) or John Caldwell (the American Ambassador in Tehran) to whom he reported.
[389] Shedd (1922), *The Measure of a Man*, p. 243.

One of the most dramatic events in this stage of the war occurred on July 8, 1918. A British surveillance airplane flew over the College compound and landed in a safe area outside Urumia, away from enemy forces. The plane, piloted by a British lieutenant named K.M. Pennington, was then approached by a mob of people from Urumia, fascinated by the sight of a magical flying machine.[390]

Pennington had come at the request of the American government to inquire about the state of the American missionaries, with whom communications had been cut off for months. More importantly, he had come to bring news about British military plans and wanted to coordinate with the leaders of the militia that were defending Urumia. He also brought along personal and official mail addressed to the missionaries. Pennington flew out the next day with an understanding that a contingent of Urumia's Assyrian-Armenian militia would break through the encirclement of Urumia to meet up with the British forces coming from the southeast. They would meet in the village of Sain Kala, located to the south of Lake Urumia. There, they would receive arms, supplies, and funds from the British, and return to Urumia to continue their defense of the city. The expectation was that British reinforcements would arrive in Urumia in about three weeks.

Agha Petros, a Turkish-born Assyrian teacher, turned military commander, organized and led this force.[391] However, the departure of his forces from Urumia was delayed, and they reached Sain Kala late. By then, the British troops had withdrawn from the area. The British were therefore unable to supply his men with the promised supplies and support. With Agha Petros and many of his men away from Urumia, by the end of July, the defensive forces in Urumia could no longer hold back the Ottoman and Kurdish troops surrounding the city.

---

[390] Coan (1939), *Yesterdays in Persia and Kurdistan*, p. 268.

[391] Agha Petros was an Assyrian, born in Turkey and educated in the American mission schools in Urumia. He returned to Turkey for a while and eventually came to Urumia as a servant of the Ottoman government. Upon the entry of Russian forces to Urumia, he took on the role of commanding the militia.

References and Related Readings

Ghazvinian, John (2021). *America and Iran: A History, 1720 to the Present.* New York: Alfred Knopf.

Kasravi, Ahmad (1998). *Eighteen Year History of Azerbaijan.* Tehran: Saad Moaser Publishing. Farsi manuscript reprint.

Shedd, Mary Lewis (1922). *The Measure of a Man: The Life of William Ambrose Shedd, Missionary to Persia.* New York: Gordon H. Doran Company.

van Bruinessen, Martin (2006). "A Kurdish Warlord on the Turkish-Persian Frontier in the Early Twentieth Century: Isma'il Agha Simko", in Touraj Atabaki (ed.), *Iran and the First World War: Battleground of the Great Powers.* London: I.B. Tauris, pp. 69-93.

Wigram, W. A. (1920). *Our Smallest Ally.* London: Society for Promoting Christian Knowledge.

Yacoub, Joseph (2016). *Year of the Sword: The Assyrian Christian Genocide.* Translated by James Ferguson. Oxford: Oxford University Press.

Zirinsky, Michael (2002). "American Presbyterian Missionaries at Urmia during the Great War," *La perse et la grande guerre,* Oliver Bast (ed.), Tehran: Institut Francais de Recherche en Iran, pp. 353-372.

Chapter 34

THE EXODUS

William Shedd's third wife, Mary Lewis Shedd, kept a detailed log of the 1918 re-occupation of Urumia by the Ottoman forces and their Kurdish allies. In her book, *The Measure of a Man*, she provided a unique inside perspective of the refugees' flight out of the city. Her detailed accounts are graphic and heart wrenching, and some have been included in this chapter with additional commentary. According to her, on July 31, 1918, in the afternoon, news came of the movement of the forces encircling Urumia. The refugees began to contemplate flight. The native Christians of Urumia felt that they too needed to leave alongside the Christian refugees who had all these months flocked into their town. If the Ottoman and Kurdish forces entered Urumia, there would be no reason to believe that they would treat the native Christians any better than they would treat the refugees.

By the early morning hours of the next day, preparations for a mass flight from the city were being made. These included the stocking up of food and supplies needed for the journey. Since contact with the outside world was not possible, those in Urumia were unaware that Agha Petros had not been able to make contact with the British in Sain Kala. Instead, they assumed that by leaving Urumia, they would meet up with the militia under his command. Their hope was to receive protection from the militia and British forces within a few days of leaving Urumia.

With the exception of Shedd and his wife, all the American missionaries decided to remain in Urumia. Most were so ill from the various diseases they had contracted on the Mission grounds, that they could not withstand the physical challenges of the long journey. Shedd felt that his leadership would be needed to guide the thousands of refugees to safety. Also, since he was now an American diplomat and Turkey was officially at war with the United States, he would be considered as enemy by Turkish forces, and would be treated as such if captured. For Shedd and his wife, remaining in Urumia could cost them their lives.

The exodus began at 7:30 in the morning. The timing was right since, within three hours, Urumia was overtaken by the Turkish forces and their Kurdish allies. The American missionaries that remained were placed under arrest at the hospital compound. The line of refugees on the road was miles long. By the third day, as they were leaving the southern shores of Lake Urumia, they came under attack in the back end of the convoy. The attacks continued throughout the exodus. On several occasions, Shedd had to organize the men to serve as rearguards to protect the tail end of the caravan.

Near East Relief Ambulance Accompanying the Refugees in Flight (c. 1918)

Refugees Fleeing Urumia (c. 1918)

In describing the exodus, Shedd's wife wrote: "The road was steep, our horses were done out, bullets were flying all about us, one almost grazed Dr. Shedd's face. It looked as if we should have to leave everything and run for our lives while our pursuers stopped to loot."[392] The extent of human suffering is well-documented in her book. Stories are told of families breaking up on the way, with ill and aging family members left behind. Hunger, illness, and inability to move on affected thousands:

> One of my school-girls told me afterwards that when she reached the river at this place, pursued by those demons and unable to carry both her children, she held one child over her head and waded through the river. Looking back she saw that it was too late to return for the other one and he was left sitting there on the opposite bank. The memory of her deserted baby haunted her day and night.[393]

---

[392] Shedd (1922), *The Measure of a Man*, p. 265.
[393] Ibid., p. 264.

The refugee caravan's movement into various areas was not welcomed by the locals in the villages they passed. The locals themselves felt they were being invaded by an unwelcomed flock of humanity. Therefore, support, food, and sympathy were hard to find. In some cases, the tensions with the locals in the villages that the convoy passed through resulted in the outbreak of more violence and suffering. Being unwelcomed and vulnerable, the misery of the experience of the refugees due to hunger, disease, and fatigue continued. Shedd's wife wrote:

> When the firing at the front ceased, that desperate jumble of humanity began frantically to move forward; it was pandemonium. Many carts and wagons were discarded with little children and old women left sitting in them, too stupefied to stir. Many completely lost their heads and did not know what they were doing. Hundreds left their food and went hungry for days.[394]

The caravan eventually reached the Sain Kala region, where a British army camp of about two hundred British soldiers was located. The camp soon came under attack, and additional men among the refugees were needed to join the fighting force. Some of the attackers were locals who were reacting to the pillaging that some of the outlaw elements of the fleeing refugees had inflicted on the local villages.

It was at this point, a few hours after having arrived at the British army camp that Shedd began to feel ill. The diagnosis by one of the doctors was that it was cholera. To alleviate the symptoms, the doctor administered calomel.[395] However, rest was not an option as the camp was still under attack, and the convoy had to continue moving forward. Shedd was put in a rested position in the back of a carriage accompanied by his wife. They passed the British camp and kept on advancing overnight. The British camp helped block any advancing forces seeking to harm the refugee convoy.

Despite receiving medication, Shedd continued to experience symptoms such as pain and convulsions, saying: "I never was so tired

---

[394] Ibid., p. 264.

[395] A commonly used purgative in the nineteenth century for a wide range of diseases including influenza, tuberculosis and cholera.

in all my life."[396] Shortly after, he lost consciousness and never regained it. The carriage stopped, and the entire refugee caravan passed on and cleared the location where he and his wife were sheltered. The British camp and forces behind them were still being attacked, and the carriage had to continue to move forward overnight. William Ambrose Shedd passed away in the early hours of August 7th.[397] To bury him, a shallow grave was dug out on the side of the road as described by his wife:

> A little farther on, with a small adz and fingers, they dug a
> shallow grave, and with the canvas from the cart for a shroud,
> we laid him there. Dr. Yonan read the burial service and a cross
> was cut on the rock beside the grave. It seemed impossible to
> go off and leave him there in that unfriendly land, but there
> could be no tarrying.[398]

Nearly a month after leaving Urumia, the caravan finally completed the 400-mile journey and reached the city of Hamadan. It is estimated that about 20,000 people died on the way.[399] Most of the approximately 50,000 refugees who survived were housed in a refugee camp in the outskirts of Hamadan. They were then moved to the Baqubah camp to the north of Baghdad, where they were protected by the British and received shelter, food, and medical care.[400]

Of the several hundred refugees who had not joined the exodus and had stayed back in Urumia on the Mission grounds, nearly half died due to disease. The American missionaries who had stayed back in Urumia were first interned by the Ottomans and then sent to Tabriz in

---

[396] Shedd (1922), *The Measure of a Man*, p. 269.

[397] The date of William Shedd's passing is not mentioned in his biography, *The Measure of a Man*, written by Mary Lewis Shedd. However, his gravestone in Tabriz, where he was later put to rest, is engraved with August 7, 1918 as the date of his passing.

[398] Shedd (1922), *The Measure of a Man*, p. 279.

[399] Yacoub (2016), *Year of the Sword*, p. xiii.

[400] Shedd's oldest daughter, Susan, who was in America at the time of the exodus, eventually returned to serve at orphanages setup for the children who were orphaned during the exodus. Her experience and those of the orphaned children are captured in a touching novel by William Shedd's granddaughter, Celia Barker Lottridge, in a book titled *Home is Beyond the Mountains*. Another book by William Shedd's second daughter (Margaret) titled *Hosannah Tree* is a novel based on the life and experiences of William Shedd.

early October. The Ottoman forces remained in control of Urumia until the end of October of 1918, at which point the treaty of Mudros called for their removal from Urumia.

Mary Lewis Shedd returned to Sain Kala in 1919 to find her husband's grave and recover his remains. Urumia was still in a state of turmoil in 1919 and unsafe for travel. It was impossible to visit the Seir cemetery, where many of William Shedd's missionary colleagues and family members had been laid to rest. Therefore, his final resting place was the Armenian Cemetery in Tabriz, close to where Howard Baskerville had been laid to rest nearly a decade earlier.

William Ambrose Shedd's Resting Place in the Armenian Cemetery of Tabriz (c. 2021)

References and Related Readings

Daniel, Robert L. (1970). *American Philanthropy in the Near East: 1820-1960*. Athens, OH: Ohio University Press.

Lottridge, Celia B. (2010). *Home is Beyond the Mountains*. Toronto: Groundwood Books.

Naayem, Joseph O.I. (1921). *Shall This Nation Die?* New York: Chaldean Rescue.

Shedd, Margaret (1967). *Hosannah Tree.* Garden City, NY: Doubleday & Company.

Shedd, Mary Lewis (1922). *The Measure of a Man: The Life of William Ambrose Shedd, Missionary to Persia.* New York: Gordon H. Doran Company.

Werda, Joel E. (1924). *The Flickering Light of Asia or the Assyrian Nation and Church.* Published by the author.

Yacoub, Joseph (2016). *Year of the Sword: The Assyrian Christian Genocide.* Translated by James Ferguson. Oxford: Oxford University Press.

Zirinsky, Michael P. (1993). "Render Therefore unto Caesar the Things Which Are Caesar's: American Presbyterian Educators and Reza Shah," *Iranian Studies*, 26: 337-356.

Chapter 35

A RETROSPECTIVE ON
WILLIAM AMBROSE SHEDD

The life of William Ambrose Shedd is unique among Urumia's American missionaries and the greater body of all the American missionaries who served in Persia. After his passing, the Urumia Mission's activities came to a halt for many years. Shedd was one of a handful of Americans who were born in Persia to American missionary parents. He traveled back-and-forth between Persia and America and experienced the contrasts and overlaps in human nature, fears, and desires between the two countries.

When examining his words and the results of his labors, it is clear that Shedd was most interested in practicality and found little use for theoretical abstractions. As Robert Speer stated, he "would not give his life to the satisfaction of intellectual tastes" but would rather dedicate his life to helping the needy.[401] His emphasis on practicality was evident in one of his letters, from his younger days, while he was a senior at Marietta College:

> Now that I am a man in years, I suppose that I ought to have a
> fixed purpose and aim in view. If I were to follow my own
> inclinations, I should go ahead and study some branches and
> settle down as teacher or college professor (if I could get such a

---

[401] Shedd (1922), *The Measure of a Man*, p. viii.

place) and live a rather inactive life. But I suppose I ought to do what will do the most good, and there are certainly many reasons why I should go to Persia.[402]

Shedd was considerably more open-minded on matters of faith than many others in his line of work. While a theology student at Princeton University, he openly contemplated converting out of Presbyterianism and becoming an Episcopalian. Later in life, while observing the horrors of the violence in the Salmas-Khoi region, he questioned how the pain and agony brought onto an innocent person can be explained by a loving and giving God. The fact that in his correspondences and writings, he openly acknowledged having such questions reflects an inquisitive and active mind that was not bound by the typical restrictions of expression or tradition. His faith, however, clearly served as his guide in dealing with life's difficult questions.

Shedd also believed in the need for the enforcement of justice and assuring social equity through an officially sanctioned force. Given the unstable social and political environment of Urumia, especially in the two decades leading to the First World War, the need for countering the harm done to innocent people by violent elements blinded by bigotry, bias, and religious hatred was quite evident to him. As a member of the Legal Board of the Syrian Evangelical Church, the poor enforcement of rulings by Persian courts was a matter with which he had first-hand experience. This, too, in his mind, justified enforcement powers, as evident in his own writing:

> If I were an autocrat in Persia, I should wish a small but effective army. Then I should try to bring about two reforms. One would be the gradual introduction of religious liberty and the other would be the establishment of courts whose decisions would be final, except by appeal in certain cases to a higher court.[403]

Interestingly, his views regarding enforcement of legal rulings by the courts were formed at approximately the same time as Morgan Shuster's views. As described in chapter 30, Shuster was an American citizen invited by the Persian Parliament to serve as the Treasurer of Persia in 1911. His concern was regarding a completely different matter: that of tax collection. Despite the differences in the concerns of

---

[402] Ibid., p. 47.
[403] Ibid., p. 85.

the two men, Shuster also strongly believed in establishing a small army of enforcement officers, purely dedicated to the important task of tax collection, which he attempted to organize.

The two men had never met nor corresponded on this issue, but both had arrived at the same conclusion. Shuster believed that such a force would be needed to prevent the country's limited wealth from disappearing due to widespread corruption. Shedd had also recognized the need for a similar force for ensuring that the rulings by Qajar courts on matters related to religious minorities are respected and not ignored. In both cases, Shedd and Shuster felt a need for strong-armed enforcement to encourage moral behavior since, in their view, the alternative would have been chaos. In both cases, they did not have access to the force and resources that they deemed necessary, and had to escape with their lives from their respective spheres of operation (Tehran for Shuster and Urumia for Shedd). For both men, in their absence, chaos followed.

Another unique aspect of Shedd was his mixing of missionary and diplomatic roles. He took on this duality of roles due to his initial belief that an authoritative hand as an official representative of America in Urumia would be instrumental to providing aid for the thousands of refugees in need. However being both a missionary and a diplomat at the same time placed him in a difficult position, which instead of expanding his abilities, restricted him. Furthermore, with his role as the administrator of Near East Relief funds and the partial use of these funds to support the militia defending Urumia against the Ottoman encirclement of Urumia, additional conflicts of interest challenged him. The Mission's support of the Christian militia had resulted in increased tensions with the local Moslem population of Urumia.[404] Reflecting on the challenges of being both a missionary and a diplomat, Shedd wrote the following in a letter addressed to Robert Speer at the Presbyterian Board of Foreign Missions in February of 1918:

> I am, as you know, acting at Mr. Caldwell's request as American
> Vice Consul in an honorary capacity. This has brought up
> rather acutely questions of the relation of the Mission to these

---

[404] In the long-term, these tensions also restricted the ability of the Mission to restart its operations in Urumia after the end of the First World War, as elaborated by Zirinsky (1993), "Render Therefore unto Caesar the Things Which Are Caesar's: American Presbyterian Educators and Reza Shah," pp. 340-341.

affairs and also questions of personal duty. It is not very clear to me what the right thing is. My position in the community is such and I have such close relations with the people that it is very difficult for me to have the amount of detachment that seems to be expected of either a missionary or a consular officer. I am not able to look at the questions of public safety or the status of the Syrian people as an outsider might consider these questions. So I hardly know what the right course is in the matter. I think that the official position has been of assistance the past month or two to the community and has enabled me to serve. I do not think that it has done the mission cause any harm either; but I do not think that the connection is one to be maintained for a great while.[405]

Shedd's other writings from that time period, cited in his biography by Mary Lewis Shedd, reflect similar expressions of hesitation:

Of course I am thinking a good deal about the questions raised by my assuming the duties of Vice-Consul here, and I am about ready to believe that it is a mistake altogether.... We are in a very delicate and dangerous situation here that makes it difficult to be bound by the sort of policy that seeks to avoid any criticism or conflict, and there is too much at stake to make it possible to play an altogether cautious game.... If the Vice-Consulship will enable me to do some service in protecting American lives and property, and also serve the community by helping secure peace, I am ready to sacrifice a good deal for it, but if it will hamper me by restricting my influence, without increasing my opportunity for service, I shall ask to be released.[406]

His expressions of doubt were due to the fact that he had to officially place America's diplomatic priorities ahead of the Urumia Mission's local responsibilities. The diplomatic role limited his freedom to dialogue and negotiate with those of influence in the highly polarized and militarized environment of Urumia. Furthermore, once America officially entered the First World War, he was increasingly viewed as an enemy by Ottoman sympathizers in Urumia. This put his life at risk, making it necessary for him and his wife to escape alongside the

---

[405] Archives of the Presbyterian Historical Society, Philadelphia. Shedd Family Archives, RG 19-0504

[406] Shedd (1922), *The Measure of a Man*, p. 229.

thousands of refugees upon the invasion of Urumia in the summer of 1918, which eventually resulted in his illness and death. In that sense, his life and death highlight the clear lines that separate missionary work from diplomatic work and put into question the ability to serve both universes at the same time.

Similar to many of the other American missionaries in Urumia, Shedd was a prolific writer. He had great intellectual interests in the area of comparative religion and authored a book on the relationship between early Islam and the Oriental Churches. This book, titled *Islam and the Oriental Churches*, was a compilation of lectures he had delivered while visiting Princeton University. In it, he examined the early interactions between Eastern Christians and the first followers of Islam.

A unique perspectives advocated by Shedd was the need for Westerners to have a scientifically correct understanding of the Oriental mind before they begin to advocate for Western values. He believed that Western Orientalists, diplomats, and missionaries need to take a research-based approach in understanding the East. He emphasized the importance of distinguishing between Islam as a religion and Moslems as individual followers of that religion. He also encouraged a respectful, inquisitive, and anthropological approach for developing a full understanding of the Moslem world. He often spent considerable time with Urumia's locals, to individually inquire about their faith and spiritual views. The range of people he spoke with about faith included dervishes, clergy, laborers, the young and the old. He believed that without such understanding, it would be impossible to create a meaningful dialogue with Persians:

> How superficially we have reached the spirit and the mind of Persia. We must some of us, take time from the grind and machinery to get to closer quarters with people and by loving controversy and fellowship, find out their beliefs and their struggles.[407]

His death and the aftermath of the devastations brought to the region due to the First World War made such a line of inquiry impossible. It is a loss to humanity that the line of inquisitive thinking that he advocated for, over a century ago, has been forgotten by some

---

[407] Ibid., p. 109.

Orientalists and foreign policymakers in the West today. American formulation of an Iranian policy, be it led by Republicans or Democrats, without truly understanding the Persian mindset, can have irreversibly damaging long-term outcomes for both the United States and Iran. The recent decades of turmoil in the region have demonstrated this unfortunate fact, the traces of which were evident in Shedd's writing well over a century ago.

References and Related Readings

Guilak, Hooshang (2011). *Fire Beneath the Ashes: The United States and Iran: A Historical Perspective 1829-1947.* Xlibris Publishing.

Kinzer, Stephen (2010). *Reset: Iran, Turkey and America's Future.* New York: Henry Holt and Co.

Said, Edward W. (1994). *Culture and Imperialism.* New York: Vintage Books.

Said, Edward W. (1979). *Orientalism.* New York: Vintage Books.

Shedd, Mary Lewis (1922). *The Measure of a Man: The Life of William Ambrose Shedd, Missionary to Persia.* New York: Gordon H. Doran Company.

Shedd, William A. (1904). *Islam and the Oriental Churches: Their Historical Relations.* Philadelphia: Presbyterian Board of Publication and Sabbath-School Work.

Zirinsky, Michael P. (1993). "Render Therefore unto Caesar the Things Which Are Caesar's: American Presbyterian Educators and Reza Shah," *Iranian Studies,* 26: 337-356.

Chapter 36

REFLECTION

The Americans of Urumia were a truly unique group. They arrived nearly two centuries ago with an intense desire to aid the Assyrian Christians of the region. They achieved a great deal by establishing an extensive school system, introducing innovations in public health, and elevating the economic and social status of the Assyrians. They were driven individuals whose intentions were pure and non-political. Many left their homes in America to live, labor, and die in a remote land. Some were born in Urumia, as children of American missionaries, and chose to stay and labor there instead of returning to their ancestral homeland.

Optimism and Risk-Taking

In addition to their drive and commitment, the Americans of Urumia were energized by a sense of optimism and risk-taking in facing seemingly impossible odds. Their willingness to accept risks was empowered by their firm belief that God would be on their side. It enabled them to endure unimaginable physical and emotional hardships and move forward under circumstances in which others may have paused or retreated.

Faith-based optimism guided many of their accomplishments. The influence of faith in risk-taking was evident in their writings and their recollection of the chances they knowingly took with their own lives and those of others. It was evident when Perkins, experiencing a crippling illness, decided to board a ship leaving Boston for the Orient in 1833, knowing full well that he could die on that ship because of it. It was also evident when Grant decided to join the ABCFM's Mission to the Nestorians, believing that God would take care of his motherless children while he would be thousands of miles away.

While faith may have empowered the missionaries' risk-taking tendencies, a related possibility is that it may have also caused some clouded judgments. The vision of the early American missionaries in Urumia was informed by the ideals of the Second Great Awakening. These ideals demanded the missionaries to evangelize to the world, and in doing so carry out seemingly impossible tasks in remote, uncharted lands. The ABCFM engaged in a massive effort to set up educational, medical and evangelical services for a wide range of aid recipients around the globe.

The urgency of America's mission to the world was further elevated by the immediacy of apocalyptic expectations, which had been approximated by some to take place in the middle of the nineteenth century. The fact that no apocalypse materialized as had been predicted put into question the appropriateness of using an apocalyptic mindset to rush evangelical mandates. Despite the doubts about the timing of the apocalypse, the fervor of the Second Great Awakening for the evangelization of the world guided the American missionaries' mindsets in Urumia and elsewhere for decades, first under the leadership of the ABCFM and later under the umbrella of the Presbyterian Board of Foreign Missions. The resulting momentum in Urumia empowered monumental advancements among the people that the Mission served, often under difficult, dangerous, and inhospitable circumstances.

American Exceptionalism

The early American missionaries, such as Perkins and Grant, arrived in Urumia with the view that the Assyrians lacked literacy and knowledge of Christian values. The missionaries' writings, intended primarily for American readers who were the ABCFM's potential financial donors, may have exaggerated the weaknesses they saw. Many of the faults they had identified could arguably have been found in any society, anywhere in the world. The negative tone in which the Assyrians were depicted in the early writings of the first missionaries arriving in Urumia may have been motivated by the need to emphasize the urgency of the work to American readers.

The Urumia missionaries may have been partially affected by a sense of American exceptionalism by questioning the appropriateness of practicing Christianity in any way other than that of American Protestants. It is no surprise that Urmia's American missionaries found themselves in conflict with the Anglicans, the Catholics, and the Russian Orthodox Church at various times. These conflicts manifested in a range of ways, from mild expressions of discontent in the missionaries' personal correspondences, to formal appeals to Persia's royal courts, local government officials, or the Assyrian patriarch for limiting competing denominations' scope of operations.

A sense of American exceptionalism was also evident in some of the simplest matters of communication, such as how to address the population that the missionaries had come to serve. During the first few decades of the Mission's operations, the missionaries insisted on using the term "Nestorian" when, in fact, the Assyrians themselves preferred not to be called that due to the historically derogatory connotations attached to it. Fully aware of this concern, the missionaries continued to use "Nestorian" and only in later years began to use "Assyrian" and "Syrian" in their communications.

This form of cultural insensitivity may have potentially clouded the judgment of the Mission throughout this time. It was evident in Grant's seemingly unintentional entanglement in the power grab contested between the Assyrian patriarch and the Kurdish chiefs in eastern Turkey in the 1840s. It was also evident in Cochran's insistence on the arrest of the thirteen tribesmen associated with the 1904 murder of Labaree, when it was simply impossible to arrest them as they had already escaped across the Ottoman border. This was an insistence which he had to backtrack from, once he recognized the depth of the retribution norms which were part of the tribal cultures of the region, making it impossible to seek justice based on American norms.

What Works in America May Not Work in Persia

What may have appeared to the missionaries as the right thing to do from an American perspective often had dramatically unexpected results in these foreign lands where the norms of behavior were so different. The resulting confusion, with which missionaries such as Grant and Cochran wrestled, demonstrated that what may have appeared to work in America eventually may have turned out to be inapplicable to Persia. On several occasions, the Urumia missionaries found this out the hard way. Their American missionary colleagues in other parts of the world seemed to have encountered similar challenges in achieving adaptation to local norms.[408]

The need for greater sensitivity toward the local norms challenged the early missionaries deployed to Persia, and eventually resulted in a recognized need to adapt. For example, while in the early writings of the missionaries, we find passages such as: "The guiding hand of Providence thus pointed us to the Nestorians as the proper medium through whom to reach the Mohammedans," this approach was abandoned early on due to the uniqueness of Persia and Islam's guidance on religious conversion.[409] The idea that Persia's Assyrians could be the means for launching a long-term campaign to convert Moslems was openly contested by others in the Christian world. Proselytizing to Persia's Moslems was also carefully studied and refuted by the American missionary James L. Merrick.

As the American missionaries soon learned, the notion of converting the world to Christianity, at the heart of the mandates of the Second Great Awakening, was uniquely inapplicable to Persia, as the laws of Islam strictly and unambiguously forbid such conversions. It is, therefore, no surprise that the records for the Urumia mission station reveal no mass conversion of the local Moslem population and no programmatic effort by the missionaries to encourage such conversions.

---

[408] See, for example, Salt (2002), "Trouble Wherever They Went: American Missionaries in Anatolia and Ottoman Syria in the Nineteenth Century."

[409] Perkins (1861), *Missionary Life in Persia*, p. 104.

An Impactful Mission

In the eight decades concluding with the end of the First World War, the Urumia mission station achieved remarkable results in improving public health and literacy. On the education front, the early missionaries were heavily involved in establishing a written form of the spoken Syriac dialect of Urumia. This accomplishment allowed them to use the modern Syriac script, which they had developed, in their educational initiatives, delivered through nearly one hundred schools in Urumia and surrounding regions. The Mission also established a printing press, which further empowered their literacy programs and educational initiatives.

In addition to accomplishments related to public education, groundbreaking advancements in public health were introduced to Persia through the Mission. Grant's arrival in 1835 introduced Western medical practices into the area, as he was exceptionally generous in sharing his methods and tools with Persian physicians. Austin Wright and other American missionary physicians coming to Urumia continued to introduce innovative American medical practices to Persians.

The Mission is also credited for establishing Iran's first medical college through Cochran's vision and labor. Due to his work, improvements in medicine and medical education were introduced to Persia, as he constructed Persia's first medical college, the Westminster Hospital of Urumia, in 1882. The educational work of the Mission also focused on higher education for the general public in fields other than medicine. The offered curriculum covered Western languages, chemistry, commercial arithmetic, blacksmithing, and carpentry.

In later years, the Mission also developed programs focused on modern agricultural methods. This was a significant contribution, given the largely agrarian economy of the Urumia region. Through the agriculture curriculum, efficient farming methods were introduced by the Urumia mission station to Persia. American vegetables and fruits were also introduced to Persia through this program and the Urumia mission station's aid to local farmers. These included tomatoes, potatoes, sweet corn, strawberries, raspberries, and several American apple species.[410] The "College" compound on which the hospital and other Mission facilities were constructed eventually transformed into a public institution for higher education and is now the campus of Iran's Urumia University.

It is important to acknowledge that the scale and long-term impact of Urumia's American missionary operations discussed in this book was simply impressive. Dozens of missionaries served there starting from 1835, many deserving their own biographies and life recognition. However, biographies have been written for only a handful. It is unfortunate that limited space does not allow for detailed elaboration on the work of missionaries other than the four profiled in this book.[411]

During the years of the First World War, the Mission protected thousands of refugees fleeing the Assyrian and Armenian Genocides.[412] The multiple generations of the descendants of these refugees number in the millions, and for many, their lineage can be traced back to the College compound in Urumia. As such, the impact of the Urumia mission station goes far beyond what was achieved in the first eight decades with respect to education and healthcare. One of the most significant human contributions of the Mission is the survival of the segment of the of Assyrian and Armenian populations whose ancestors had found refuge on the Mission grounds nearly a century ago.

Furthermore, the educational services of the Mission elevated the literacy level of Urumia's population. The replication of these services elsewhere in Persia by other American mission stations resulted in the establishment of some of Persia's best educational institutions. Many of the graduates of these schools were able to attend colleges and universities in the West, creating accomplished immigrant communities in the United States, Canada, Europe, and elsewhere in the world.

---

[410] For additional details on the Mission's contributions to Persian agricultural practices, see Coan (1939), *Yesterdays in Persia and Kurdistan*, pp. 227-231.

[411] For a comprehensive list of American missionaries who served in Persia, interested readers are encouraged to consult the Appendix in Karimi (1975).

[412] The Assyrian genocide is often referred to as *Sayfo*, meaning the "year of the sword". Consult Gaunt (2006) and Yacoub (2016) for related details.

An Unhappy Ending

Despite the accomplishments of the Urumia mission station before and during the First World War, its revival after the war was significantly delayed. In early 1919, Harry Packard, a senior missionary physician, returned to Urumia, intending to restart the Urumia mission station's activities. In order to provide security protection for the Mission compound, he had hired Kurdish guards. This, along with the fact that Packard had been at the head of the Assyrian police force controlling the city during the previous year's civil war in Urumia made him an unwelcome presence in the city.

In late May of 1919, riots in the city in protest to Packard's presence resulted in the destruction of what was left of the Mission compound and the death of hundreds of refugees. Packard and his family had to be rescued by Persian government forces and escaped from the city. It was not until 1923 that the Mission could safely return to Urumia.[413] However, the return of the Urumia mission station was to be short-lived and in 1933, by order of Reza Shah, the Urumia station was shut down, and American missionary activities had to refocus on other civilian centers in Persia.[414] The Shah's order ended nearly a century of American missionary presence in Urumia.

A Glimmer of Hope

Although the Urumia mission station's operations came to an end, new American mission stations had already been modeled after it in other Iranian cities: Tehran (1872), Tabriz (1873), Hamadan (1881), Resht (1881), Qazvin (1906), Kermanshah (1910), and Mashad (1911). Each of these mission stations continued to directly or indirectly serve millions of Iranians over the decades. Advancements in public education and public health, which were achieved in Urumia, were

---

[413] Zirinsky (1993), "Render Therefore unto Caesar the Things Which Are Caesar's: American Presbyterian Educators and Reza Shah," pp. 340-341.

[414] Ibid., p. 341. Note that by then, the Qajar era had ended, Reza Shah had become Persia's new ruler, and Urumia was renamed Rezaiyeh after him (in 1926). He was concerned that by allowing the Mission to continue operating, it would embolden Assyrians' desire for recognition as a minority group and increase tensions among the diverse groups in the Urumia region.

replicated throughout Iran as a result of the establishment of these stations.

Given that the American mission stations were primarily supported through private donations from American citizens, they helped in the formation of strong bonds between Iranians and Americans during the first half of the twentieth century. During that time, the Iranian public viewed America as the most trustable and caring Western nation. However, these sentiments would diminish significantly after the CIA-orchestrated coup d'état of 1952 and the 1979 Islamic Revolution.

Nevertheless, traces of the positive sentiments remain in place even today. Reflecting on the Americans of Urumia, one noteworthy fact is that in honor of Dr. Joseph Plumb Cochran, the home he lived in has been retained in its original form by Urumia University. This is a testament to the fact that if anything is to be learned from America's early experience in Urumia, it is the bonding strength of humanitarian initiatives. Education, relief work, and public health initiatives created bonds that have lasted centuries and have overcome deeply embedded differences. It is these bonds that need to be revisited and re-strengthened for us to achieve a peaceful state between the United States and Iran.

Dr. Joseph P. Cochran's Former Home Located on the Current Campus of Urumia University (c. 2021)

References and Related Readings

Coan, Frederick G. (1939). *Yesterdays in Persia and Kurdistan.* Claremont, CA: Saunders Studio Press.

Gaunt, David (2006). *Massacres, Resistance, Protectors: Muslim-Christian Relations in Eastern Anatolia during World War I.* Piscataway, NJ: Gorgias Press.

Joseph, John (1961). *Nestorians and their Muslim Neighbors.* Princeton: Princeton University Press.

Karimi, Linda C. (1975). *Implications of American Missionary Presences in 19th and 20th Century Iran.* Masters Dissertation. Portland State University.

Knight, George R. (1993). *Millennial Fever and the End of the World: A Study of Millerite Adventism.* Nampa, ID: Pacific Press.

Perkins, Justin (1861). *Missionary Life in Persia: Glimpses of a Quarter of a Century of Labors among the Nestorian Christians.* Boston: American Tract Society.

Said, Edward W. (1994). *Culture and Imperialism.* New York: Vintage Books.

Salt, Jeremy (2002). "Trouble Wherever They Went: American Missionaries in Anatolia and Ottoman Syria in the Nineteenth Century", *The Muslim World,* Vol. 92, 287-313.

Wilsey, John D. (2015). *American Exceptionalism and Civil Religion: Reassessing the History of an Idea.* Downers Grove, IL: IVP Academic.

Yacoub, Joseph (2016). *Year of the Sword: The Assyrian Christian Genocide.* Translated by James Ferguson. Oxford: Oxford University Press.

Zirinsky, Michael P. (1993). "Render Therefore unto Caesar the Things Which Are Caesar's: American Presbyterian Educators and Reza Shah," *Iranian Studies,* 26: 337-356.

SOURCES OF PHOTOGRAPHS, SKETCHES, AND MAPS

Page	Contents	Source
Cover	Urumia mission station group photograph	Shedd Family Papers, 16-0623, Box 2, Folder 2, ID 139047, Presbyterian Historical Society, Philadelphia, PA.
2	Map of Persia / Urumia mission field	Shedd (1922), *The Measure of a Man*, centerpiece.
4	Photograph of Justin Perkins	Shedd Family Papers, 16-0623, Box 2, Folder 4, ID 139058, Presbyterian Historical Society, Philadelphia, PA.
5	Urumia and surrounding regions	Laurie (1863), *Woman and Her Saviour in Persia*, frontispiece.
7	Urumia plain photograph	Shedd Family Papers, 16-0623, Box 2, Folder 3, ID 139075, Presbyterian Historical Society, Philadelphia, PA.
9	Urumia mission station group photograph	Shedd Family Papers, 16-0623, Box 2, Folder 2, ID 139047, Presbyterian Historical Society, Philadelphia, PA.
12	Assyrian family photograph	Shedd Family Papers, 16-0623, Box 2, Folder 6, page 9 of photo album, Presbyterian Historical Society, Philadelphia, PA.
13	Assyrian village photograph	Shedd Family Papers, 16-0623, Box 2, Folder 6, page 33 of photo album, Presbyterian Historical Society, Philadelphia, PA.
22	Sketch of the Kurdish mountains	Wigram & Wigram (1911), *The Cradle of Mankind*, page 158.
31	Photo of mountain village	Shedd Family Papers, 16-0623, Box 2, Folder 6; page 7 of photo album, Presbyterian Historical Society, Philadelphia, PA.
33	Regional map of Nestorian Settlements	Laurie (1856), Dr. *Grant and the Mountain Nestorians.* Frontispiece.
36	Nestorian church photograph	Shedd Family Papers, 16-0623, Box 2, Folder 6, page 13 of photo album, Presbyterian Historical Society, Philadelphia, PA.
52	View of Urumia	Yohannan (1916). *The Death of a Nation*, page 147.
54	Assyrian family in Urumia	Shedd Family Papers, 16-0623, Box 2, Folder 3, ID 139080, Presbyterian Historical Society, Philadelphia, PA.
56	Flooded rice fields	Shedd Family Papers, 16-0623, Box 2, Folder 6, page 49 of photo album, Presbyterian Historical Society, Philadelphia, PA.
56	Photo of village of Seir	Thomas Kirkpatrick Papers, 12-1222, SPP 111; c.1911; Photo taken by Thomas L. Kirkpatrick. Presbyterian Historical Society, Philadelphia, PA.
61	Image of Justin Perkins	Perkins (1861), *Missionary Life in Persia*, frontispiece.
72	Mar Yohannan sketch	Perkins (1843), *A Residence of Eight Years*, page 172.
75	Mission seminary sketch	Perkins (1842), *A Residence of Eight Years*, page 157.
76	Students in Kurdish mountains	Shedd Family Papers, 16-0623, Box 2, Folder 5, ID 139048; Photo taken by Louise Wilbur Shedd, Presbyterian Historical Society, Philadelphia, PA.

Page	Contents	Source
76	Village school children	Shedd Family Papers, 16-0623, Box 2, Folder 3; ID 139063, Presbyterian Historical Society, Philadelphia, PA.
83	Urumia mission station printing press	Shedd Family Papers, 16-0623, Box 2, Folder 6; page 125 of photo album, Presbyterian Historical Society, Philadelphia, PA.
95	Sketch of Judith Grant Perkins	*The Persian Flower* (1853), frontispiece.
109	Sketch of Asahel Grant	Laurie (1853), *Dr. Grant and the Mountain Nestorians,* frontispiece.
118	Class in the Female Seminary	Shedd Family Papers, 16-0623, Box 2, Folder 6; "Turkey and Iran Photo Album," page 63, Presbyterian Historical Society, Philadelphia, PA.
118	Fiske Seminary graduate and her students	Shedd Family Papers, 16-0623, Box 2, Folder 5, ID 139088. Photo taken by Louise Wilbur Shedd. PHS, Philadelphia, PA.
129	Kurdish fighters	Ryder (1925), *The Demarcation of the Turco-Persian Boundary*, page 228.
129	Kurdish mountain passes	Shedd Family Papers, 16-0623, Box 2, Folder 6, page 24 of photo album, Presbyterian Historical Society, Philadelphia, PA.
131	Sketch of Mosul	Wigram & Wigram (1911), *The Cradle of Mankind,* page 80.
132	Regional map related to Grant's visits	Laurie (1853), *Dr. Grant and the Mountain Nestorians,* frontispiece.
134	Sketch of entrance to Amadia	Wigram & Wigram (1911), *The Cradle of Mankind,* page 321.
135	Photo of mountain Nestorian home	Shedd Family Papers, 16-0623, Box 2, Folder 6; Photo album, page 22, Presbyterian Historical Society, Philadelphia, PA.
136	Sketch of Mar Shimon Abraham	Yohannan (1916), *The Death of a Nation,* page 113.
142	Photo of Zab River	Shedd Family Papers, 16-0623, Box 2, Folder 6; page 3 of photo album, Presbyterian Historical Society, Philadelphia, PA.
151	Nestorian church congregation	Shedd Family Papers, 16-0623, Box 2, Folder 6; page 18 of photo album, Presbyterian Historical Society, Philadelphia, PA.
155	Nestorian fighter	Shedd Family Papers, 16-0623, Box 2, Folder 6, page 15 of photo album, Presbyterian Historical Society, Philadelphia, PA.
158	Map of villages in Hakkari region	Laurie (1853), *Dr. Grant and the Mountain Nestorians,* frontispiece.
184	Village of Dizza	Shedd Family Papers, 16-0623, Box 2, Folder 6; page 17 of photo album, Presbyterian Historical Society, Philadelphia, PA.
201	Portrait of Joseph Plumb Cochran	Speer (1911), *The Hakim Sahib.* frontispiece.
211	Urumia wheat market	Thomas Kirkpatrick Papers, 12-1222, SPP 111;ID: 12-1222_02_014; Presbyterian Historical Society, Philadelphia, PA.
214	Westminster Hospital of Urumia	Presbyterian Historical Society, Philadelphia, PA: NT8.2 Ur8cp; ID: 33382.
216	Interior view of the College compound	Shedd Family Papers, 16-0623, Box 2, Folder 2, ID 139081, Presbyterian Historical Society, Philadelphia, PA.

Page	Contents	Source

BIBLIOGRAPHY

Ainsworth, William F. (1842). *Travels and Researches in Asia Minor, Mesopotamia, Chaldea, and Armenia.* London: John W. Parker.

Ameer, John Pierre (2008). *Assyrians in Yonkers.* Piscataway, NJ: Gorgias Press.

Ameer, John Pierre (1997). *Yankees and Nestorians: The Establishment of American Schools Among the Nestorians of Iran and Turkey, 1834-1850.* Doctoral Dissertation. Harvard University.

Badger, George P. (1852). *The Nestorians and their Rituals.* London: Joseph Masters.

Barton, James L. (1930). *Story of Near East Relief.* New York: MacMillan Co.

Barton, James L. (1908). *Daybreak in Turkey.* Boston: The Pilgrim Press.

Bassett, James (1890). *Persia: Eastern Mission.* Philadelphia: Presbyterian Board of Publication and Sabbath-School Work.

Becker, Adam H. (2015). *Revival and Awakening: American Evangelical Missionaries in Iran and the Origins of Assyrian Nationalism.* Chicago: University of Chicago Press.

Benite, Zvi (2013). *The Ten Lost Tribes: A World History.* Oxford: Oxford University Press.

Bernstein, Peter (2006). *Wedding of the Waters: The Erie Canal and the Making of a Great Nation.* New York: W.W. Norton & Company.

Bird, Isabella L. (1891). *Journeys in Persia and Kurdistan.* London: John Murray.

Browne, Edward G. (1910). *The Persian Revolution of 1905-1909.* Cambridge: Cambridge University Press.

Browne, Edward G. and Hassan Javadi (2008). *Letters from Tabriz: The Russian Suppression of the Iranian Constitutional Movement.* Odenton, MD: Mage Publishers.

Bryce, Viscount (1916). *The Treatment of Armenians in the Ottoman Empire.* London: Hodder and Stoughton.

Burrow, T. (1973). "The Proto-Indoaryans," *The Journal of the Royal Asiatic Society of Great Britain and Ireland,* No. 2, pp. 123-140.

Coakley, John F. (1995). "Edward Breath and the Typography of Syriac," *Harvard Library Bulletin,* 6(4), 41-64.

Coan, Frederick G. (1939). *Yesterdays in Persia and Kurdistan*. Claremont, CA: Saunders Studio Press.

Cubberley, Ellwood P. (1919). *Public Education in the United States*. Boston: Houghton Mifflin.

Curzon, George N. (1892). *Persia and the Persian Question*. London: Longmans, Green & Co.

Daniel, Elton L (2012). *The History of Iran*. Santa Barbara: Greenwood.

Daniel, Mooshie G. (1901). *Modern Persia*. Toronto: The Carswell Co. Ltd.

Daniel, Robert L. (1970). *American Philanthropy in the Near East: 1820-1960*. Athens, OH: Ohio University Press.

Davidson, Roderick (1956). "The Hatt-i-Humayn of 1856 and the Climate of its Reception," in *Reform in the Ottoman Empire (1856-1876)*. Princeton: University Press.

Elder, John (1960). *History of the American Presbyterian Mission to Iran: 1834-1960*. Literature Committee of the Church Council of Iran, Philadelphia, PA.

Elton, Daniel. L. (2012). *The History of Iran*. Santa Barbara, CA: Greenwood.

Emhardt, William and George M. Lamsa (1926). *The Oldest Christian People*. Eugene: Wipf & Stock.

Farrokh, Kaveh (2011). *Iran at War*. London: Osprey Publishing.

Fiske, Fidelia (1870). *Mary Lyon: Recollections of a Noble Woman*. London: Morgan, Chase and Scott.

Fraser, David (1910). *Persia and Turkey in Revolt*. Edinburgh: William Blackwood and Sons.

Gaunt, David (2006). *Massacres, Resistance, Protectors: Muslim-Christian Relations in Eastern Anatolia During World War I*. Piscataway, NJ: Gorgias Press.

Ghazvinian, John (2021). *America and Iran: A History, 1720 to the Present*. New York: Alfred Knopf.

Goldschmidt, Arthur, and Ibrahim Al-Marashi (2019). *A Concise History of the Middle East*. New York: Routledge.

Grant, Asahel (1841). *The Nestorians, or, The Lost Tribes*. London: John Murray.

Grant, Asahel (1837). "An Appeal to Pious Physicians," In A.C. Lathrop's *Memoir of Asahel Grant*, Boston: M.W. Dodd, pp. 203-216.

Guilak, Hooshang (2011). *Fire Beneath the Ashes: The United States and Iran: A Historical Perspective 1829-1947.* Xlibris Publishing.

Harmelink, Herman (1967). "The Ecumenical Relations of the Reformed Church in America," *Journal of Presbyterian History*, Vol. 45, No. 2, pp. 71-94.

Hopkirk, Peter (1992). *The Great Game: The Struggle for Empire in Central Asia.* Tokyo: Kodansha International.

Hurewitz Jacob C. (1956). *Diplomacy in the Near and Middle East: A Documentary Record 1914–1956.* Princeton: Van Nostrand.

Hutchison, William R. (1993). *Errand to the World: American Protestant Thought and Foreign Missions.* Chicago: The University of Chicago Press.

Joseph, John (1961). *Nestorians and their Muslim Neighbors.* Princeton: Princeton University Press.

Jwaideh, Wadie (2006). *The Kurdish National Movement: Its Origins and Development.* Syracuse: Syracuse University Press.

Karimi, Linda C. (1975). *Implications of American Missionary Presences in 19th and 20th Century Iran.* Masters Dissertation. Portland State University.

Kasravi, Ahmad (1998). *Eighteen Year History of Azerbaijan.* Tehran: Saad Moaser Publishing. Farsi manuscript reprint.

Keddie, Nikki R. (2012). *Qajar Iran and the Rise of Reza Khan.* Costa Mesa, CA: Mazda Publishers.

Keddie, Nikki R. (1981). *Roots of Revolution: An Interpretive History of Modern Iran.* New Haven: Yale University Press.

Kinzer, Stephen (2010). *Reset: Iran, Turkey and America's Future.* New York: Henry Holt and Company.

Knight, George R. (1993). *Millennial Fever and the End of the World: A Study of Millerite Adventism.* Nampa, ID: Pacific Press.

Lancaster, Joseph (1821). *The Lancastrian System of Education.* Baltimore: Lancastrian Institute.

Lathrop, A.C. (1847). *Memoir of Asahel Grant, M.D.* New York: M.W. Dodd.

Laurie, Thomas (1863). *Woman and Her Saviour in Persia.* Boston: Gould and Lincoln.

Laurie, Thomas (1853). *Dr. Grant and the Mountain Nestorians.* Boston: Gould and Lincoln.

Lawrence, T.E. (1935). *Seven Pillars of Wisdom*. Garden City: Doubleday, Doran & Company.

Layard, Austen H. (1867). *Nineveh and its Remains*. London: John Murray.

Layard, Austen H. (1854). *A Popular Account of Discoveries at Nineveh*. London: John Murray.

Leavy, Margaret R. (1992). *Looking for the Armenians: Eli Smith's Adventure, 1830-1831*. New Haven: The Connecticut Academy of Arts and Sciences.

Lewit, Robert T. (1963). "Indian Missions and Antislavery Sentiment: A Conflict of Evangelical and Humanitarian Ideals," *The Mississippi Valley Historical Review*, Vol. 50, No. 1, pp. 39-55.

Luke, Harry C. (1925). *Mosul and its Minorities*. London: Martin Hopkinson & Company.

MacCulloch, Diarmaid (2011). *Christianity: The First Three Thousand Years*. New York: Penguin Books.

McKenna, Rebecca T. (2017). *American Imperial Pastoral: The Architecture of US Colonialism in the Philippines*. Chicago: University of Chicago Press.

Malick, David G. (2008). *The American Mission Press: A Preliminary Bibliography*. ATOUR Publications.

McDowall, David (2007). *A Modern History of the Kurds*. New York: I.B. Tauris & Company.

McLoughlin, William G. (1973). "Indian Slaveholders and Presbyterian Missionaries, 1837-1861," *American Society of Church History*, pp. 535-551.

Miller, Duane M. (2017). "Anglican Mission in the Middle East up to 1910," in *The Oxford History of Anglicanism*, Rowan Strong (ed.). Oxford: Oxford University Press, pp. 276-295.

Missionary Herald (1826). "Christians Called Chaldeans," pp. 120-121. Published by the *American Board of Commissioners for Foreign Missions*, Boston, MA.

Murre-van den Berg, Heleen (1999). *From a Spoken to a Written Language: The Introduction and Development of Literary Urmia Aramaic in the Nineteenth Century*. Leiden: Nederlands Instituut Voor Het Nabije Oosten.

Murre-van den Berg, Heleen (1996). "The Missionaries' Assistants: The Role of Assyrians in the Development of Written Urmia Aramaic," *Journal of the Assyrian Academic Society*, 10(2), pp.3-17.

Perkins, Henry Martyn (1887). *Life of Rev. Justin Perkins, D.D.: Pioneering Missionary to Persia*. Chicago: Woman's Presbyterian Board of Missions of the Northwest.

Perkins, Justin (1865). *The Beloved Physician: A Sermon Occasioned by the Death of the Rev. Austin H. Wright, M.D.* New York: Edward Jenkins.

Perkins, Justin (1861). *Missionary Life in Persia: Glimpses of a Quarter of a Century of Labors Among the Nestorian Christians.* Boston: American Tract Society.

Perkins, Justin (1853). *Our Country's Sin: A Sermon Preached to the Members and Families of the Nestorian Mission at Oroomiah, Persia on July 3, 1853.* New York: H.B. Knight

Perkins, Justin (1843). *A Residence of Eight Years in Persia Among the Nestorian Christians.* Andover: Allen, Morrill & Wardell.

Platt, Mary S. (1915). *The War Journal of a Missionary in Persia.* New York: The Board of Foreign Missions of the Presbyterian Church in the U.S.A.

Ponafidine, Emma C. (1932). *My Life in the Moslem East.* Indianapolis: The Bobbs-Merrill Company.

Potts, Daniel T. (2017). "Achievement and Misfortune: On the Life and Death of Friedrich Eduard Schulz (1799-1829)," *Journal Asiatique*, 305(2), pp. 249-270.

Preston, Diana (2001). *The Boxer Rebellion: The Dramatic Story of China's War on Foreigners That Shook the World in the Summer of 1900.* New York: Walker & Company.

Rankin, William (1895). *Memorials of Foreign Missionaries of the Presbyterian Church, U.S.A.* Philadelphia: Presbyterian Board of Publication and Sabbath Work.

Rockwell, William W. (1916). *The Pitiful Plight of the Assyrian Christians in Persia and Kurdistan.* New York: American Committee for Armenian and Syrian Relief.

Ryder, C.H.D. (1925). "The Demarcation of the Turco-Persian Boundary in 1913-14," *The Geographical Journal*, 66(3), pp. 227-237.

Said, Edward W. (1994). *Culture and Imperialism.* New York: Vintage Books.

Said, Edward W. (1979). *Orientalism.* New York: Vintage Books.

Salt, Jeremy (2002). "Trouble Wherever They Went: American Missionaries in Anatolia and Ottoman Syria in the Nineteenth Century," *The Muslim World,* Vol. 92, pp. 287-313.

Shafaq, S.R. (1976). "Howard Baskerville," in Ali Pasha Saleh (ed.), *Cultural Ties between Iran and the United States.* Tehran: Bistopanj-e-Sharivar.

Shedd, Mary Lewis (1922). *The Measure of a Man: The Life of William Ambrose Shedd, Missionary to Persia.* New York: Gordon H. Doran Company.

Shedd, William A. (1912). *The Life of John Haskell Shedd.* Unpublished manuscript.

Shedd, William A. (1904). *Islam and the Oriental Churches: Their Historical Relations.* Philadelphia: Presbyterian Board of Publication and Sabbath-School Work.

Shojadel, Nadereh (2020). "Typology of the Historical Assyrian Churches in Urmia," *Journal of Critical Reviews,* 7(19), pp. 9238-9250.

Shuster, William Morgan (1912). *The Strangling of Persia.* New York: Century Company.

Smith, Stephen A. (2002). *The Russian Revolution: A Very Short Introduction.* Oxford: Oxford University Press.

Speer, Robert (1911). *The Hakim Sahib.* New York: Fleming H. Revell Company.

Speer, Robert (1898). *Missions and Politics in Asia.* New York: Fleming H. Revell Company.

Stewart, John (1928). *Nestorian Missionary Enterprise: The Story of a Church on Fire.* Edinburgh: T.&.T. Clark.

Stoddard, David T. (1855). *Grammar of the Modern Syriac Language.* New Haven: American Oriental Society.

Sykes, Percy (1969). *A History of Persia.* New York: Barnes & Noble.

Taylor, Gordon (2009). "Deep Waters: Life and Death in the Perkins Family: 1834-1852," *Journal of Assyrian Academic Studies.*

Taylor, Gordon (2008). *Fever & Thirst: An American Doctor Among the Tribes of Kurdistan, 1835-1844.* Chicago: Academy Chicago Publishers.

The Persian Flower: A Memoir of Judith Grant Perkins. Boston: John P. Jewett and Company. Published anonymously in 1853.

Thompson, Joseph P. (1858). *Memoir of the Rev. David Tappan Stoddard, Missionary to the Nestorians.* Boston: American Tract Society.

van Bruinessen, Martin (2006). "A Kurdish Warlord on the Turkish-Persian Frontier in the Early Twentieth Century: Isma`il Agha Simko," in Touraj Atabaki (ed.), *Iran and the First World War: Battleground of the Great Powers.* London: I.B. Tauris, pp. 69-93.

Werda, Joel E. (1924). *The Flickering Light of Asia or the Assyrian Nation and Church.* Published by Joel Werda.

Wigram, W. A. (1920). *Our Smallest Ally.* London: Society for Promoting Christian Knowledge.

Wigram, W. A. (1910). *An Introduction to the History of the Assyrian Church or the Church of the Sassanid Persian Empire, 100-640 A.D.* London: Society for Promoting Christian Knowledge.

Wigram, W. A. and E.T.A. Wigram (1914). *The Cradle of Mankind.* London: Adam and Charles Black.

Wilsey, John D. (2015). *American Exceptionalism and Civil Religion: Reassessing the History of an Idea.* Downers Grove, IL: IVP Academic.

Wilson, Samuel G. (1895). *Persian Life and Customs.* New York: Fleming H. Revell Company.

Yeselson, Abraham (1956). *United States-Persian Diplomatic Relations: 1883-1921.* New Brunswick: Rutgers University Press.

Yacoub, Joseph (2016). *Year of the Sword: The Assyrian Christian Genocide.* Translated by James Ferguson. Oxford: Oxford University Press.

Yohannan, Abraham (1916). *The Death of a Nation.* New York: Knickerbocker Press.

Zirinsky, Michael (2002). "American Presbyterian Missionaries at Urmia during the Great War," *La perse et la grande guerre,* Oliver Bast (ed.), Tehran: Institut Francais de Recherche en Iran, pp. 353-372.

Zirinsky, Michael P. (1993). "Render Therefore unto Caesar the Things Which Are Caesar's: American Presbyterian Educators and Reza Shah," *Iranian Studies,* 26: 337-356.

INDEX

AUTHOR'S BIOGRAPHY

Hooman Estelami is a professor at the Gabelli School of Business, Fordham University in New York City. He is the author of several books, including *Marketing Strategy*, *Marketing Turnarounds*, *Simplified Business Research Methods*, and *Marketing Financial Services*. Estelami is the editor-in-chief of the *International Journal of Bank Marketing* and previously served as the associate co-editor of the *Journal of Product and Brand Management*. His research has appeared in over 50 journal articles, for which he has received multiple prestigious awards. Using primary, secondary and archival data, Estelami has studied and published on a range of topics from customer protection and pricing to the history of US-Iran economic relations and American missionary presence in Persia during the nineteenth century. He received his Ph.D. in business from Columbia University, his MBA from McGill University, and his BA from Coe College.

Made in United States
North Haven, CT
05 August 2022

22269821R10215